MATHEMATICS FOR INNUMERATE ECONOMISTS

Gavin Kennedy

MATHEMATICS FOR INNUMERATE ECONOMISTS

MATHEMATICS FOR INNUMERATE ECONOMISTS

Gavin Kennedy

Holmes & Meier Publishers, Inc.
New York

First published in the United States of America 1982 by
Holmes & Meier Publishers, Inc.
30 Irving Place, New York, N.Y. 10003

Copyright © 1982 by Gavin Kennedy

All rights reserved

Library of Congress Cataloging in Publication Data

Kennedy, Gavin.
   Mathematics for innumerate economists.

   Bibliography: p.
   Includes index.
   1. Economics, Mathematical. 2. Mathematics.
I. Title.
HB135.K47   1981   510'.24339   81-13337

ISBN 0-8419-0777-3   AACR2
     0-8419-0789-7 (pbk)

Printed in Great Britain

Contents

PREFACE		ix
ONE	FOR WHOM THE COURSE TOLLS	1
	1.1 Introduction	1
	1.2 For Whom then?	2
	1.3 The Mathematics Mountains	3
	1.4 Do's and Don't's	4
TWO	EQUILIBRIUM RULES, OK?	6
	2.1 Introduction	6
	2.2 The Neoclassical Idea	6
	2.3 On Equilibrium	8
	2.4 Some Kit	8
	2.5 The Foothills	11
	2.6 For the Notebook	13
THREE	WALK – DON'T RUN!	14
	3.1 Introduction	14
	3.2 The Executive's Tale	14
	3.3 The Cognoscenti	15
	3.4 Harmless Ghosts	17
	3.5 Some Fragile Flowers	19
	3.6 Madame Notation	21
	3.7 In Full Bloom	22
	3.8 For the Notebook	24
FOUR	THE MARCH OF THE MULTIPLIERS	26
	4.1 Introduction	26
	4.2 Rock Bottom	26
	4.3 The Famous Forty-Five	28

	4.4	The Multiplier	30
	4.5	Plus Taxes	32
	4.6	More Multipliers	33

FIVE NEXT TO NOTHING   37
    5.1 Introduction   37
    5.2 On the Terrors of Notation   37
    5.3 Mind your P's and Q's   38
    5.4 Second Best to a Tangent   41
    5.5 The Brewer's Tale   43
    5.6 The Dee Why Dee Ecks Show   46
    5.7 For the Notebook   49

SIX THE DANCE OF THE DERIVATIVES   51
    6.1 Introduction   51
    6.2 Take your Partners   51
    6.3 The Power Reel   52
    6.4 The Publisher's Tale   55
    6.5 The Owner's Tale   55
    6.6 An Elastic Example   57
    6.7 Robinson's Reel   58
    6.8 The Product Reel   59
    6.9 Another Elastic Example*   60
    6.10 More Elasticity!   63
    6.11 The Trainer's Tale*   63
    6.12 For the Notebook   66

SEVEN PEAKS, VALLEYS AND LEDGES   68
    7.1 Introduction   68
    7.2 Memory Joggers   68
    7.3 A (Long) Tale of Two Averages   69
    7.4 Take Seconds   74
    7.5 The Prophets' Trail   76
    7.6 For the Notebook   81

EIGHT THE CAMP OF THE CURLY DEES   84
    8.1 Introduction   84
    8.2 Down Memory Lane   85
    8.3 Bring on the Curly Dees!   87
    8.4 The Professors' Tale   89
    8.5 Some Familiar Results   92
    8.6 Badges of Rank*   95
    8.7 For the Notebook   97

*These sections are more difficult and can be missed on a first reading.

Contents

NINE	**CLIMBS OF THE CURLY DEES**	98
	9.1 Introduction	98
	9.2 Paths and Contours	98
	9.3 The Total Diffs	100
	9.4 Three Swift Climbs	100
	9.5 Total Dees	103
	9.6 Curly Dee Meets Leaning Lambda*	106
	9.7 For the Notebook	111
TEN	**FROM SCENES LIKE THESE**	113
	10.1 Introduction	113
	10.2 Hunting for Zeros	113
	10.3 Summits, Valleys and Passes	115
	10.4 A Brief Encounter with the Summing Sids*	119
	10.5 The Way Ahead	125
	10.6 Selected Ideas on Further Reading	125
	10.7 Mathematics for Numerates?	127
REFERENCES		129
INDEX		132

FOR JOHN VAIZEY

Preface

This book originated in lectures on remedial mathematics given ten years ago at Brunel University to first-year social science students. Professor (now Lord) Vaizey gave me the assignment, presumably on the principle that poachers make good gamekeepers, because I was (and happily remain) a mathematical simpleton.

Much of the book — roughly Chapters 5 to 9 — has been given informally for the past six years to individual students at the University of Strathclyde in a 'calculus for idiots' form. Within its limitations the course achieves its objectives: the students' fear of mathematics is overcome, and their new-found confidence helps them cope with their economics. This underlines a point I have long maintained — that, if the approach is sympathetic and light-hearted enough, the innumerate will respond and make progress towards numeracy.

Many colleagues and former students contributed to the approach adopted. Lord Vaizey has been a major source of encouragement since I first joined his department as a lecturer. Professors Tait, Furness, Bain and Clunies-Ross at the University of Strathclyde have generously turned a blind eye to my activities in the mathematics underground (though they are entirely without blame for my approach!) and the course will, I hope, continue to develop (perhaps proceeding to include elementary econometrics and introductory axiomatic choice theory). I am particularly grateful to Kim Swales who read through the text and drew my attention to obscurities and to many outright errors. Professor David Simpson also read the manuscript and made useful suggestions. But any faults and errors that remain are, of course, my own.

Patricia, Florence, Beatrice and Alexander have tolerated my wanderings over the Mathematics Mountains with their usual patience. One day soon I shall take the children with me on an expedition there, knowing that an introduction to numeracy will enable them to avoid learning economics the hard way.

Morningside, Edinburgh   G.K.
1981

ONE

For Whom the Course Tolls

1.1 Introduction

I had a growing feeling in the later years of my work at the subject that a good mathematical theorem dealing with economic hypotheses was very unlikely to be good economics: and I went more and more on the rules — (1) Use mathematics as a shorthand language, rather than as an engine of enquiry. (2) Keep to them till you have done. (3) Translate into English. (4) Then illustrate by examples that are important in real life. (5) Burn the mathematics. (6) If you can't succeed in (4), burn (3). This last I did often.

Alfred Marshall

Economists have not kept to Marshall's rules. Mathematics has become an 'engine of enquiry' in all branches of economics. The results can be seen in the academic journals: very few articles confine themselves to purely literary statements and many are almost entirely mathematical. Textbooks make mathematical statements which assume that students are numerate as well as literate.

The trend has accelerated over the past decade. Compare two well-known intermediate microeconomics textbooks written within six years of each other: Ferguson's *Microeconomic Theory* [1969, revised edition] and Koutsoyiannis's *Modern Microeconomics* [1975, first edition]. Ferguson has a few mathematical derivations as footnotes in the last chapters of his book. Koutsoyiannis, on the other hand, brings formal mathematics right into the text from the start and supplements these with footnotes. The only concession she makes to the innumerate student is the use of a different typeface for the mathematics.

Innumerates can still qualify in economics, but the trend is firmly towards a mathematically based discipline. Indeed, as in a marathon, there is a gap between front runners and back markers. Kelvin Lancaster claimed in 1969 that 'traditional elementary price theory texts are at least a generation behind advanced theory in content and approach' and Walsh [1970] demonstrated this by using elementary properties of point sets, in place of calculus, to derive familiar theorems in microeconomics without the many restrictive assumptions of traditional theory.

How confident, in these circumstances, can an innumerate economist feel about employment prospects? If the mathematics used by the professsion is being revolutionised faster than it is being diffused among students, we have a form of built-in obsolescence.

Not all economists were worried by the trend towards mathematical reasoning. Indeed many welcomed it. Peston, for example, [1969] believed that the antipathy to a mathematical approach produced professional journals 'full of a great deal of meaningless controversy which might have been avoided if economists had understood how to formulate a model and put its conclusions to the test' [p. vii].

Unfortunately, mathematical competence has not purged the journals of all 'meaningless controversy' — in the opinion of some it has encouraged it! — but the main point must be accepted that mathematics has done much to make explicit what is involved in many areas of economic theorising. Generally it has been more of a benefit than a burden, though the pendulum may have swung a trifle far: instead of a theory without measurement, we may have created measurement without theory.

Many leading economists expect their readers to be numerate. Peacock and Shaw, for example, in *The Economic Theory of Fiscal Policy* [1976, revised edition, p. 5] assert:

> It is a sign of the revolution in economics education that we can state with some confidence that a student who has grasped the elements of mathematical economics should have no difficulty with following this text.

But what if the student has not 'grasped the elements of mathematical economics'? For example, if you don't understand what they mean by

$$dY = \frac{\partial Y}{\partial \theta} d\theta + \frac{\partial Y}{\partial \phi} d\phi$$

there would be little point trying to read Peacock and Shaw, because they assume that you can cope with Total Differentials.

1.2 For Whom then?

This book is for students who have realised rather late in their study of economics that some acquaintance with mathematics would benefit them. In general, they won't have much time to allocate to additional work — they may even be entering their final undergraduate year, or their first graduate term.

Having decided to allocate some (even only a little) time to mathematics, they may still have doubts about its eventual pay-off (either in an understanding of the subject or in improved prospects of a job). But they shouldn't waste too much time worrying about results, particularly if their time constraint has become critical.

It should be made clear perhaps that this is not a *textbook* in the conventional sense, nor a comprehensive survey of mathematical economics. It is an introduction to the fringes of mathematics and is unashamedly aimed at *innumerate economists*: it presumes nothing about previous mathematics. But it does assume that the reader has some economics. I conceive of him as someone who has completed intermediate level economics and wants a swift tour to get a feel of the subject without the formality of course work. The economics student has an enormous advantage here over others. His knowledge of literary economics involves (literally!) scores of implicitly mathematical ideas. By using his economics he can make relatively swift progress, because he already understands the mathematics implicit in economics. Many students who have mastered difficult ideas in economics, and produce good tutorial essays on complicated concepts involving several interlocking variables, also claim that mathematics is a closed book for them. The verbal reasoning they have to employ to reach a high standard in economics often involves notions which are far more difficult than much of the mathematics in this book.

The innumerate's aversion to mathematics must be the result of poor, if not downright bad, teaching. No single book or course of lectures can turn him into a wizard mathematical economist. The aim here is more modest. He won't reach the Frontier reading this book (and, anyway, the mathematics it covers is already well short of the frontier of recent work in point sets). But he may be able to follow 'what's going on' in the kind of textbooks and journal articles that he will be required to read to complete his course.

I encourage the view, anathema to purists — and they are right, of course — that a rigorous understanding of mathematics isn't necessary if you wish to find your way around the literature, any more than a degree in fine art is necessary if you wish to find your way around the Louvre. You don't need to know Ohm's Law to switch on a light — you only need to know where the switch is. The location of the switch isn't always immediately apparent, as anybody knows who has stumbled round a strange bathroom midway through a party! You sometimes have to work at finding the switch, and this is as true for mathematics as it is for light switches in strange bathrooms. I assume that the reader is motivated enough to work tolerably hard at finding the mathematical switches which will throw some light on those problems in economics most open to a mathematical approach.

Scepticism is understandable; many numerates do 'speak with forked tongues'. They promise bread and they give you a stone. They hold your hand for the first chapter and then shoot off into the clouds. This text doesn't do that. It sticks with you, all the way, because it is written by one of *you*, not one of *them*!

1.3 The Mathematics Mountains

Mathematics is like a mountain range. Down in the plains, where most of us live, we see the mountains only at a distance. The foothills are a little nearer, but they are covered with Number Plants which grow in great profusion, emitting soporific doses of tedium whenever an innocent mind passes nearby. Many of the mountains are permanently covered in Clouds of Notation, and you have to rise to great heights to have any chance of appreciating the beauty of their points — and for many of them, even that is fruitless.

Some people spend a lifetime exploring in the mountains — some few leave the plains and are never seen by ordinary people again. Many who do return after a prolonged sojourn suffer from an affliction of the tongue — they make sounds but cannot be understood. This impediment is apparently induced by overdoses of Complexity, a draught that flows in abundance in these mountains.

Almost everybody living in the plains knows about the Mathematics Mountains and a few have been to the foothills, where humourless people prowl about chanting things of an incredibly boring nature, which is more than normal people can stand. If — and this is rare — you *can* stand the boredom, you may not be able to take the surge in adrenalin as they launch into chorus chants of 'Algebra!', 'Quadratics!', and 'Cosines and Secants!' After dark there are new terrors to be endured. Night riders (thinly disguised mathematics teachers) order their cowed and quivering victims about mercilessly: 'Square that hypotenuse!', 'Drop your Perpendiculars!', 'Collect those Terms!', 'Cross Multiply!', and 'No, no you idiot, you've got it wrong again!'

Getting beyond the foothills into the mountains is no easy matter. The only way is through Passes, and these are patrolled by Pass Holders, a faceless cartel if ever there was one, who harry and hassle you, and make you perform a devilishly cunning trick: you must tell them about items in the Knowledge Box *without* seeing them beforehand. And, unless you are at least fifty per cent right they won't let you pass.

The pass holders let you try the trick only once a year. Some people try time and time again. Others who pass soon return to the plains having seen all the Mathematics Mountains they feel are good for them. But most people have experienced such disasters and humiliations in or near the passes that they forsake the mountain trail for ever. They are convinced, and convince others, that the Mathematics Mountains are not really a proper place for nice people.

This text can be thought of as a guide book. Its author has explored parts of the Mathematics Mountains and discovered that most of the people who thrive there are really quite kindly when you get to know them. They indulge in the behaviour they are famous for only because they don't know any better (it is how they were initiated themselves), though a few do genuinely believe that the plains people deserve the treatment they get — 'Those who anticipate humiliations should experience them!'

The secret of making serious mathematicians leave you alone is really very simple. The one thing they can't abide is sloppiness, or, as they express it, *lack of rigour*. Hence, in your trek in the mountains, whenever a real mathematician approaches you, all you have to shout is: 'No rigour here!' The effect is amazing. All card-carrying members of the Mathematicians Union take to their heels at the first sight of lack of rigour, let alone at the sound of its proclamation as a principle.

Necessarily, this expedition is a short one. It sticks closely to a chosen path. Wandering off the path is not advisable, as there are bands of Marauding Mathematicians on the loose who will torment you with mind-boggling lectures. As with the sex life of the rhinoceros (of interest only to another rhinoceros), the lectures of Marauding Mathematicians aren't really of any relevance to you. Also, unfortunately, much of the natural beauty of the Mathematics Mountains will have to be missed on this trek. Nor can we take time out to watch the antics of distant Troops of Mathematical Terms. Sometimes we must jump from peak to peak, missing out the fascinating valleys below; at other times we move along the valley floor with our heads down and no glances up the slopes around us.

1.4 Do's and Don't's

First you must overcome the feeling of horror at the sight of a page of mathematical symbols. You can help yourself here by not flicking through this book to the end, because, unlike a detective story, it offers no clues that way. You may even endanger the expedition. Read through the text, without too much skipping, at whatever pace you find most comfortable. A regular twenty- to forty-minute session is much better than infrequent reading bouts of several hours — they will become less frequent and shorter if you attempt too much at a time.

Try to avoid simply 'reading' through the examples. Write them down, including the working. Nine-tenths of the innumerate's problem with mathematics is due to premature verbalising of the mathematical symbols. Only accomplished mathematicians can 'read' symbols like the text of a book. These symbols are a shorthand for long verbal expressions. To help you cope with the problem, I have verbalised mathematical statements below each example in italics. A page of mathematics can be intimidating if you try to apply a literary skill to a non-literary form. If you realise this, your anxiety about symbols will diminish. Ironically, because we are exploring new territory, the mathematics pages look even more intimidating than they usually are. In advanced texts only the main mathematical steps are summarised; the reader 'fills in' the connecting steps himself. Here, we fill in *every step* in a manipulation to make certain that you follow the argument, though there is a cost in a more frightening visual appearance — but as an economist you will understand the inescapable consequences of trade-offs!

There is a great deal of literary exposition in the text. This is both deliberate and necessary. It is *deliberate* because it is an alternative to endless pages of mathematics — this way everybody will be able to recognise *something* on each page. It is *necessary* because we are using the body of economic theory to illustrate mathematical concepts and manipulations.

You should have no difficulty with the economics — it is pitched somewhere between A-level and a first-year degree course — though on some topics you may well be a trifle rusty. You can use your economics to learn something about mathematics. And if you aren't too sure about something in the economics, look it up in your textbook.

The economics examples are highly simplified, as you will soon notice. When mathematics is introduced it is discussed extensively in the text (each step of the manipulation is given). There is no absolutely rigid way to tackle a problem in mathematics, and if the method in the text is different from your own preference use the method you find most suited to your needs.

You will note the absence of foot-and-note-disease. This is also a deliberate policy decision. Footnotes have their place in many books but here they would distract the reader. The general principle applied has been to eliminate anything which couldn't justify a place in the text itself.

Reference is made to the literature, and you will find the details in the bibliography. Author and date of publication are given in the style of most academic journals. A central aim of the text is to enable readers to use the literature, and to this end suggestions are made which will be within your competence as you complete each topic.

Mathematics lends itself to a single 'right' answer and an infinite number of 'wrong' ones. Getting wrong answers can be demoralising. But while we oughtn't to make a virtue of inaccuracy, we must remember that this book is a Guide to the Subject not a Treatise on Mastering Mathematical Skills. Don't be dismayed by unfulfilled, and probably unattainable, standards of perfection; this is a clear case of optimisation being better than maximisation!

TWO

Equilibrium Rules, OK?

2.1 Introduction

No matter how close to grief you come in your economics, you already know, probably without realising it, a great deal of mathematics. Much of the economic theory which is taught today in the classroom owes its origins to the work of mathematically-minded economists. Marshall, in the words of Schumpeter [1954], 'was careful to banish his mathematics from the surface of his argument', and generations of students worked through his *Principles* without realising their 'obligations to the mathematically trained minority' of the discipline. Of the thirteen front-rank economists of the new marginalist, or neoclassical, school at the turn of the century, ten were competent mathematicians. Indeed, the neoclassical school, with its new theories of value and distribution, was basically the application of the calculus to economics. If you understand the neoclassical theories of value, you effectively understand the principal ideas of the calculus. The next chapters will demonstrate this to you. In this chapter we will begin the Quest for the Calculus with a look at the mathematical implications of equilibrium ideas in economics.

2.2 The Neoclassical Idea

Since the so-called Marginal Revolution (1870–90), mainstream economics has been dominated by equilibrium analysis. The textbook theories of resource allocation, household demand, rewards to factors and market structure, for example, have been formulated as problems of equilibrium. The classical economists (Smith, Ricardo, Malthus, Mill and the dissident, Marx) were more concerned with the rate of growth of aggregate output and its distribution among the classes of society than with what we know today as microeconomics.

Smith (1723–1790) defined *political economy* as a study of the 'nature and causes of the wealth of nations'. By wealth he meant the absolute size of, and growth in, what we think of today as national income. Ricardo (1772–1823) considered that the 'principal problem' was to 'determine the laws which regulate' the distribution of the 'whole produce of the earth'. Marx (1818–1883) concentrated on the distribution problem, and founded his political economy on the drive to capital accumulation and the exploitation of labour.

Some Marxists claim that marginalism was a weapon of the class struggle against the ideas of Marx. If you aren't familiar with the relativist and absolutist interpretations of the impetus for new ideas in economics you should read through the papers in Black, Coats & Goodwin [1973] and chapter 8, 'The Marginal Revolution', in Blaug [1968, second edition]. For a relativist view, you may sample Robinson and Eatwell [1973].

Jevons, Menger, Walras and Marshall introduced marginalism into economics, and whatever conclusions are drawn about their motives (though a conspiratorial interpretation of their work grossly overestimates the importance their theories had in their day to an audience wider than their students) it must be agreed that they have had a lasting impact. Association of the new marginalism with utilitarian philosophy, however, proved less lasting. The most important thing about Marginal Utility is the adjective not the noun. Utilitarianism gave way to modern microeconomics. It had to. 'If one is a utilitarian in philosophy,' wrote Hicks [1939], 'one has a perfect right to be utilitarian in one's economics. But if one is not (and few people are utilitarians nowadays), one also has a right to an economics free of utilitarian assumptions' [p. 18].

For pedagogical reasons, all modern texts include an exposition of utility theory; the neoclassical texts to introduce the *Equimarginal Principle* and the radical texts for criticism. In a utility theory framework, the Equimarginal Principle can be summarised neatly:

> A consumer with a given budget faces various goods, each with a given price, How will the consumer allocate his budget? Assuming that the consumer seeks something called utility from the goods consumed, it follows that income will be spent to acquire the largest possible amount of utility purchaseable with the given budget. The consumer's utility is maximised when the marginal unit of expenditure contributes the same increment in utility. For this to occur, a transfer of expenditure from one good to another must contribute less utility from an extra unit of the other good than the last unit of the original good. (Such a transfer will reduce total utility because the consumer gives up more utility than is gained.) Total utility is maximised when the marginal utilities of the purchased goods are proportional to their prices.

The consumer is in a state of equilibrium when utility is maximised and utility is maximised when the equimarginal principle applies.

The equimarginal principle is the corner stone of neoclassical equilibrium economics. Since Marshall's day, it has been extended across allocative problems generally. As it has been extended it has become more abstract, leading Kaldor [1972] to make a strong criticism of post-War trends:

> [Neoclassical equilibrium involves] propositions which the *pure* mathematical economist has shown to be valid only on assumptions that are manifestly unreal — that is to say, directly contrary to experience and not just 'abstract'. In fact, equilibrium theory has reached the stage where the pure theorist has successfully (though perhaps inadvertently) demonstrated that the main implications of this theory cannot possibly hold in reality; but has not yet managed to pass his message down the line to the textbook writer and the classroom [p. 1240].

Strong stuff, indeed.

Kaldor's target is the Set Theoretic approach of Debreu [1959], about which Walsh [1970] is so enthusiastic. In Walsh's view the General Equilibrium axioms scientifically establish the theory which Kaldor considers irrelevant. Debreu denied that the logically true implications of the axioms are relevant for a real world; he established by abstract reasoning the conditions under which a price system would be in general equilibrium. For this to occur, demand and supply of factors and products would have to be determined simultaneously.

General Equilibrium Theory is an integral part of neoclassical economics. It developed, largely on the continent, in parallel with Marshall's Partial Equilibrium Theory. Both theories apply maximising behaviour under constraints in a perfectly competitive environment. The main difference lies in the number of variables allowed into the analysis. Marshall takes the price and quantity of a *single* commodity, while general equilibrium takes the price and quantities of numerous commodities, incomes of consumers and production functions of firms, and attempts to specify the conditions under which the total system will be in equilibrium.

Walras [1874] made a heroic attempt to develop mathematical tools for a general equilibrium solution, but the practical applications of his results were less obvious than those that Marshall [1890] achieved. Typically, Cournot [1838] recognised that for 'a complete and precise solution of the partial problems of the economic system, it is inevitable that one must consider the system as a whole'. But the more abstract the analysis the more unrealistic it is.

2.3 On Equilibrium

A pendulum at rest is in equilibrium. When it oscillates it tends to return to rest. Small movements on either side of its rest position will gradually diminish in swing until it comes to rest again. Unless some force is applied to the pendulum it will remain at rest. Machlup [1958] defined equilibrium as 'a constellation of selected interrelated variables so adjusted to one another that no inherent tendency to change prevails in the model which they constitute'. The important thing about equilibrium in an economic model is its property of 'no inherent tendency to change'.

Equilibrium is a property of the model, not a description or conclusion about the real world. Hence equilibrium economics is an analytical device, designed to highlight certain relationships between variables and how they react upon each other when movement occurs from one equilibrium position to another. By starting with the related variables at rest and introducing a disturbance, the next position of rest must occur when all the effects of that disturbance on the variables has been completed. When the equilibrium positions are compared, we can be sure that the changes in the variables have occurred exclusively as a result of the disturbance. In the first position of equilibrium there is no inherent tendency to change. Hence any change must be caused by the introduction of the disturbance. In the next position of equilibrium all the tendencies to change have worked themselves through [Machlup, 1952, pp. 6–7].

Economists are not the only people who work with models. A map is a model. Car and aircraft designers use models in wind tunnels. These physical models contrast with the conceptual models used by economists (though some enterprising lecturer a few years ago marketed a physical model of an economy, complete with tubes, a hydraulic pump and some coloured liquid, and Irving Fisher (1892) for his PhD designed an hydrostatic mechanism which used water levels to prove the existence of utility).

Perfect competition is a model consisting of specific assumptions. Demand and supply models involve a large number of specific assumptions about rationality and utility maximisation in households and diminishing returns and profit maximisation in firms. Such models may be represented verbally, graphically or mathematically. The presumption made about mathematical models is that they are likely to be less ambiguous than literary models. This improves understanding of the relationships between the variables, provided, of course, we remember, before operational conclusions are drawn, that the real world involves complex time-lags which are not incorporated in timeless comparative statics.

The great strength of a mathematical model is its dependence upon general laws of mathematical manipulation. The designer cannot 'make up' rules to suit arbitrary or predetermined conclusions. The manipulations are derived from the accepted science of mathematics and can be tested by anybody with a knowledge of, and competence in, the science.

2.4 Some Kit

To get into shape for the more arduous

2. Equilibrium Rules, OK?

slopes ahead we shall begin our expedition to the Mathematics Mountains with a walk in the foothills. Just as it is foolhardy to go climbing without sensible preparation, so it isn't very clever to attempt even the gentle slopes without some specially prepared kit. But in contrast to the Army where new recruits are issued with every item of kit in one session (much of which does not fit!), here we requisition only those items we need for each itinerary.

The first item of our kit is known as a *variable*. This is an incredibly versatile piece of equipment: it can take on innumerable values and identities. You may know of some of its guises from economics: *price* is a variable, *profit* is a variable, *unemployment* is a variable, *national income* is a variable, and so on. Variables are most interesting when they are related in some way to each other.

The next piece of kit is known as a *constant*. Shackle [1973, p. 27], leaving no room for improvement, gave a brilliant analogous definition of a constant:

> The throttle of a motor-cycle engine can be open to various degrees, and the engine will accordingly propel the machine at more or less speed, but the bore and the stroke of the engine, and its gear ratios, will remain the same, and these constant design features will determine the precise effect of opening the throttle to this or that extent. Evidently when we look at a different type of motor-cycle we may find a different set of 'constant' design features.

Hence, a constant doesn't change for a specific relationship but may change for another one. This doesn't make a constant a variable. Once the constant is specified, it holds the same value whatever changes take place in the variables within the given relationship.

During this first excursion we shall have to use our variables and constants a great deal. We use them to keep our balance as we walk along the extremely narrow pathways of the foothills. If we lose our balance at any point we shall slip down the muddy banks, to our acute embarrassment. To achieve a firm foothold anywhere in the foothills (and other places besides) we simply have to create a piece of apparatus known to mathematicians as an *equation*. This is done by combining variables and constants together into specific relationships. Once the equation has been formed, there is no danger of our losing balance, provided we remember some absolutely simple rules for walking with equations.

Equations consist of two parts: a Left Hand Side (LHS) and a Right Hand Side (RHS). A simple gadget known as an Equals Sign ($=$) joins them together. No equation is complete without one, but equations only work if you remember never to load up the LHS with more than you load the RHS (and, of course, vice versa). In fact we might as well make clear the most important rule about equations:

> *Anything you do to one side you must always do to the other.*

Whatever else you forget for the moment, you must never forget that rule. Your equilibrium depends upon it.

Equations come in *three* basic models and you should be familiar with them.

Variables, we have said, are most interesting when they are related to one another in some way. For instance, if we said that national income (Y) consists of two variables, consumption (C) and investment (I), and nothing else, we would be *identifying* the components of national income. We could write this out as:

National income consists of, or is equal to, consumption and investment.

Or, to save ink, we could put it into symbols:

$$Y = C + I \qquad [1]$$

Similarly, we could state that profit (π)

consists of the difference between two variables, revenue (R) and cost (C). In words this would be written

> *Profit is equal to the difference between revenue and cost.*

or, using symbols,

$$\pi = R - C. \qquad [2]$$

And, again, we could say that if the money supply (M) is multiplied by the velocity (V) of its circulation it will be identically equal to prices (P) multiplied by the number of transactions (T). In words we have

> *Money times velocity equals prices times transactions.*

In symbols, we have

$$MV = PT. \qquad [3]$$

All these statements have been written in the form of equations. The Left Hand Side (LHS) is defined as being *identically equal* to whatever is on the Right Hand Side (RHS). For this reason these types of equations are known as *identities* and are sometimes given a special Equals Sign: ($\equiv$). In an identity we define what a variable consists of.

The next most common form of an equation is known as a *behavioural*, or *functional*, *equation*. You will find plenty of these in the Mathematics Mountains. They are used when a behavioural relationship between variables is assumed. For example, if we assert that when the price variable takes a specific value it *causes* the quantity variable to take on a specific value, we are making an assumption about the linked behaviour of price and quantity. When we use symbols to state the behavioural relationship we often add a simple gadget to the equals sign. Writing the price-quantity behavioural relationship in words we get

> *The quantity* (Q) *demanded is dependent upon the price* (P).

But in symbols we are not saying that quantity is *equal* to price, we are saying that quantity is *dependent* upon price, which is something entirely different. When something is dependent upon something in mathmatics it is a *function* (f) of it. Thus, in symbols we write

$$Q = f(P) \qquad [4]$$

> *Quantity demanded is a function of price.*

Other examples of behavioural equations probably spring readily to mind. From macroeconomics we have: employment (N) is a dependent upon output (O), which in symbols is written

$$N = f(O). \qquad [5]$$

And output is dependent upon effective demand (D):

$$O = f(D). \qquad [6]$$

In equilibrium economics the important equation is the *equilibrium condition*. No model is complete without it. It is almost as important as maintaining your balance, because without the equilibrium condition your trek into the foothills will have no purpose and you will get hopelessly lost, or — just as bad — waste your time. It isn't enough to identify the composition of the variables, nor even to assert some behavioural relationship between them. It is the equilibrium condition of the variables that counts. Once the equilibrium conditions have been specified, you can use the model to explore the territory through which you intend to pass.

The most obvious example of an equilibrium condition can be taken from the simple economics of a market. For equilibrium to exist in a market there should be no tendency for the quantity demanded (D) to be different from the quantity supplied (S). In words we write

> *Quantity demanded equals the quantity supplied.*

2. Equilibrium Rules, OK?

In symbols this becomes

$$D = S. \qquad [7]$$

Another example, from macroeconomics, is the equilibrium condition for a national income: intended savings (S) equal intended investment (I). In symbols, we write

$$S = I. \qquad [8]$$

If [8] obtains, there will be no inherent tendency for national income to change.

2.5 The Foothills

Our first excursion takes us to some fairly gentle slopes. You will practise using your new kit in the field. You will also pick up one or two simple dodges when you see what clever things you can do with equations. But stick to the rules laid down by your guide. They may seem somewhat patronising to some of you, but when the going gets a good deal tougher it is the strivers who thrive and the pompous too-clever-by-half types who need mountain-rescue operations.

The main thing to remember about an equation is its balancing property. If it doesn't balance it isn't an equation. Only for as long as each side of the equation remains equal will it continue as an equation. Therefore *whatever you do to one side you must always do to the other*.

Take the theory of the firm, for example, and remember that the Average Revenue (AR) of the firm is found by dividing Total Revenue (TR) by the Quantity of Output sold (Q). In words:

Average revenue equals total revenue divided by quantity sold.

And in symbols:

$$AR = \frac{TR}{Q}. \qquad [9]$$

You will also remember that total revenue is found by multiplying the quantity sold by the price (p) per unit. This also can be written as

$$TR = Qp \qquad [10]$$

Total revenue equals quantity times price.

Equation [9] states that average revenue consists of two variables: total revenue (TR) and quantity (Q) and the RHS of equation [10] consists of two variables, quantity (Q) and price (p). By inspection you will note that the variable total revenue (TR) appears in both equations — it is on the RHS of [9] and the LHS of [10] — and that variable Q also appears in both equations — on the RHS of [9] and [10]. This may have some relevance.

If we wanted to find a relationship between average revenue (AR) and price (p), how would we set about it? Well, as average revenue appears in [9] but not [10] and price appears in [10] but not [9] it is clearly necessary to get both variables into the same equation. To do this we use a dodge known in the trade as *substitution*. You should note carefully how it is done, because you never know when you may have to use it.

Substitution requires that one variable is replaced by another variable exactly equal to it (so as not to disturb the balance of the equation). The variable, total revenue, in [9] is defined in [10]: $TR = Qp$. If we substitute in [9] something from [10] exactly equal to the variable in [9] we don't alter the balance of the equation at all. Therefore we can rewrite for the RHS of [9] the substituted variable from [10]:

$$AR = \frac{Qp}{Q} \qquad [11]$$

Average revenue equals the quantity sold times price divided by the quantity sold.

Equation [9] has not been imbalanced by the substitution in any way, but we have brought the variable average revenue into the same equation as price. Equation [11] now states the relationship between average revenue and price.

The RHS of [11] has the variable Q above the line and the same variable below the line. You can follow the next step easily, if you haven't spotted it already, by asking yourself what you would do if your tutor told you he had multiplied your essay mark by ten and simultaneously divided it by ten? Would you have cause for celebration or not? Hardly, because you are no better (or worse) off by such a manipulation:

To multiply and divide a variable by the same number does not alter the value of the variable.

This is a most useful dodge, obvious as it may appear at the moment. It allows you to *eliminate* the variables concerned without upsetting the balance of the equation (which, you must must always remember, is the major objective of the exercise). When we eliminate the variable Q from [11],

$$AR = \frac{Qp}{Q} \qquad [11]$$

we get

$$AR = p \qquad [12]$$

Average revenue equals price.

You know, from your economics, that this is correct.

There is always more than one way to the top, and this is especially true in the Mathmatics Mountains, where there are innumerable ways up a trail — if you know how. Suppose, this time, we take equation [10]

$$TR = Qp \qquad [10]$$

Total revenue equals quantity times price

and divide both sides by the variable Q. Because we are doing to one side exactly what we are doing to the other, the balance of the equation remains undisturbed:

$$\frac{TR}{Q} = \frac{Qp}{Q}. \qquad [13]$$

From your first steps along the trail you will remember that a variable multiplied and divided by the same term must remain exactly the same. If it isn't altered in value, then the multiplier-divider term can be eliminated without affecting the balance of the equation. Hence [13] becomes

$$\frac{TR}{Q} = p \qquad [14]$$

Total revenue divided by quantity equals price.

On inspection of the LHS of [14] you will notice that it is the same as the RHS of [9] and anything that is equal to a variable may be substituted in its place, which permits us to write

$$AR = \frac{TR}{Q} \qquad [9]$$

and substituting [9] into [14] we get

$$AR = p \qquad [15]$$

Average revenue equals price.

This is exactly what we achieved earlier.

The mathematics of these simple operations can be summarised:

*If you treat both sides of an equation exactly the same, then the balance of the equation is undisturbed.

*You may substitute for any variable in the equation an exactly equal variable without disturbing the equation.

*In fact, in general, if you take something away from one side you must take it away from the other; if you add something to one side you must add it to the other; if you multiply one side you must multiply the other by the same amount, and if you divide one side by something you must divide the other by the same amount.

*A number multiplied and divided by the same number remains the same.

2. Equilibrium Rules, OK?

Therefore the multiplier and divider can be eliminated without upsetting the balance of the equation.

You deserve a short rest here on your first hike into the foothills. It is a good idea to look back over the trail and see what territory you have covered. For those of you who have seen the trail before and would like a slight change in scenery it might be an idea for you to peruse, though not necessarily to learn by rote, some rules out of the Mathematicians' Highway Code. These can be noted down in some convenient place and called up for service when, and only when, you require them.

2.6 For the Notebook

The number system has some common laws governing addition, subtraction, multiplication and division. A few of these laws are summarised here for reference.

It doesn't matter in what order two numbers are added together:

$$a + b = b + a.$$

It doesn't matter how numbers are grouped when they are to be added together:

$$(a + b) + c = a + (b + c).$$

It doesn't matter in what order two numbers are multiplied together:

$$a \cdot b = b \cdot a.$$

It doesn't matter how numbers are grouped when they are to be multiplied together:

$$a(b \cdot c) = (a \cdot b)c.$$

If two numbers are to be summed and then multiplied by a third number, this is equivalent to multiplying each number separately by the third number and summing the result:

$$a(b + c) = ab + ac.$$

THREE

Walk–Don't Run!

3.1 Introduction

You have begun your ascent from the plain. But for a little while yet the good views are obscured by undergrowth, and you will have to put up with some not very interesting walks until we get clear of the scrub line. But it isn't all boring and dreary — far from it. Nor is it endless effort. Your guide will show you the swiftest pathways up the gentle nursery slopes to the more open country ahead. You will also be issued with some more kit to use with your equations, and because some of it is a wee bit cumbersome you are advised to walk along the chosen paths and not run up them.

3.2 The Executive's Tale

One of the rewards of walking in the Mathematics Mountains is the opportunity it provides to meet people from all sectors of the economy. You will find everyone very inquisitive and eager to converse with you. Mainly this can be put down to their need to have someone solve the little (and sometimes big) problems they face in running their businesses, or households — and, sometimes, the country's entire economy. Economists who are familiar with the Mathematics Mountains can earn fees from those searching for solutions to their problems (some of which they got from taking the advice of other economists).

On a recent walk the author was accosted by an Executive who wanted to motivate a sales force. Industrial selling requires the sales engineers to be out in the field on their own visiting potential clients. Direct supervision of their work effort is impractical. If they get up late, go home early, have long lunches and hourly coffee breaks, and practise poor inter-personal relations with clients — in other words don't try very hard — the result is reflected in the volume of sales of the company's products. The Executive had tried two policies with the sales force but neither had worked.

The first solution tried was a 'No sales — no pay' 'carrot'-type policy: the sales engineers got paid only when they sold products to customers. But the plan was abandoned when a sales engineer, failing to make any sales for a month, died of starvation. To avoid the unfortunate publicity associated with this unintentional tragedy the company adopted a 'Sell or be sacked' 'stick'-type policy: if a sales engineer wasn't making sales the consequent dismissal occurred long before malnutrition set in. But this policy too was abandoned when, in a bad week, three quarters of the sales force were sacked by the company's computer which had been programmed to issue dismissal notices if sales targets weren't met. The ex-employees sued the company for 'unfair dismissal' and won thousands in compensation.

What the Executive wanted was a payment system which would motivate the sales engineers to seek new business without starving or being sacked in a bad month.

The answer was a Remuneration Package (a fancy executive name for wages) which combined a basic minimum salary with a sales commission. When this was put to the Executive he insisted that a picture be drawn of the system so that it could be properly presented to the sales force (executives call a lecture with graphs a Presentation). In no time at all the system was illustrated and the Executive rushed off to the weekly sales meeting (some organisations spend more time meeting than working).

You can see the graph which was drawn for the Executive in Figure 3.1. It makes a

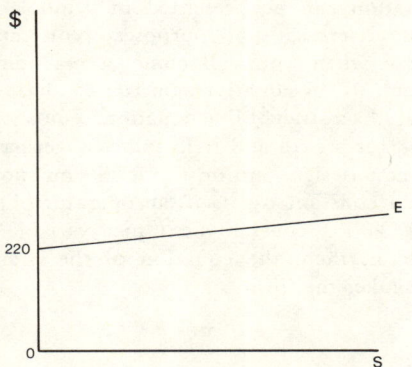

Figure 3.1

visual statement of the proposed payment system. The most appealing aspect of the graph is that it rises upwards from left to right. This alone could motivate a beneficiary, providing the ascent wasn't too arduous. To discover what is involved in the system we need some additional verbal information.

The remuneration package consists of two elements: a fixed basic salary (say, $220 a week) and a commission on sales of, say, 10 per cent of value. With your equation kit you can put that into symbols with a little help. If the gross earnings of the sales engineer are represented by E we can write down the LHS of the equation:

$$E =$$

Earnings equals (something).

We know what earnings are made up of: basic salary (B) and commission (C). This gives us the RHS:

$$E = B + C \qquad [1]$$

Earnings equals basic salary plus commission.

We have been told what both B and C consist of: $B = \$220$ and $C = 10\%$ of sales value (S). This gives us

$$E = 220 + 10\% \, S. \qquad [2]$$

In Figure 3.1 the vertical axis (the one going upwards) measures the money value of the earnings in dollars, the horizontal axis (the one running across the page) measures sales value.

The sales engineer gets $220 salary even if he sells nothing that week. Hence at zero sales (shown as the extreme left hand of the horizontal axis) the earnings value on the vertical axis is 220. If sales are made, the company increases earnings by 10 per cent of sales value. Thus, for every unit of sales value, the earnings line rises by one tenth (= 10 per cent), or, alternatively, for every ten units of sales earnings rise by one unit. The earnings line slopes upwards in the ratio of one unit vertically for ten units horizontally. This slope may motivate. If, for instance, it is 2 pm on a wet Friday and the sales engineer has made nine sales so far in the week, the trip across town may be a lot more attractive when the value of the tenth sale is regarded as a 'Home Run'.

3.3 *The Cognoscenti*

In economics you have to draw graphs hundreds of times whether you understand the mathematics of co-ordinate geometry or not (remember you don't need to know Ohm's Law to switch on a light!). Figure 3.1 showed a graph of the sales engineer's earnings and we shall pause for a moment to consider some points about this particular type of graph.

The first thing to note about the graph is that it is a straight line. Not all graphs are straight lines. But until we get well on with our quest for calculus we shall concentrate upon straight lines (which tend to congregate in the foothills, while their more elaborate cousins thrive in the rarified air of the mountains). The symbolic representation of the particular straight line in Figure 3.1 is given in equation [2]:

$$E = 220 + 0.10\, S. \qquad [2]$$

Straight-line equations consist of six bits, and these should be noted, in case you have to order up a spare part some time.

In all equations there are three main elements: the LHS, the Equals Sign and the RHS. The LHS in this case consists of a single term (E) followed by the equals sign (=). The RHS has four important bits in it. First, there is the constant: (220). No matter what happens, this always remains the same, which is why it is called a constant! Next, there is the operator sign (+) which tells you what to do to the two terms in the RHS (in this case add them). Then follow two bits together: a constant (0.10, which is a decimal alternative to 10 per cent) and a variable (S). The relationship between these two bits is absolutely crucial to the straight line. The constant tells you the *rate* at which the variable increases the LHS or (E). Thus when we say in Figure 3.1 that for every ten units of S there is a one unit increase in E, we are actually stating how far up the vertical axis we travel for every unit move along the horizontal axis. This is the *slope* of the line.

There are foothills all around us with different slopes. Some are very steep. For every step we take up these we rise much further than we would on the hills with flatter slopes. On the steeper slopes the constant which multiplies the variable is going to be bigger in value than on the shallower slopes. If, instead of 10 per cent commission, the sales engineers received 25 per cent, it would mean that for every unit increase in sales (movement along the horizontal axis) they would add more to their earnings (move higher up the vertical axis). The equation for a 25 per cent commission would read

$$E = 220 + 0.25\, S. \qquad [3]$$

Hence the constant next to the variable in straight-line equations determines the size of the contribution which that variable makes to the total on the LHS of the equation and, graphically, determines the relative steepness (or *slope*) of the straight line.

The six bits that make up a straight-line equation can be presented in symbols for general recognition purposes (you never know when you will come across one of them). If an equation consists of these six bits, it is a straight-line equation. You should look for a LHS and RHS joined together by an equals sign, and on the RHS you should see a constant by itself, an operator (+) or (−), and a constant next to a variable. In general, then, the equation of the straight line takes the form

$$y = a + bx \qquad [4]$$

where y is the variable measured on the vertical axis, a and b are constants and x is the variable measured on the horizontal axis. To find how the value of y is changed by a change in the value of x, equation [4] tells us to multiply x by the constant b and add the result to the constant a.

A well-known Italian family, whom you will get to know in these parts, are the Cognoscenti, who insist on enobling things with Titles. They are so charming (so Italian!), that no matter how much you resist, you too, like everybody else, will soon be imitating them.

Sr. Cognoscento's title for the constant a in the straight line (or, as he calls it, *linear*) equation is the Intercept Constant. If you hear somebody using that title in future you should know what they are referring to, even if you don't know what they are talking about.

If the constant a is greater than zero, as it is in Figure 3.1, it will appear up the vertical

3. Walk—Don't Run!

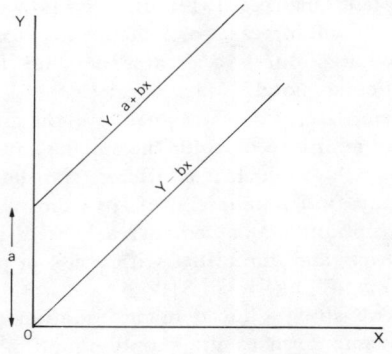

Figure 3.2

axis to show where the straight line begins. Sometimes, the constant *a* is zero, and graphically this will be represented by the straight line starting at the origin. You can get a visual example of this in Figure 3.2.

3.4 Harmless Ghosts

Before entering a new neck of the woods, we must caution you. To give some atmosphere we will quote a distinguished American citizen:

> Every beginning student of economics is (or should be) repeatedly warned of the hypothetical nature of the functional relations between the variables. There are no 'observable' supply and demand functions — unless one means merely the chalk symbols which the teacher produces on the blackboard for students to observe. All the values of the functions are imagined; the supply function assigns hypothetical quantities offered in the market to hypothetical prices paid, and the demand function assigns hypothetical quantities demanded to these prices, but since the prices and quantities are hypothetical only, they cannot be observed by anybody . . . The so-called statistical supply and demand curves have not really been 'observed'; they are the result of highly imaginative computations from data recorded at different times under different conditions and manipulated on the basis of unverifiable assumptions which range from 'plausible' to 'contrary to fact'. [Machlup, 1976, p. 547]

As long as this caution is remembered, the manipulation of hypothetical supply-and-demand curves should prove to be fairly harmless. You need to get more practice in manipulating equations and, as long as you don't start believing that ghosts exist in the real world, supply-and-demand equations are a safe topic of conversation for dark nights around a camp fire or for late night reading in an empty house.

What will induce a supply of extra output? Because extra output involves higher costs of production, elementary theory asserts that a price covering these incremental costs will be required if suppliers are to respond. The relationship between the variable price and the variable supply is assumed to be positive: if price rises supply rises, if price falls supply falls. A positive relationship of this kind can be represented graphically by an upward sloping line, such as in Figure 3.3.

One of the curiosities of economics (at least to mathematicians) is the convention, since Marshall, of placing the price variable on the vertical axis and the quantity variable

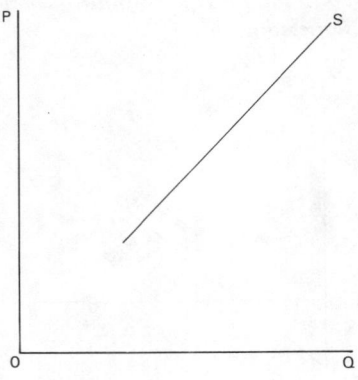

Figure 3.3

on the horizontal axis. Mathematicians place the *dependent* variable (the one which changes in response to the other variable) on the vertical axis and the *independent* variable (the one which changes on its own account) on the horizontal axis. If this was applied to economics we would have price on the horizontal axis (it being independent) and quantity on the vertical axis (it being dependent) as in Figure 3.4. In economics, however, the inertia of Marshallian convention continues, though every now and then an author makes a stand for scientific conformity and reverses them as we do here for the convenience of exposition.

The straight-line supply curve in Figure 3.4 has the familiar features previously discussed. The intercept constant $-a$ (see what I mean by the Cognoscenti's influence!) starts the line off on the vertical axis and cuts the horizontal axis some distance from the origin. The economic relevance of this is that the offer price for the output will have to be at least as much as a/b before any output is supplied. The supply line rises from left to right, starting at the intercept $-a$. Its slope is determined by the size of the constant b. The straight line equation of Figure 3.4 is the standard type and could be written

$$Q = -a + bP \qquad [5]$$

Quantity supplied equals the intercept constant plus price multiplied by the slope constant.

In plain language, [5] tells us by how much supply will increase for a change in price.

What induces a greater demand for a particular good? Marshall designated 'one general law of demand', namely, 'the greater the amount to be sold, the smaller must be the price at which it is offered in order that it may find purchasers; or, in other words, the amount demanded increases with a fall in price, and diminishes with a rise in price' [*Principles*, bk. 3, ch. 3].

The straight-line demand equation takes the same form as the supply equation [5]. It can be written as

$$Q = a - bP \qquad [6]$$

Quantity demanded is equal to the intercept constant minus the price variable multiplied by the slope constant.

In plain language [6] tells us by how much demand will change for a change in price.

A graphical version of a straight-line demand curve is shown in Figure 3.5. You already know that it slopes downwards from left to right. If you look closely at [6] you will note that the slope constant b is prefixed with a negative $(-)$ and not with a positive $(+)$ as in [5]. The price variable has to have a negative sign because the 'law of demand' requires that when price falls, demand will rise, and when price rises, demand will fall. In other words the change in the dependent variable, quantity, is the *opposite*

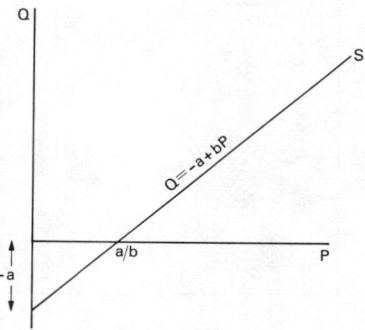

Figure 3.4

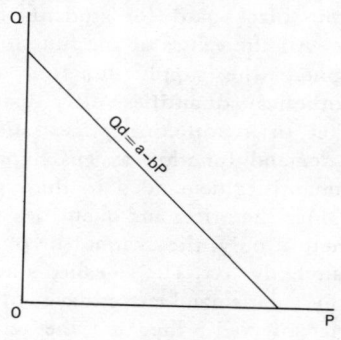

Figure 3.5

of the change in the independent variable, price.

If you inspect Figure 3.5 for a moment you will note that the intercept constant a starts the demand curve off from a relatively high point on the vertical axis. Consider the economics of this: at a zero price there is a high demand for the good. As price rises a positive but falling amount of the good is demanded, until at some high price a zero quantity is demanded. This can be seen in Figure 3.5, where the demand curve reaches the horizontal axis. At zero price there is always an excess demand for an economic good (remember that at zero price there will be a zero amount supplied) and at some positive price there will be an excess supply (zero amount demanded).

3.5 Some Fragile Flowers

One of the earliest plants to catch the fancy of economists in the foothills of the Mathematics Mountains is the apparently robust bloom of Market Equilibrium. There is no doubt that the market equilibrium variety are very impressive — they are also usually the first plants newcomers handle, and, like first love, they are seldom forgotten. But remember, in what follows they are composed of two ghosts — and two ghosts do make a difference.

From our theory we know that the market clearing price is the price at which the quantity supplied is exactly equal to the quantity demanded. This conclusion rests on the Marshallian assumption of *ceteris paribus* (other things being equal). Demand-and-supply functions isolate the price and quantity variables from all the other possible influences upon demand and supply. Marshall vigorously defended this assumption but wasn't unaware of the dangers in reading too much into it. '[When] the study of some group of tendencies,' he wrote, 'is isolated by the assumption *other things being equal*: the existence of other tendencies is not denied, but their disturbing effect is neglected for a time. The more the issue is thus narrowed, the more exactly it can be handled; but also the less closely does it correspond to real life. Exact and firm handling of a narrow issue, however, helps towards treating broader issues, in which the narrow issue is contained, more exactly than would otherwise be possible' [1890, bk. 5, ch. 5].

Marshall noted that 'violence' could be done when too wide a scope was given to the *ceteris paribus* assumption. Modern critics have commented that there may be 'no way of knowing whether a discrepancy between theory and facts refutes the theory or merely shows that *ceteris* were *imparibus*' [Hollis & Nell, 1975].

Comparative statics, you will remember, concerns itself only with equilibrium positions. It is timeless. The equilibrium price is determined instantly — the time lapse between two equilibrium states is zero, or, which amounts to the same thing, there is an infinite velocity of adjustment. For expository purposes, we often explain the adjustment process between different equilibria by slipping time into the adjustment process. Your textbook explains how a disequilibrium moves back to equilibrium when the price/quantity relationship is disturbed. If price is too 'high', the argument usually goes, there will be an excess supply (supply exceeds demand) and this will lower the market price; if price is too 'low' there will be an excess demand (demand exceeds supply) and this will raise the price. Only when price equates supply with demand will an equilibrium be reached.

In a strictly timeless model no sales or purchases will occur until the equilibrium price is reached. This has led to some quite extraordinary models of the market clearing process, with an 'auctioneer' calling out prices and checking the supply-and-demand quantities until, through constant re-contracting, he discovers the prices that will clear all the markets simultaneously. Fortunately it is only a model; otherwise there could be mass starvation while the market clearing prices were sought. It also assumes that there is no 'dissimulation and the objectionable arts of higgling' [Edgeworth, 1881, p. 30]. Everybody is absolutely honest, or at least the auctioneer has perfect information. This eliminates a real world feature of the market place, namely, the attempts by the buyer to ascertain 'the lowest price at which the seller is willing to part with his object, without disclosing, if possible, the highest price, which he, the buyer, is willing to give' [Jevons, 1871, p. 134].

Having entered the caveats we can approach market equilibrium with a spring in our step. Cast a glance at Figure 3.6 for an example of a graphical model of market

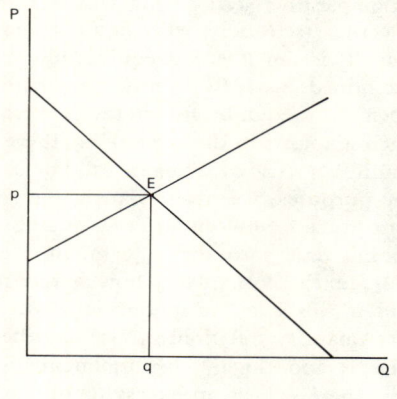

Figure 3.6

equilibrium. You have seen and drawn hundreds of them before. But this time we shall look a little closer into their construction, using simple straight-line equations and some manipulation of the variables and constants.

The market clearing price is defined as the intersection of the (hypothetical) supply-and-demand curves. Unless, and until, the intersecting price is reached, there will not be an equilibrium in the market. The equilibrium condition is defined as the equality of the amount demanded with the amount supplied. In symbols, we write this as an equation:

$$Qd = Qs \qquad [7]$$

Quantity demanded equals quantity supplied.

In Figure 3.6 we have two straight lines, and we can assume that we know their equations. Suppose that, in a particular market, the quantity hypothetically demanded of a good is given by the equation

$$Qd = 10 - 3p \qquad [8]$$

Quantity demanded equals 10 minus three times the price.

We could also suppose that the quantity supplied is given by the supply equation

$$Qs = -4 + 4p \qquad [9]$$

Quantity supplied is equal to minus 4 plus four times the price.

The manipulation to find the equilibrium price is quite simple. The equilibrium condition tells us that at equilibrium the quantity supplied equals the quantity demanded. As we have two equations for these quantities we can put them into [7] by substitution. This will give us

$$Qd = Qs \qquad [7]$$

and by substitution

$$10 - 3p = -4 + 4p. \qquad [10]$$

Equation [10] has an unknown, the value of p, and four known constants. We can discover the value of the unknown because there is one point at which the quantities demanded and supplied are the same: at the point of intersection of the two straight lines. To find the value of the unknown we have to 'solve' the equation. There is more than one way to do this and the one selected is extremely simple.

The first thing we do is to collect the like terms together. Equation [10] has numbers and the unknown price variable on both sides, and ideally we want all the numbers on one side and the unknown variables on the other. We apply the first rule of equations: to keep a balance, whatever is done to one side must be done to the other.

Add 4 to both sides to eliminate it from the RHS:

$$10 + 4 - 3p = -4 + 4 + 4p.$$

Now carry out the arithmetic to reduce the equation:

$$14 - 3p = 4p.$$

Next, add $3p$ to both sides to eliminate it from the LHS:

$$14 - 3p + 3p = 4p + 3p$$

giving

$$14 = 7p.$$

To get a value for the unknown variable in this equation we must divide both sides by 7. This will give

$$\frac{14}{7} = \frac{7p}{7}$$

Though the answer may be obvious, it is worthwhile with simple examples to walk rather than run until you have the confidence to master the more complex equations — where the answer won't be obvious.

A number multiplied and divided at the same time by another is equal to itself, and this takes care of the RHS and the arithmetic of the LHS equals 2, giving

$$2 = p.$$

At the market clearing price of $p = 2$ we have an equilibrium between the quantity demanded and the quantity supplied. What quantity will be supplied and demanded at this price? This can be found by substitution of $p = 2$ into equations [8] and [9]:

$$Qd = 10 - 3p \qquad [8]$$
$$= 10 - 3(2)$$
$$= 10 - 6$$
$$= 4$$

and

$$Qs = -4 + 4p \qquad [9]$$
$$= -4 + 4(2)$$
$$= -4 + 8$$
$$= 4.$$

Thus, the market is cleared when the price is 2 and the quantity is 4.

3.6 Madame Notation

The market equilibrium model we have just worked through is a very simple one. It also rests on the fragile foundation of hypothetical straight-line demand-and-supply schedules and the concept of stable equilibrium. Disturbances may occur, and the resulting oscillations are supposed to bring things back to equilibrium. Marshall, typically, cautioned against too rigid a view of stable equilibrium. He suggested that rather than conceiving of equilibrium as analogous to a string swinging like a pendulum, we should think of it as a string hanging in the 'troubled waters of a mill-race, whose stream was at one time allowed to flow freely, and at another partially cut off' and the person holding the string swung it 'partly rhythmically and partly arbitrary' because the 'demand and supply schedules do not in practice remain unchanged for a long time together, but are constantly being changed; and every change in them alters the equilibrium amount and the equilibrium price, and thus gives new positions to the centres about which the amount and the price oscillate' [*Principles*, 1890, bk. 5 ch. 3].

It is well to remember in what follows that you must keep your feet on the ground; otherwise you may fall victim to Mathematician's Palsy — a paralytic suspension of belief in things as they are in the real world.

The next section of the trail definitely isn't suitable for running. You are advised to walk — briskly if you must — even though you may be tempted to skip and run ahead. There is still a lot of undergrowth to cut through and we have to work our way steadily up the trail to be ready for tomorrow's spectacular event: the March of the Multipliers.

The first thing we start with is the market equilibrium model we have been admiring up to now but in its *general* rather than a specific form. Instead of using straight-line equations with numbers and an unknown (such as in [8] and [9]) we want to take a general statement of the model using letters representative of the specific terms which a particular model would require if it was to be solved for equilibrium. Such a model is set out below:

$$Qd = Qs \qquad [7]$$

$$Qd = a - bp \qquad [11]$$

$$Qs = -c + dp. \qquad [12]$$

The letters a, b, c and d represent the constants (which the Cognoscenti insist on calling 'parametric constants' or 'parameters'); a and $-c$ are the intercept constants and b and d are the slope constants of the straight lines. A graph representing these equations is shown in Figure 3.7.

The Cognoscenti have a French friend, Madame Notation, who, with Gallic persistence, runs a franchise operation supplying symbols and typefaces to mathematicians. Some of her material is extremely handy and time saving and we are in the market for a couple of them right now. Whenever we want to indicate that something is greater than something else we use the notation: $>$; and if it is smaller we use: $<$. This is merely a symbol to save writing it out in longhand.

In elementary economics we normally assume that the demand curve is negatively sloped. This means that the slope constant b has a negative sign in front of it.

3.7 In Full Bloom

We will set to work on the market equilibrium model. This will complete today's little hike and bring us to a good spot for tomorrow's parade. But remember, it is only a model, not the real world.

The mathematical steps we take are exactly the same as in the arithmetical example above. We put the RHS of the demand equation equal to the RHS of the supply equation, by substituting [11] and [12] into [7]. This gives us

$$a - bp = -c + dp. \qquad [13]$$

Each side of [13] consists of a constant and a variable multiplied by a constant. Taking this one step at a time, we start to collect like terms together, by adding c to both sides:

$$a - bp + c = -c + c + dp.$$

This eliminates c on the RHS and gets it over to the LHS, to give

$$a - bp + c = dp. \qquad [14]$$

Now eliminate bp from the LHS by adding bp to both sides:

$$a - bp + bp + c = dp + bp$$

giving

$$a + c = dp + bp \qquad [15]$$

We now have two terms on the RHS with the variable p common to them both. We can rewrite this side without altering in any

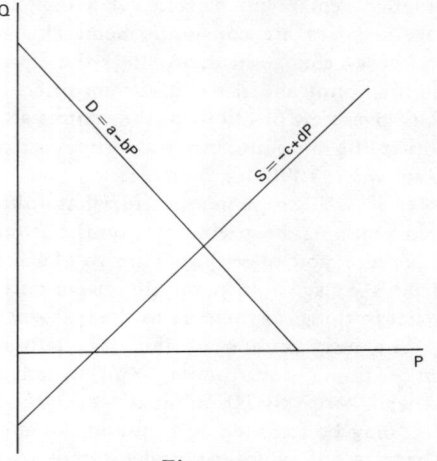

Figure 3.7

3. Walk—Don't Run!

way its value, which, therefore, leaves the equation in balance. If we put the constants d and b in brackets and place the variable p outside the bracket, we inform those interested that each term in the brackets is to be multiplied by the term outside the bracket, thus, because

$$dp + bp = p(d + b)$$

putting this into [15] gives

$$a + c = p(d + b). \qquad [16]$$

We haven't finished collecting terms because there are constants on both sides of [16]. Again, taking each step separately, we collect the constants on to the LHS by dividing both sides by $(d + b)$:

$$\frac{a + c}{d + b} = p\frac{(d + b)}{(d + b)}.$$

Because a number divided by itself is equal to 1, the RHS reduces to the variable p, giving

$$\frac{a + c}{d + b} = p.$$

By convention (and one convention is as good as another) the unknown variable is normally written on the LHS of an equation, so we write our concluding equation as

$$p = \frac{a + c}{d + b} \qquad [16]$$

Price is equal to the sum of the intercept constants divided by the sum of the slope constants.

This, of course, is some mouthful and on its own doesn't appear to mean very much. We can try it out with the earlier arithmetic example and see what happens.

Equations [8] and [9] were

$$Qd = 10 - 3p \qquad [8]$$

$$Qs = -4 + 4p. \qquad [9]$$

Identifying the constants for substitution in [16] we have: $a = 10$; $b = 3$; $c = 4$ and $d = 4$:

$$p = \frac{a + c}{d + b} \qquad [16]$$

$$= \frac{10 + 4}{3 + 7}$$

$$= \frac{14}{7}$$

$$p = 2.$$

This is exactly what we arrived at in the arithmetical example. The manipulation appears to be general for these types of straight-line schedules.

What about the quantity variable at market equilibrium? This too can be found by using a general equation in terms of the parameter constants. The manipulation is no more difficult than what you have just done, though the result *looks* a lot more cumbersome.

We start with [11]:

$$Qd = a - bp$$

and substitute into it the equivalent of the price variable in constants from [16]:

$$Qd = a - b\left[\frac{a + c}{d + b}\right]. \qquad [17]$$

We could stop here and use this expression to find the equilibrium quantity, but we want to practise some more manipulation before setting up camp for the night. We use a little dodge to expand the equation. You have already been introduced to it: a number multiplied and divided by another remains the same, because this is the equivalent of multiplying by one. We shall treat the constant a in this way:

$$Qd = a\frac{(d + b)}{(d + b)} - b\frac{(a + c)}{(d + b)}.$$

This gives us two terms on the RHS, each divided by the same bracketed expression

$(d + b)$. No change has taken place in the value of the a constant because $(d + b)/(d + b) = 1$ and a number multiplied by 1 is itself. You will agree it is a crafty dodge!

The RHS can now be rewritten, without changing anything, so as to make explicit the sharing of the common denominator (that is Sr. Cognoscento's name for the bit below the line — he calls the bit above the line the *numerator*):

$$Qd = \frac{a(d+b) - b(a+c)}{(d+b)}. \quad [18]$$

We can also carry out some further expansion to the RHS by multiplying out the bracketed expressions (in mathematics we are always either expanding or simplifying expressions, depending on what our intentions are):

$$Qd = \frac{ad + ab - ba - bc}{(d+b)}.$$

The terms $+ab$ and $-ba$ cancel out, because a minus number added to its positive self equals zero (you will see in your notebook that $ab = ba$). This means we can reduce this equation to

$$Q = \frac{ad - bc}{d + b}. \quad [19]$$

The equilibrium quantity demanded (or supplied) equals the difference between the demand intercept constant multiplied by the supply slope constant and the demand slope constant multiplied by the supply intercept constant, all divided by the sum of the supply and demand slope constants.

There can be no doubt that this is another mouthful! If we don't watch it, we shall become as incoherent as some of the mathematicians we meet — and we have hardly started up the hills! You can see why you are advised *not* to try to read equations off the page. Even if you get it right verbally, it is unlikely to mean much.

Equation [19] is the general equation for finding the equilibrium quantity in simple straight-line demand-and-supply schedules. We can test it with our earlier example. When the constants are substituted into [19] we get

$$Q = \frac{(10)(4) - (3)(4)}{(4) + (3)}$$

$$= \frac{40 - 12}{7}$$

$$= 4.$$

As we already know, the market is cleared when the price is 2 and the quantity demanded and supplied is 4.

3.8   *For the Notebook*

You can jot these notes down and refer to them when you need to. There is no need to memorise them before proceeding up the trail.

Rules for negative and unlike signs

*The absolute *value of a number is its face value*: 6 and -6 have the same absolute value, i.e. six. Mme. Notation denotes the absolute value of a number by placing it between two vertical lines: $|6|$. When we consider a number's absolute value we ignore the sign prefixed to it (remembering that the $+$ sign is generally not specified in most contexts but is taken for granted while the negative sign is almost always specified).

*To multiply unlike signs, multiply the absolute values of the numbers and prefix the result with a negative sign:

$$-a \times +b = -ab$$
$$-2 \times +4 = -8.$$

*To divide unlike signs, divide the absolute numbers and prefix with a negative sign:

3. Walk—Don't Run!

$$\frac{-a}{+b} = -\frac{(a)}{(b)}$$

$$\frac{-10}{+2} = -5.$$

*To multiply like signs, multiply the absolute values of the numbers and prefix with a positive sign:

$$-a \times -b = +ab$$

$$-2 \times -3 = +6.$$

*To divide like signs, divide the absolute values of the numbers and prefix with a positive sign:

$$\frac{-a}{-b} = +\frac{a}{b}$$

$$\frac{-6}{-3} = +2.$$

*To add like signs, add the absolute value of the numbers and prefix with the original sign:

$$(-a) + (-b) = -(a+b)$$

$$(-2) = (-3) = -5.$$

*To add unlike signs, find the difference between the absolute values of the numbers and prefix with the sign of the largest number:

$$(-9) + (+6) = (9-6) = -3$$

$$(-6) + (+9) = (9-6) = 3.$$

Rules for inequalities

*A constant may be added to or subtracted from each side of an inequality. If

$$a < b$$

then

$$a + d < b + d.$$

*Each side of an inequality may be multiplied by a non-zero positive constant. If

$$a < b$$

then

$$ad < bd.$$

*If each side of the inequality is multiplied by a non-zero negative constant, then the direction of the inequality is reversed. If

$$a < b$$

then, if d is negative (<0)

$$ad > db.$$

*Each side on the inequality may be raised to a positive power. If $(a, b > 0)$ and

$$a < b$$

then, where n is positive (>0)

$$a^n < b^n.$$

*If each side of the inequality is raised to a negative power the direction of the inequality is reversed. If $(a, b > 0)$ and

$$a < b$$

and if n is negative power (<0), then

$$a^{-n} > b^{-n}$$

i.e.

$$\frac{1}{a^n} > \frac{1}{b^n}.$$

FOUR

The March of the Multipliers

4.1 Introduction

At this point you may be feeling somewhat number-drunk. It has been a long climb through scrubland. True, you have met a couple of nice people, Sr. Cognoscento and Mme. Notation, and you have seen some dodges and manipulations (and dodgy manipulations!). However, the work today is taken at an entirely different pace, because you don't need to do anything except sit back and watch a parade pass before you. Every contingent on the parade you have seen before (in your economics) and you have covered the mathematics on the trail. Why then, you may ask, are we bothering? The answer is simple. *You need the practice*, and as an alternative to going over and over additional examples from market equilibrium (which, you will agree, could become a trifle tiresome) we shall switch scenery, so to speak, from the scrubland of microeconomics to the 'commanding heights' of macroeconomics.

First, we must describe the scenery which acts as a backdrop to the parade. The March of the Multipliers nowadays is what TV producers call a Family Show, though when it was first put on, back in the 1930s, it raised more than one nervous eyebrow among the Guardians of Good Taste and Stability.

4.2 Rock Bottom

In classical economics the volume of money determined the absolute price level and relative prices were determined by demand and the costs of production. Full employment, if it was considered at all, was assumed through the instantaneous adjustment of wages and prices. Therefore the quantity of money didn't influence decisions about real outputs, and governments couldn't increase employment or output by injecting money into a less than full-employment economy. From Keynes's *General Theory* [1936] the possibility of equilibrium at less than full employment gradually became the conventional wisdom. Recently there has been a decline of confidence in 'Keynesian' prescriptions (there is also some confusion as to what is or is not 'Keynesian'). The new consensus appears to be that the 'Keynesians' oversold macroeconomic 'fine tuning'.

Hansen [1953] remains the best blow-by-blow introduction to Keynes [1936], and Robinson's essay 'Marx, Marshall and Keynes' [1978] should be read by those who think they understand the Keynesian revolution. An excellent antidote to the old consensus about Keynes will be found in Hutchinson [1978], 'Demythologising the Keynesian Revolution: Pigou, wage cuts and the General Theory.'

Part of the enthusiasm for 'Keynesian' models among teachers was the ease with which the workings of the economy could be transcribed into simple mathematical models which were relatively easy to teach and not much more difficult to grasp. The multipliers paraded before you in the following pages are, it should be said, heroi-

4. The March of the Multipliers

cally simplified versions of a real economy. No claims for their realism need be entertained for a moment. The sole reason for their inclusion is the practice they provide in simple mathematics.

The multipliers march at rock bottom. It is rock bottom because the economy is simplified down to three variables only: income, consumption and investment. By income is meant the money value of production in a month, a year, or whatever. People acquire income from collaborating to produce goods and services. At rock bottom there are only two things that can be done with income: first it can be spent on consuming things needed for life or for enjoyment, and secondly it can be saved; i.e., set aside for future consumption. As all income is used in either of these two ways, we can write out the following identity:

$$Y = C + S \qquad [1]$$

Income consists of consumption expenditure plus saving

where Y is income, C is consumption and S is saving.

As income arises entirely from collaborating in production and some income is *not* spent on consumption, what happens to the production which is not consumed? At rock bottom we approach the answer from the production side by distinguishing between those goods and services which are intended for consumption and those intended for producing future outputs. Goods for producing future outputs are what economists mean by investment; they include buildings, machinery, work in progress, education and training. We know who buys consumer goods, but who buys investment goods? The entrepreneurs and managers of production organisations (firms). As all output consists of consumption goods and investment goods we can write the following identity:

$$Y = C + I \qquad [2]$$

Output consists of consumption goods plus investment goods

where Y is total output, C is consumption output and I is investment output.

Equations [1] and [2] have common terms, Y and C. The money value of output is identical with the money value of income. The money spent on consumption equals the money value of consumption output. Therefore the equality of equations [1] and [2] must turn on the equality of the amount not-consumed out of income (i.e. saved) and the money value of the output intended for future production (i.e. investment). *If* savings are equal to investment, at rock bottom we must have

$$S = I \qquad [3]$$

Savings equal investment.

Savers are a sub-set of all income receivers (not all income receivers save) and investors (the entrepreneurs) are also a sub-set of all income receivers, but it doesn't follow that the two sub-sets are identical. The managers don't canvass the individual opinions of all savers. It would be impractical to do so. They make their investment decisions independently of the decisions of income receivers to save. What influences them in their decisions is of great interest to economists, but for the moment you can accept that these are probably different from the influences on savers.

The identity betwen saving and investment is only true in a special sense. They are equal *ex post* (Latin for something akin to 'in the event' — a Cognoscenti in-word!); they need not be equal *ex ante* ('before the event'): the *intentions* of savers not to consume needn't match the *intentions* of investors to acquire future output capacity. Indeed, why should they? The *ex ante* inequality is highly significant for economics. The difference between the 'best laid schemes' of investors and savers kicks the rock bottom model into life, because somehow the inequality of intentions has to be reconciled with the absolute necessity of the equality of the eventual outcome. Somebody, somewhere, sooner or later, has to adjust to the fact that their intentions are going to be frustrated.

Disequilibrium will occur when intentions and outcomes are different. If actual output ('in the event') is greater than the sum of consumption and investment expenditure (i.e., if $Y > C + I$), there will be an unintended (and unexpected) increase in the stock of goods held by suppliers. These unsold goods become unintentional investment in this time period for the next time period. If the goods are not being sold it means that savings are higher than anticipated by investors and these savings are exactly matched ('after the event') by unintended investment in stocks.

Investors holding unintended stocks adjust their behaviour by reducing their flow of output. This causes a drop in employment incomes for those no longer required to produce output, and this in turn revises the savings intentions of those affected by the cut backs, some of whom will have to draw on past savings (i.e., dis-save). In doing so, they reduce total savings in the economy and thus bring actual savings into line with intended investment.

Similarly, if actual output is smaller than intended spending on consumption and investment, there will be an unintended disinvestment of stocks held by firms. Suppliers will hold insufficient goods to meet the unanticipated demand, manifested by queues waiting outside their shops. If they had extra output available they could sell it and this causes them to revise their investment plans upwards. They hire more factors, including income-earning labour, and the formerly unemployed stop dis-saving and start spending again out of current income. As their incomes are restored, they revise their decisions about saving.

Keynes believed that there was no reason to suppose that if equilibrium was reached it would coincide with full employment.

4.3 The Famous Forty-Five

Consumption is directly related to the amount of income available to consumers: if income rises, consumption rises and if income falls, consumption falls. Cognoscenti entitle this the *Consumption Function*. At rock bottom the relationship between consumption and income is assumed to be represented by a straight-line equation. One of the first banners we will see at the head of the march will be one emblazoned with the symbols

$$C = a + bY \qquad [4]$$

Consumption consists of some minimum constant (a) *plus a proportion* (b) *of Income* (Y).

You will recognise [4] as the equation of the straight line from yesterday's walk. It has been graphed in Figure 4.1. The intercept constant *a* is positive, and it starts the consumption line off from a point up the vertical axis because even at zero income there is still some consumption out of past income (savings) or borrowing (other people's savings). The slope constant (to the Cognoscenti: the slope *parameter*) has exactly the same role as it had in the supply-and-demand equations — it determines the slope of the straight line. In this case it tells us by how much consumption will increase for an increase in income, or, visually,

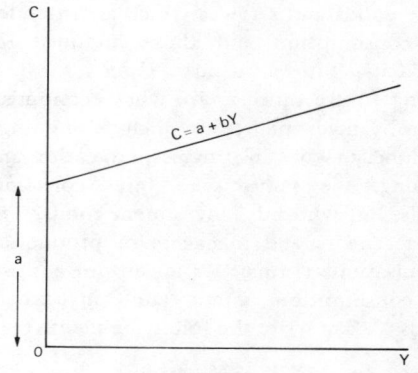

Figure 4.1

4. The March of the Multipliers

how much vertical movement there is for any given horizontal movement. From your economics you will recognise the slope constant as the Marginal Propensity to Consume, and if you don't the Cognoscenti will remind you.

In macroeconomics you have drawn numberless '45-degree' diagrams and you are therefore (whether you realise it or not) familiar with some basic ideas in geometry, because the diagram uses simple geometry to represent the relationship between consumption and income. If the consumer spends all available income, consumption is equal to income ($C = Y$). This state of affairs can easily be represented by two sides of a square, as in Figure 4.2. The 45-degree diagonal covers all points of equality between income and consumption. But if the consumer spends only a proportion of available income there must be an inequality in the length of sides representing income and consumption ($C < Y$). As consumption is less than income, the side representing consumption is smaller than the side representing income. This is why a rectangle's diagonal is an ideal representative of the consumption function (Figure 4.3). The consumption line in Figure 4.1 has a shallower slope than the 45-degree line. We know, by comparing the relative slopes of the various functions with the 45-degree marker, what is being assumed about the relative sizes of consumption and income.

The diagramatic apparatus which spread throughout the textbooks after the Keynesian revolution, though it wasn't developed by Keynes himself, helped hundreds of thousands of students to understand 'Keynesian' economics, though probably few except the specialists read the *General Theory* [1936] itself. This is a pity because, though a difficult book it has a unique style which makes it well worth the trouble to storm through the difficult bits. Consider the following extract:

> The fundamental psychological law, upon which we are entitled to depend with great confidence both *a priori* from our knowledge of human nature and from the detailed facts of experience, is that men are disposed, as a rule and on average, to increase their consumption as their income increases, but not by as much as the increase in their income . . . it is also obvious that a higher absolute level of income will tend, as a rule, to widen the gap between income and consumption. For the satisfaction of the immediate primary needs of a man and his family is usually a stronger motive than the motives towards accumulation, which only acquire effective sway when a margin of comfort has been attained. These reasons will lead, as a rule, to a greater *proportion* of income being saved as real income increases. But whether or not a greater proportion is saved, we take it as a fundamental psychological rule of any modern community that, when its real income is increased, it will not increase its consumption by an equal *absolute* amount, so that a greater absolute amount must by saved, unless a large and unusual change is occurring at the same time in other factors [1936, bk. 3, ch. 8].

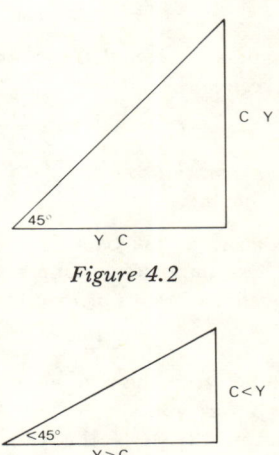

Figure 4.2

Figure 4.3

For Keynes the gap between income and consumption was a rule of economic life and, indeed, 'the stability of the economic system essentially depends on this rule prevailing in practice'. Something must fill that gap and for Keynes that role was allotted to investment. Managers purchase output for a purpose other than consumption. The economy requires that investment increase to fill the gap between consumption and rising real incomes, and, for investment to increase, consumers must increase their savings out of income. The consumers' efforts to increase their consumption out of their rising incomes stimulates managers and entrepreneurs to raise output to a new level and in the process the incomes which are generated provide the margin of saving that covers the increased investment. The 'Keynesian' *multiplier* 'tells us by how much their employment has to be increased to yield an increase in real income sufficient to induce them to do the necessary extra saving, and is a function of their psychological propensities' [1936, ch. 10].

At rock bottom we don't need an investment function, and investment is taken as being previously determined before the march. The Cognoscenti insist on entitling variables determined outside the model *exogenous variables*, and notation franchisers usually insist on identifying them with a bar over the letter $\bar{I}$, or with a zero subscript next to it: I_0. While we show due deference to the Cognoscenti family and like to have a good business relationship with the franchisers of notation, we baulk at cluttering up the pages with bars and subscripts.

4.4 The Multiplier

The concept of the multiplier was first introduced into economics by Kahn [1931], and you can read Keynes' early stab at it in 'Can Lloyd George Do It?' (written with Hubert Henderson) [1929]. The multiplier device answered the question posed by a group of economists working at Cambridge in the early 1930s: what was the consequential change in employment induced by a change in net investment in public works? Some increase in employment followed from the expectation that the receivers of incomes from the public works project spent *some* of their incomes on consumption goods. Some income is saved because not all income is consumed. Income that is spent becomes income for sellers of consumption goods. They too spend *some* of their new income. Each round of expenditure creates another round of income for sellers, each of whom spends *some* and saves the rest. The amount passing on as income gradually declines, because at each round some of it is saved. Eventually the amount to be passed on diminishes towards zero. A limit is set on the number of rounds of expenditure by the amount saved at each round. If a great deal is saved, the additional expenditures in the economy, and, therefore the additional employment generated by the public works, will be less than if only a little is saved. The marginal propensity to save determines the extent of the additional employment from net investment.

We are now ready for the first contingents in the March of the Multipliers. As the first banners hove into sight you will recognise them both:

$$Y = C + I \qquad [2]$$

Income is defined as consumption plus investment.

$$C = a + bY \qquad [4]$$

Consumption is a straight line function of income.

Tucked away at the back is a smaller, but nevertheless important, banner proclaiming the Exogenous Origins of Investment:

$$I = I_0. \qquad [5]$$

You should write the manipulation down as it passes before you.

Equation [2] uses the variable C (for consumption) to define income (Y) and in [4] C is itself declared to be a function of

4. The March of the Multipliers

Y. We will use this information to produce a new banner:

$$Y = a + bY + I \qquad [6]$$

Income is equal to the intercept constant plus a proportion of income added to investment.

If you were quick — and you have to be to see the March of the Multipliers — you will have noticed that the variable C has been substituted out of [2] by the RHS of [4]. This hasn't altered the balance of equation [2] because what was taken out, C, is exactly the same as what was put in, $a + bY$. Equation [6] is now composed of two variables, Y and I, instead of three, Y, C and I.

The next steps of the rock-bottom multiplier contingent were introduced in yesterday's walk. We use the standard 'collect-like-terms' dodge and get the Y variables on to the LHS of the equation by taking bY from both sides:

$$Y - bY = a + bY - bY + I$$

which gives, when the arithmetic is completed

$$Y - bY = a + I. \qquad [7]$$

We now have two Y terms on the LHS which we rewrite into a standard form (of great versatility in these kinds of manipulation). We use the dodge that a number outside a bracket tells us to multiply the terms inside the bracket. In [7] there are two Y terms multiplying *two* other terms. It may not be obvious, but if you think about it for a moment you will see the logic of this statement. Remember: $(b \times Y)$ is the same as bY, and $(Y \times 1)$ is the same as Y (because a number times 1 equals itself!). Therefore

$$Y - bY = Y(1 - b)$$

and this allows us to rewrite [7]

$$Y(1 - b) = a + I. \qquad [8]$$

There is a reason for using this little dodge which we shall see in the next step. A great deal of mathematical manipulation uses the rules of mathematics to rewrite expressions into forms more suitable for manipulation than their original form. You are *not* expected to rediscover these dodges yourself, nor to think of them in the first place. Mathematical specialists have done all the work you are likely to need in your economics. You are treading well-worn paths.

Equation [8] is now suitable for further adjustment to eliminate the constant terms on the LHS, thus isolating the Y term. To make sure that the equation remains in balance we divide both sides by $(1 - b)$:

$$Y \frac{(1 - b)}{(1 - b)} = \frac{a + I}{(1 - b)}$$

giving

$$Y = \frac{a + I}{(1 - b)} \qquad [9]$$

Income equals the sum of the intercept constant and investment, divided by the fraction formed when the slope of the consumption function is taken away from one.

The slope of the consumption function (b) is the Marginal Propensity to Consume (*MPC*) and what is not consumed is saved, hence, taking b from 1 will give the Marginal Propensity to Save (*MPS*):

$$(1 - b) = (1 - MPC) = MPS.$$

The RHS of [9] tells us to divide the numerator (the bit on top) by the denominator (the bit below). A fraction actually consists of two elements: the denominator, which identifies the fraction, and the numerator, which tells you how many of them there are. In the case of, say, 3/4 we have a denominator of /4, and we can see from the top line that there are three of them:

$$3/4 = (1/4) \times 3.$$

Analogously, the RHS of [9] can be rewritten

$$\frac{a + I}{(1 - b)} = \frac{1}{(1 - b)} \times (a + I).$$

This is how it appears in the textbooks. The term $1/(1-b)$ is known as the 'Keynesian' multiplier. Now, remember that $(1-b)$ is a fraction, because b is a number less than one, and therefore the result of taking b from 1 (finding the value of the MPS) must produce another fraction. If a fraction is divided into 1, which is the meaning of $1/MPS$, we get what Cognoscenti call the *reciprocal*.

Now you know why the 'Keynesian' multiplier is known as the reciprocal of the marginal propensity to save! If the MPS is 1/4 then the MPC is 3/4 [because $(1-3/4) = 1/4$] and the multiplier will be 4 (because 1 divided by 1/4 is 4); likewise, if the MPS is 1/3 the multiplier will be 3, if 1/2 it will be 2 and if 1/10 it will be 10, and so on.

If we know what the MPC is we also know what the MPS is at rock bottom and if we know the MPS we know by how much income will increase for any given injection of investment.

4.5 Plus Taxes

The rest of the march is an elaboration of the rock-bottom model but with no additional mathematics. You can skip through what follows if you feel secure in the manipulation of equations of this type – you may wish to work through it in greater detail at a second read. If not, carry on making notes on what passes before you.

The step up from the rock-bottom model introduces a government sector financed by taxation. Income taxation alters the disposable income of households. Instead of Y they get what is left after taxation T is taken off. Governments spend the income they collect (and often much more besides) and this adds a new category to total expenditure. We now have $C + I + G$, where G is government expenditure.

The identity equation is the same as before:

$$Y = C + I + G \qquad [10]$$

Total expenditure equals the sum of consumption, investment and government expenditures.

In the new model there are two leakages from aggregate demand out of income: saving and taxation. If the identity is to hold, we need an equal injection of expenditure in the form of investment and government to offset the leakages of savings and taxation. In the rock-bottom model $S = I$ had to hold at equilibrium giving

$$S + T = I + G \qquad [11]$$

Savings plus taxation equals investment plus government.

The new model can be written out formally as an identity [10], an equilibrium condition [11], a behavioural equation for consumption [4] and with statements of the exogenous origins of I, T and G:

$$Y = C + I + G \qquad [10]$$
$$S + T = I + G \qquad [11]$$
$$C = a + bY \qquad [4]$$
$$I = I_0$$
$$T = T_0$$
$$G = G_0.$$

We will have to adjust equation [4] because in its present form it refers to consumption as a function of the total income of consumers and not the disposable income of taxpayers. But rather than keep creating new notation (whatever the protests from the franchiser) we will state the adjustment and revert to using [4] as it is:

$$Y' = Y - T \qquad [12]$$

Disposable income equals income minus taxation.

We can now proceed to establish the multiplier for a model which includes a government sector.

The steps will be familiar to you (I hope!).

4. The March of the Multipliers

First, we substitute [4] (as adjusted in [12]) into [10]:

$$Y = a + b(Y-T) + I + G$$

and then collect terms by taking $b(Y-T)$ from both sides:

$$Y - b(Y-T) = a + b(Y-T) - b(Y-t)$$
$$+ I + G$$

giving

$$Y - b(Y-T) = a + I + G. \quad [13]$$

The LHS has Y and T terms together and we want to separate them before taking the T term over to the RHS. We do this by multiplying the bracketed terms by $-b$, remembering that T also has a negative sign, and this will give a positive result:

$$Y - bY + bT = a + I + G. \quad [14]$$

If we take bT from both sides we will eliminate $+bT$ from the LHS and still keep the equation in balance:

$$Y - bY + bT - bT = a + I + G - bT$$

giving

$$Y - bY = a + I + G - bT.$$

The LHS can now be simplifed as before into $Y(1-b)$:

$$Y(1-b) = a + I + G - bT$$

and dividing both sides by $(1-b)$ we get

$$Y = \frac{a + I + G - bT}{1 - b}. \quad [15]$$

This looks fairly fearsome compared with a rock-bottom multiplier but, like a lot of mathematics, it isn't half as bad as it looks. In its conventional form we have

$$Y = \frac{1}{1-b}(a + I + G - bT) \quad [16]$$

Income equals the intercept constant plus the sum of investment and government expenditure minus a proportion of the amount taken in taxation, all multiplied by the 'Keynesian' multiplier.

The economics of the term $-bT$ will be clearer if you remember that taxation reduces total income but doesn't reduce consumption by the same amount, because some of the income would have been saved anyway.

The effect of taxation on the multiplier will depend on the marginal propensity to consume. The smaller the *MPC* the more taxation will shift private savings to the government and the more this will increase the employment effects of government expenditure. You can now try Hansen 'The Marginal Propensity to Consume and the Muliplier' [1953, ch. 4].

4.6 More Multipliers

It is time for you to meet one of the many Greeks who have a differentiated product in popular notation. This one is called *Delta* and looks like this: Δ. He is used instead of 'change in' and he turns up all over the shop. Let him show what he can do when he is deployed to demonstrate some multipliers.

We begin with the 'Keynesian' multiplier

$$Y = \frac{1}{1-b}(a + I) \quad [9]$$

and Figure 4.4 which is a standard 45-degree income determination diagram from your textbook. Suppose for some exogenous reason the amount of investment increases from I to I^*. This raises the consumption/investment schedule from $C + I$ to $C + I^*$ and equilibrium income from Y to Y^*. The increase in investment causes a rise in income. The amount by which investment increases is given by the difference between I^* and I, and this is represented by the 'change in' I, or ΔI. Similarly, the amount by which income increases is given by the difference between Y^* and Y, or 'change in' Y: ΔY. The ratio between these two magnitudes is

$$\frac{\Delta Y}{\Delta I} \quad [17]$$

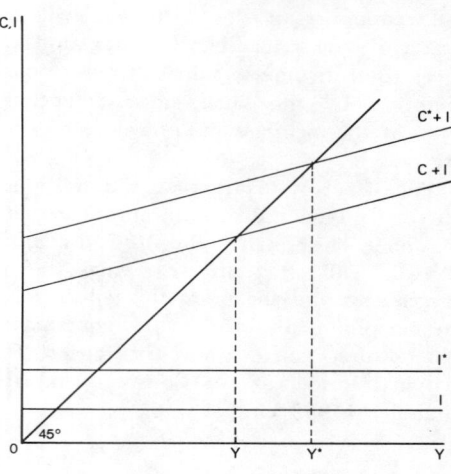

Figure 4.4

and this is the 'investment multiplier', often given the symbol k.

We find this investment multiplier by going to work on [9]:

$$Y = \frac{1}{1-b}(a+I).$$

This gives us the amount of income Y, but what about the amount of income Y^*? This too can be set out using [9]:

$$Y^* = \frac{1}{1-b}(a+I').$$

The change in income will be the difference between these two values:

$$Y^* - Y = \frac{1}{1-b}(a+I') - \frac{1}{1-b}(a+I) \quad [18]$$

The change in income is equal to the product of the multiplier times investment level I' minus the product of the multiplier times investment level I.

The change in Y is exactly the same as ΔY (or, 'delta why') and we write this in [18]. We also note that the two parts of the RHS of [18] are multiplied by the same term

$(1/1-b)$ and we therefore write this outside a bracket indicating that the terms inside the bracket are to be multiplied by the common term. This rewrites [18] as

$$\Delta Y = \frac{1}{1-b}(a+I'-a-I).$$

The intercept a will cancel out by arithmetic $(a-a=0!)$ and we are left with

$$\Delta Y = \frac{1}{1-b}(I'-I).$$

Again, we notice that the change in investment is the same as $I'-I$, or, using delta notation, we get

$$\Delta Y = \frac{1}{1-b}\Delta I. \quad [19]$$

As usual, we tidy this up a little by getting like terms together and we do this by dividing both sides by ΔI

$$\frac{\Delta Y}{\Delta I} = \frac{1}{1-b} \quad [20]$$

which is the standard 'Keynesian' multiplier.

By now you are getting used to several mathematical manipulations. Some very complex verbal models are now open to you.

To illustrate this point let us suppose that the government decided to alter the level of taxation in the taxation multiplier [16]. What affect would this have on the level of income? The complex diagramatic exposition of this affect is shown in Figure 4.5. Equilibrium income is Y when investment is at I and government expenditures are at G. The aggregate demand function is shown by $C+I+G$. If taxes are raised, they will reduce consumption, because disposable income will fall. The consumption function is assumed to be of the type: $C = a + b(Y-T)$ and when taxes rise to T' the consumption function becomes: $C' = a + b(Y-T')$. In the diagram the new equilibrium of this (lower) function with the 45-degree line produces a lower national income of Y'.

4. The March of the Multipliers

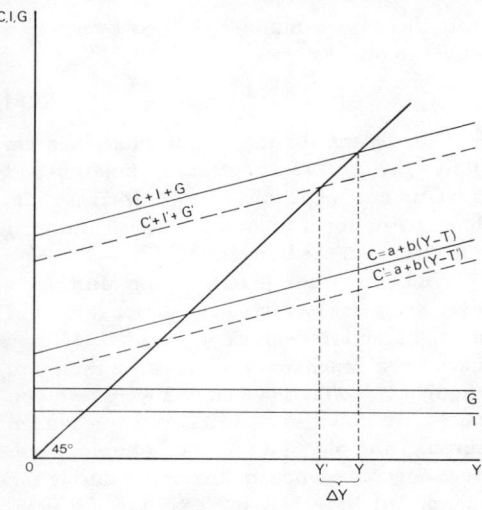

Figure 4.5

How do we derive the taxation multiplier using mathematics? One thing we don't need to do is learn any new mathematics. First, we set out [16]

$$Y = \frac{1}{1-b}(a + I + G - bT) \quad [16]$$

and write out the equation for when government increases taxation:

$$Y' = \frac{1}{1-b}(a + I + G - bT'). \quad [16']$$

The difference between these two equations will tell us the effect of the taxation increase on income. Writing them out the long way, we get

$$Y' - Y = \frac{1}{1-b}(a + I + G - bT')$$

$$- \frac{1}{1-b}(a + I + G - bT) \quad [21]$$

but we simplify this using delta notation

$$\Delta Y = \frac{1}{1-b}(a + I + G - bT' - a - I - G + bT). \quad [22]$$

Eliminating a, I, and G by arithmetic, we get

$$\Delta Y = \frac{1}{1-b}(-bT' + bT). \quad [23]$$

But $(-bT' + bT)$ is the same as $-b(T' - T)$ and we express 'change in' T, or, 'delta tee', by: ΔT. Thus, [23] becomes

$$\Delta Y = \frac{1}{1-b}(-b\Delta T). \quad [24]$$

If both sides are divided by ΔT we get

$$\frac{\Delta Y}{\Delta T} = \frac{-b}{1-b}. \quad [25]$$

The taxation multiplier is negative because when the government increases taxation it reduces disposable income. Income falls from Y to Y'. Writing out the taxation multiplier is a much shorter task than drawing a complex diagram and trying to verbalise the steps.

In a final demonstration of the ability of mathematical manipulation to bring out important consequences of economic models we shall quickly go through the famous 'balanced budget multiplier'. Again, absolutely no new mathematical work is involved, and you can do this for practice. It is also a useful theorem to know about, because it remains popular with examiners the world over (if cursed by examinees).

The impact on income of a simultaneous increase in government expenditure and taxation can be written down as the positive effect of the change in government expenditure on income and the negative effect of the taxation increase on consumption. The government multiplier is the same as an investment multiplier: the increase in expenditure is multiplied by the reciprocal of the MPS. The taxation multiplier is taken from the previous manipulation. This gives us, using delta notation,

$$\Delta Y = \frac{1}{1-b}\Delta G - \frac{b}{1-b}\Delta T. \quad [26]$$

We assume that the change in government expenditure is exactly equal to the change in taxation; i.e., that 'delta G' is equal to 'delta T': $\Delta G = \Delta T$. Hence we get a *'balanced budget'* — the government spends what it collects in taxation. For simplicity, we represent this equality by 'delta B': ΔB. Putting this into [26] gives

$$\Delta Y = \frac{1}{1-b} \Delta B - \frac{b}{1-b} \Delta B. \qquad [27]$$

Equation [27] has a common denominator $(1-b)$ and a common multiplying term (ΔB), thus it can be simplified to

$$\Delta Y = \Delta B \left[\frac{1}{1-b} - \frac{b}{1-b} \right]$$

giving

$$= \Delta B \left[\frac{1-b}{1-b} \right]$$

and, because a number divided by itself is equal to one, we get:

$$\Delta Y = \Delta B. \qquad [28]$$

The balanced-budget multiplier theorem states that an equal increase in taxation and government expenditure will increase the level of national income by the amount of the change in the budget.

Well, that's the March of the Multipliers over. The last banners have disappeared out of sight and the music has faded. It may have been much more exhausting than you thought it would be when you were told you could sit down and watch rather than go through the physical effort of climbing. You have covered no new mathematics during the march but have had some very useful practice in simple equations. Your knowledge of the economics involved will have made it a rewarding occasion. We must now move up the slopes to the higher ground and start the quest for the calculus in earnest.

FIVE

Next to Nothing

5.1 Introduction

You are about to begin the Quest for the Calculus. It is a quest most feared by innumerates, and 'yet of all the wonders that I have heard it seems to me most strange that you should fear *Calculus* — 'tis much ado about next to nothing!'

From a computational point of view the calculus is extremely easy, so the source of fear must lie elsewhere — perhaps in memories of school algebra.

There is no point in pretending that there are no baffling moments during the quest. But they are only moments, not epochs! So keep a clear head for dizzy heights and accept a little cloud fogging up the scene now and again. You have some reliable kit, specially constructed for the high ground above the foothills. And you need never be afraid of getting lost because rescue is always just a page away.

5.2 On the Terrors of Notation

Any calculus text has one or other of the following items of notation:

$$\frac{dy}{dx}$$

or

$$\int dx.$$

Far from being terrifying symbols of oppression, they are actually the quintessence of amiability, intimidating only in their simplicity. They oughtn't to alarm anybody.

In calculus, the notation 'd' means a 'wee bit of' something. Thus, 'dy' ('dee why') means a 'wee bit' of y; 'dx' ('dee ecks') means a 'wee bit' of x, and so on. Together, as 'dy/dx' ('dee why, dee ecks') we simply have a special relationship of a 'wee bit' of y and a 'wee bit' of x. That's all there is to it!

As for $\int dx$, we have notation telling us to 'sum all the wee bits of x'; i.e., all the 'dxs'. You pronounce it 'sum'. Thus, when we break down x into wee bits we use 'dx', and when we put it back together again we use '$\int dx$'.

Surely this notation is not too difficult. In fact it is so incredibly simple that you may think there is a trick somewhere, but there are no tricks. In fact calculus is simple: it is the terror it promotes that is remarkable. True, some stony-faced examiners react harshly to students who don't understand calculus, but those who chastise the innocent probably kicked cats when they were children; the majority of teachers are more gracious, because they know that it is much more difficult to explain the *why's* of calculus than the *how's*.

Fortunately, for the economics student, the *why* bit is made much more tractable. You already know the answer we shall be looking for.

To get at calculus you have to undertake some fairly lengthy, and at times perplexing detours. To stop to explain the why's and wherefore's of every step causes confusion rather than clarity. If at times you feel you are dangling on the end of a very thin rope to no good purpose, with a long fall if the rope parts, don't panic. The fuzziness with which the quest for the calculus meanders along is somewhat illusory to beginners. One minute your head is deep in the clouds, and you have little idea where you are going; the next the clouds part and the whole territory lies before you in magnificent splendour.

Your first steps take you through the minutiae of Elasticity, chosen because of its familiarity to all economics students and its usefulness as an introduction to how calculus improves the precision of economic statements. We move quickly through this familiar territory to get to the first slope. Our task is to compare an arithmetical non-calculus explanation of Elasticity with a more accurate method. Once the limitations of arithmetic are seen we can set about finding another way (the calculus) up the slopes ahead.

5.3 Mind Your P's and Q's

The concept of elasticity was implicit in classical economics and, typically, it was Cournot [1838] who got closest. The honour of making the concept explicit belongs to Marshall, who 'hit on the notion of elasticity as he sat on the roof at Palermo shaded by the bath cover in 1881'! [Keynes, 1933, p. 228]. Marshall published his first results in 1885 and provided an exposition of *point* elasticity in his *Principles* [1890, bk. 3, ch. 4 and 'Note Three' of the 'Mathematical Appendix'].

Point elasticity appeared long before the concept of *arc* elasticity, which didn't arrive till 1933, but on this climb they are introduced in reverse order, because it is the underlying mathematics that we are interested in. You can read about the development of arc elasticity in Lerner [1947] and Allen [1934; 1938]. Early innovators in this area — which spawned a great deal of interesting work — include Hicks [1932] and Robinson [1933]. Texbooks cover several

applications of elasticity concepts, including cross elasticities and income elasticities. The latter was suggested by the German statistician Ernst Engel (1821–1896) in 1857.

We make a Cognoscenti approach from the foothills with Own Price Elasticity of Supply. In words, this is defined as

Own price elasticity of supply equals the percentage change in the quantity supplied divided by the percentage change in the price.

You are no doubt familiar with it both in its symbolic form

$$e = \frac{\%\,\Delta Q}{\%\,\Delta P}$$

and in its mathematical form from your basic microeconomics

$$e = \frac{\frac{\Delta q}{q}}{\frac{\Delta p}{p}}. \qquad [1]$$

To arrive at the standard textbook definition of elasticity we will manipulate [1] using some laws of arithmetic. Note that in [1] you are told to divide a fraction $(\Delta q/q)$ by another fraction $(\Delta p/p)$, and from arithmetic we use the dodge that a fraction divided by another fraction is the same as a fraction multiplied by the *inverse* of the other fraction. Thus

$$\frac{a}{b} \text{ divided by } \frac{c}{d} \text{ equals } \frac{a}{b} \text{ multiplied by } \frac{d}{c}.$$

Applying this to [1] we get

$$e = \frac{\Delta q}{q} \div \frac{\Delta p}{p}$$

therefore

$$e = \frac{\Delta q}{q} \times \frac{p}{\Delta p}. \qquad [2]$$

We now have two fractions multiplied together, and, again, from the laws of arithmetic, we know that it doesn't matter in

5. Next to Nothing

which order the denominators are multiplied together:

$$\frac{a}{b} \times \frac{d}{c} = \frac{a}{c} \times \frac{d}{b}$$

which applied to [2] gives

$$e = \frac{\Delta q}{\Delta p} \times \frac{p}{q}. \qquad [3]$$

This, of course, is the textbook definition of elasticity:

> *Elasticity equals the ratio of the changes in quantity to the change in price multiplied by the ratio of the original price to the original quantity.*

We shall examine this more closely with the aid of graphs (or, as the Cognoscenti call it, 'coordinate geometry'). This will help to construct the apparatus needed for the first attempt up from rock bottom.

Figure 5.1 shows an upward-sloping straight-line supply schedule. We want to focus in greater detail on the construction of the term $\Delta q/\Delta p$ in [3]. Quantity is measured on the vertical axis and price on the horizontal axis (using the mathematician's convention — one convention being as good as another). The supply schedule can be represented by the general equation of a straight line $(y = a + bx)$, and we write this out using p and q for the variables:

$$q = a + bp. \qquad [4]$$

In Figure 5.1 two points, m and n, are arbitrarily marked on the supply schedule and lines drawn from these points to the axes. These lines (or 'perpendiculars') designate the price–quantity relationships of the points. Thus point m links price p' to quantity q' and point n links price p^* to quantity q^*.

What happens to supply if the offer price rises from p' to p^*? This depends on the responsiveness of supply to price changes, or, the Supply Elasticity. The graph of the supply schedule and the equation of the line $(q = a + bp)$ provide the information: simply fill in the variables and solve for the change in price. It sounds difficult, but it is actually quite easy, if a trifle cumbersome.

At point m the quantity supplied is given by the equation of the line at that point with the specific price–quantity variables written in:

$$q' = a + bp' \qquad [5]$$

and similarly, for point n:

$$q^* = a + bp^*. \qquad [6]$$

We are interested in the change in quantity; i.e., Δq, which is found by taking q' from q^*:

$$\Delta q = q^* - q' \qquad [7]$$

and as q' and q^* are defined in [5] and [6] we substitute into [7]:

$$\Delta q = (a + bp^*) - (a + bp').$$

Opening up the brackets and performing the arithmetic we get

$$\Delta q = a + bp^* - a - bp'$$
$$= bp^* - bp' \qquad [8]$$

(because $a - a = 0$).

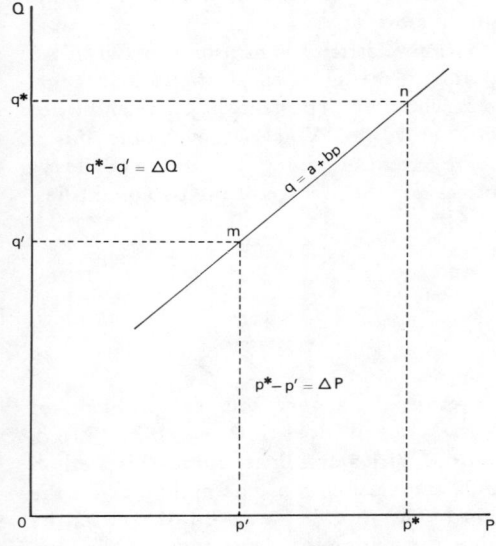

Figure 5.1

The RHS has two terms multiplied by a common term and hence can be rewritten

$$\Delta q = b(p^* - p') \quad [9]$$

but $p^* - p'$ is the 'change in price' (or Delta $p : \Delta p$), and [9] becomes

$$\Delta q = b\Delta p.$$

Dividing both sides by Δp to keep the equation in balance gives

$$\frac{\Delta q}{\Delta p} = b \quad [10]$$

The ratio of the change in quantity to the change in price is equal to the slope of the supply curve.

In a straight line the slope of the line is constant throughout its length (that's why it's a straight line!), and hence $\Delta q/\Delta p$ is a constant. Elasticity is determined by both the ratio $\Delta q/\Delta p$ *and* the original price–quantity ratio p/q. As the $\Delta q/\Delta p$ ratio is constant, it follows that the specific values of the p/q ratio change the elasticity, depending on where elasticity on the schedule is being measured from.

In the case of non-straight line (a *non-linear* curve) $\Delta q/\Delta p$ also changes for different points on the curve. In Figure 5.2 a non-linear supply schedule is graphed. A change in price from p' to p^* alters the quantity supplied, as before, from q' to q^*. But the ratio $\Delta q/\Delta p$ no longer measures the slope of the actual schedule – it is measuring the slope of the line joining the two points m and n. This line forms a chord between the two points. (A chord is a straight line joining two points on a curve from inside the curve.)

If another point, n' is taken and the ratio $\Delta q/\Delta p$ is measured the chord is even further away from the schedule than the two points, m and n. The further apart the two points representing prices, the less the resulting ratio $\Delta q/\Delta p$ corresponds to the slope of the actual schedule.

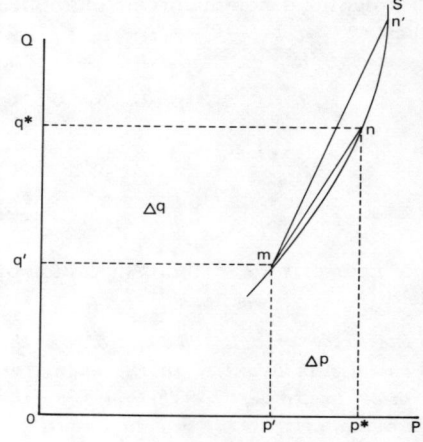

Figure 5.2

The situation on a demand schedule is no different. Remember how many times you have had to explain why elasticity alters as you move down the curve; elasticity is greater at the 'top' of the curve than at the 'bottom'. 'Price elasticity of demand depends upon the initial price and quantity, the direction of the price change and its magnitude – discuss' is a regular examination question.

When elasticity is measured between two points, it measures *arc elasticity* and it matters where you start on the curve and where you move to. You can overcome this to some extent by taking the average of the two prices and the average of the two quantities:

$$\frac{\dfrac{q^* + q'}{2}}{\dfrac{p^* + p'}{2}}. \quad [11]$$

This doesn't remove the real problem, of course, but it does improve the approximation. With a non-linear curve, this method finds the elasticity of the mid-point on the chord. The shorter the chord of course, the more the mid-point closes towards the elasticity at the original point.

5. Next to Nothing

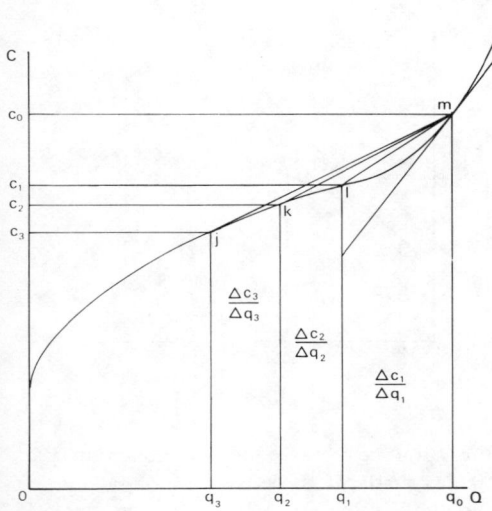

Figure 5.3

5.4 Second Best to a Tangent

If there were some means of measuring the very smallest chord between two adjacent points, a more accurate measure of price elasticity would result. The closer the two points the better. How 'close' is close? Ideally, so close that the distance between the points is 'next to nothing'.

The key to what you are looking for has already been hinted at. You need to do a lot of arithmetic and use the basic rules for handling equations, both of which are well within your capability. In Figure 5.3 the total cost curve of a firm has been graphed. At zero output there are some fixed costs incurred, and as output increases the cost curve rises steeply at first, flattens out as 'economic' output is achieved and then rises more steeply as capacity is approached.

To find the change in costs (ΔC) for a change in output (ΔQ), form a ratio

$$\frac{\Delta C}{\Delta Q}. \qquad [12]$$

This gives the slope of the line joining m to l.

Suppose the points are moved further apart to mk and mj. The cost changes are now given by

$$\frac{\Delta C_1}{\Delta Q_1}, \quad \frac{\Delta C_2}{\Delta Q_2}, \quad \text{and} \quad \frac{\Delta C_3}{\Delta Q_3}.$$

Starting with mj and moving towards ml the slopes of the chords joining the respective points get steeper. The chords joining all points from j to m get steeper in slope as the point approaches m.

If you take a fresh orange, or similar object, and put it on a table, it will touch at a *single* point of contact. Cognoscenti say that the table surface is at a 'tangent', or is tangential, to the orange. A pencil laid across the orange also forms a tangent with it. A tangent is a line touching — not cutting — a curve at one point.

A tangent has been drawn touching the point m on the cost curve. The slope of each tangent is unique (all points on the schedule have their own tangents). Now what is so interesting about the slope of the tangent at m is that it acts as a reference slope for the slopes of the chords joining points on the cost curve to m. By inspection, you will note that the slopes of the chords swing in towards the slope of the tangent as the points approach m. This is a most important result and, while it may of of obscure relevance for you at the moment, you must imprint it on your memory, because it is the key to the calculus.

You will no doubt accept, on intuition alone, that there must be a point *very very close* to m whose chord with m has almost the same slope as the tangent. If the distance between this point and m is *next to nothing*, the difference between its slope and the tangent's will also be *next to nothing*. In fact, for all practical purposes they will be the same, which is precisely how they are treated.

You are now standing on the very brink of the calculus. If this is your first time, savour the moment — you will never be the same again!

To recapitulate: as the change in quantity, ΔQ, gets smaller and smaller the slope of the chord between m and the approaching point becomes more and more like the slope of the tangent touching m.

Hold on to that idea; it has brought you to the brink and if it slips away you will go back to rock bottom. To strengthen your grip on the idea, we shall express it differently and splice in some jargon.

Instead of saying that 'Delta Q gets smaller and smaller' we can say that 'Delta Q moves towards zero'. This means the same thing: the change in quantity becomes infinitesimal as the distance between the points becomes next to nothing. Cognoscenti refer to the movement towards zero as '$\Delta C/\Delta Q$ going to its limit, or limiting value'.

The effect on the change in cost of a change in quantity which is near zero mustn't be forgotten — after all it is the change in cost we are interested in. Infinitesimal changes in output cause infinitesimal changes in cost. In our introduction to calculus notation you will recall that the calculus symbol for a 'wee change' in something is 'little delta' or 'd'. Thus the limit value of the ratio of Delta C to Delta Q can also be written as dC/dQ:

$$\underset{\Delta Q \to 0}{\text{Limit}} \frac{\Delta C}{\Delta Q} = \frac{dC}{dQ} \qquad [13]$$

As the change in quantity diminishes towards zero the limit value of Delta C by Delta Q equals dee Cee by dee Queue.

From microeconomics you know that the change in cost for a small change in quantity is defined as *marginal cost* and by mathematics we have found a way of expressing this idea.

In Figure 5.4 tangents to a firm's total cost curve have been drawn, each touching a point on the curve representing a specific output level. As the quantity increases, the slopes of the tangents get steeper. Just how steep they become depends on the shape of

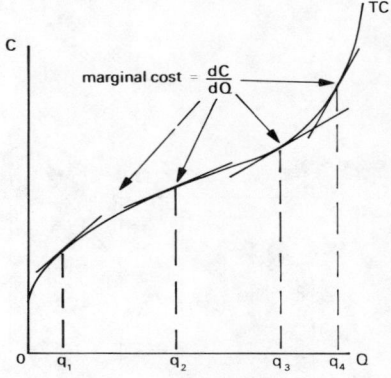

Figure 5.4

the total cost curve but, whatever its particular shape, if there is a way of calculating the limit value of $\Delta C/\Delta Q$ for any specific quantity of output we will have an accurate measure of the marginal cost of increasing output. The limiting value of $\Delta C/\Delta Q$ is dC/dQ, which is the slope of the tangent at the point on the curve and it gives the marginal cost of output at that point. The *calculus* is the means by which the limit value is *calculated*!

The same point is demonstrated in Figure 5.5 which shows a demand curve with tangents touching it at various points. Again, the slopes of the tangents change as the points correspond with higher prices (on the

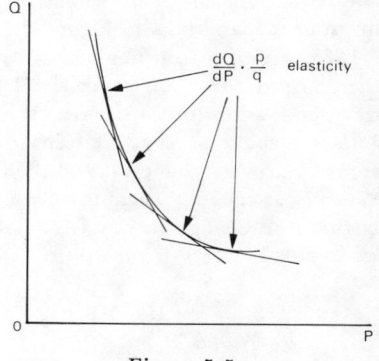

Figure 5.5

5. Next to Nothing 43

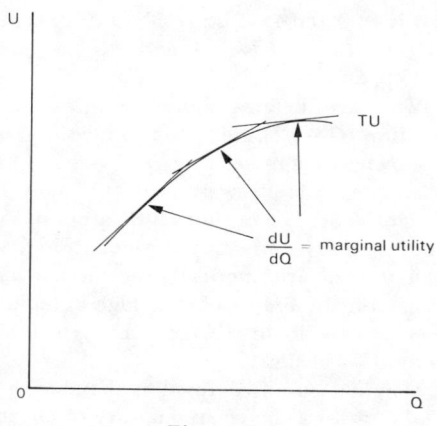

Figure 5.6

horizontal axis). The limiting value of $\Delta Q/\Delta P$ is given by dQ/dP and when these values are multiplied by p/q the coefficient of price elasticity of demand is found.

Lastly, Figure 5.6 shows the relationship between total utility and the quantity consumed of a good. The curve rises at a diminishing rate and the tangents reflect this relationship by their shallower slopes. The limiting value of $\Delta U/\Delta Q$ is du/dq, and as this diminishes as more of the good is consumed we have a neat exposition of Diminishing Marginal Utility.

There is something very promising about the limiting values of the delta ratios. *If dC/dQ, dQ/dp and dU/dQ can be calculated our economics will be given a much sharper edge.*

5.5 The Brewer's Tale

There are a number of assumptions implicit in the neoclassical theory of the firm. For example, it is assumed that the cost curves are *continuous*. This is a convenient abstraction and not a description of the real world. The neoclassical firm is not an organisation of real people but a purely abstract device for transforming inputs into outputs. Even the entrepreneur is redundant, there being nothing entrepreneurial in woodenly obeying decision rules which maximise the excess of revenue over cost (except, perhaps, the entrepreneurial initiative in getting such an undemanding job in the first place!). There has been a prolonged debate, often tedious, occasionally exciting, between critics and supporters of the neoclassical theory of the firm. The literature is now prodigious. Koutsoyiannis [1975] in 'A Critique of the Neoclassical Theory of the Firm' gives an excellent summary of the main issues, followed by several chapters on the major post-War contributions in this area.

With this caveat in mind we shall unravel the 'riddle' of dy/dx using the neoclassical theory of the firm as the catalysis. Recipes for rabbit stew start with 'First catch your rabbit', and in calculus it is no different: 'First learn how to find a value for dy/dx!' Only if this is learned will your trek in the Mathematics Mountains be worthwhile. This is the decisive moment in your climb from rock bottom. You are, if you like, spread-eagled on a rock face, hanging on like grim death, deciding whether to try to move upwards or downwards. It is a difficult position to be in and one which we face when struggling with ourselves. Instinct urges you to give in, pride pushes you on. Some give in, whether they are on a rock face, or a strict diet, or stopping smoking, or grasping calculus. Some slip a little but recover — others go over the edge, their real problem being their attitude, not their ability. For those who go on it is a triumph of character over defeatism.

Having thought this sounded somewhat sombre, you will be relieved to learn that finding dy/dx is actually fairly simple. The main requirements are patience and concentration as the argument unfolds. The mechanics of finding dy/dx are a lot easier to follow than understanding for the first time *why* the mechanical operations work. For this reason what follows is presented at a snail's pace, but you will soon be replacing the cumbersome and tedious equipment used in this section with a slim-line set of tools.

Suppose, by way of illustration, that you meet a Brewer who is anxious to ask arithmetical questions about the cost—output relationships of a brewery. He wants, for instance, to find the marginal cost of output of his beer. How could you set about helping him find the answer? We take a brewery as a hypothetical example because beer production corresponds much more closely than do cars, refrigerators and widgets to a continuous and minutely divisible flow of output. (Hence, in seeking the marginal cost of beer production, we at least make a gesture towards the assumption of continuous cost functions.)

Let us suppose that the Brewer already has some information of the cost function in the form set out in Table 5.1. The cost function shown in the table is very simple and conforms to

$$C = Q^2 \qquad [14]$$

Cost of output equals the quantity squared.

You can check this by inspecting Table 5.1 and noting that the figures under total cost always equal the square of the number under quantity. For example, at output 2.00 the cost is 4.00 and 4 is 2 squared, or 2×2; at output 3.00 the cost is 9.00 and 9 is 3 squared, or 3×3, and so on.

We have here a much simplified cost function ($C = q^2$) and this produces a graph as shown in Figure 5.7.

Suppose the Brewer wants to know his marginal cost for output levels around, say, 3,000 gallons of beer per week. First, we shall use an arithmetical procedure, which is easy on the brain-box but high in tedium. Then we will introduce an even easier method — calculus!

Marginal cost is defined as the change in total cost for a change in quantity of output. In symbols it is written:

$$MC = \frac{\Delta C}{\Delta Q} \qquad [15]$$

Marginal Cost is equal to delta C divided by delta Q.

We have to decide how big or small the measured change in output is to be. This will depend upon the need for accuracy in the measure of marginal cost because the smaller the unit of output change the more accurate the required measure.

Let us try the marginal cost of output through the range 2.50 to 3.00 in Table 5.1. The change in output is $3.00 - 2.50 = 0.50$ (or 500 gallons). The difference in cost must be the difference between the total cost of producing 3,000 gallons and the total cost of producing 2,500 gallons. These costs are read off from Table 5.1 as $9,000 minus $6,250 which equals $2,750. This means that increasing output by 500 gallons of beer when output is already at 2,500 gallons causes a rise in total cost of $2,750.

The change in cost per unit of output is found from [15]:

$$\frac{\Delta C}{\Delta Q} = \frac{2.75}{0.50}$$

$$= 5.5 \qquad [16]$$

from which we conclude that the marginal cost is equivalent to $5.50 per gallon.

Table 5.1   Cost and Output Schedule of a Brewery

Quantity '000 gallons	Total Cost '000$s	Average Cost $/gal
0.50	0.25	0.50
1.00	1.00	1.00
1.50	2.25	1.50
2.00	4.00	2.00
2.50	6.25	2.50
3.00	9.00	3.00
3.50	12.25	3.50
4.00	16.00	4.00
4.50	20.25	4.50
5.00	25.00	5.00

5. Next to Nothing

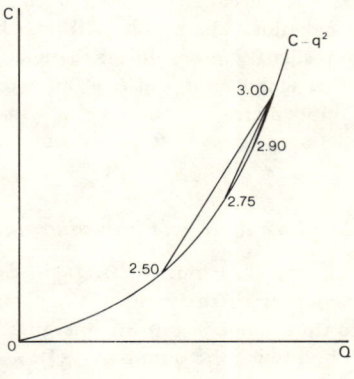

Figure 5.7

In Figure 5.7 the greater the change in quantity (delta Q) the less the measured marginal cost is representative of the true marginal cost at the point (in this case 3,000 gallons). In the above calculation the change in quantity is given from 2,500 gallons to 3,000 and therefore the manipulation brings together lower marginal costs associated with outputs near 2,500 gallons and higher marginal costs associated with outputs near 3,000 gallons. The marginal cost we are measuring in Figure 5.7 is represented by the slope of the chord from the point 2.5 and the point 3.00. The chord is clearly not the same thing as the cost curve of $C = q^2$. The greater the distance between the points on the cost curve the more the chord is going to diverge from the cost curve, and, conversely, the closer the two points the more the chord is going to approach the cost curve.

This conclusion from inspecting Figure 5.7 is the geometric representation of the inaccuracy of the measure of marginal cost of a change in output for a quantity change as large as 2,500 to 3,000 gallons. To estimate marginal cost as accurately as we can we want to get as close a change in output to 3,000 gallons as is practicable. To do this we try output changes closer to 3,000 gallons. To this end we can repeat the above arithmetic for a change in output from 2,700 to 3,000 gallons.

In Figure 5.7 the chord between 2.7 and 3.0 on the cost curve is closer to the cost curve than the chord between 2.5 and 3.0. to compare the costs we use [14]:

$$C = Q^2 \qquad [14]$$
$$= (2.7)^2$$
$$= 7.29 \qquad [17]$$

and for an output of 3 we get

$$= (3)^2$$
$$= 9. \qquad [18]$$

The difference in costs (delta C) equals [18] minus [17]:

$$9 - 7.29 = 1.71 \qquad [19]$$

and Marginal Cost is found from [15]:

$$\frac{\Delta C}{\Delta Q} = \frac{1.71}{0.30}$$
$$MC = 5.70 \qquad [20]$$

or $5.70 per gallon.

Compare [20] with [16] and note how the value of marginal cost has moved up from $5.5 to $5.7. If the same calculation is carried out for output changes of 2.95 and 2.99 with 3.00 we get the results in Table 5.2.

Table 5.2 Marginal Cost by Arithmetical Method of Output Changes near 3,000 gallons

Output change	Marginal cost $\Delta C / \Delta Q$
2.50 — 3.00	5.50
2.70 — 3.00	5.70
2.95 — 3.00	5.95
2.99 — 3.00	5.99

The trend is distinct: *the smaller the change in output at 3.00 the closer the marginal cost moves towards 6.00*. If we take a very small range of, say, from 2.995 to 3.00, we find that the marginal cost is 5.995, which is very close to 6.00.

If we take output changes close to 5.00 from Table 5.1 and use equations [14] and [15], we get the results in Table 5.3.

Table 5.3   Marginal Costs by Artithmetical Method of Outputs near 5,000 Gallons

Output change	Marginal cost $\Delta C/\Delta Q$
4.50 – 5.00	9.50
4.70 – 5.00	9.70
4.95 – 5.00	9.95
4.99 – 5.00	9.99

Exactly the same type of result appears: *the smaller the output change at 5.00, the closer the marginal cost of output approaches 10.00.*

This arithmetical method gives you a means for calculating a measure of marginal cost at various levels of output and it may be that the measures you provide will satisfy the Brewer, though he may be a trifle wary of a consultant who gives him different measures of marginal cost near the same level of output. He could say: 'Yes, Mr Economist, but what is *the* marginal cost of an extra unit of output at 3,000 gallons?' If you are very honest, you won't be able to tell him the answer — you can appeal to his sense of fair play or try the widows-and-orphans gambit and hope he will pay your fee. But if you are imaginative and do look for patterns in the normal course of events, you will have recognised that a pattern has emerged, even if, as yet, you can't explain it. You could say: 'Mr Brewer, it is clear to me, from the cost function information you have provided ($C = Q^2$), that the marginal cost of output for any level of output is twice the quantity level — in other words, if output is Q, then marginal cost is 2Q.'

5.6   The Dee Why Dee Ecks Show

You won't be surprised to learn that the result achieved in your consultancy job with the Brewer has great significance in the quest for the calculus. The result will now be restated in slightly more formal language, at the end of which you will read an astonishing announcement.

The Brewer's cost function was given by

$$C = Q^2 \qquad [14]$$

Cost is equal to quantity squared.

As the change in output (delta Q) got smaller (approached zero) the ratio of the change in costs to the change in output (marginal cost) approached twice the quantity (2Q): as

$$\Delta Q \to \text{zero}$$

$$\frac{\Delta C}{\Delta Q} = 2Q. \qquad [21]$$

But what have we done when we take delta Q to its limit value of next to nothing? Why, *nothing less than found its* dC/dQ! *This is truly an astonishing and most welcome conclusion.* We have found the RHS of

$$\underset{\Delta Q \to 0}{\text{Limit}} \frac{\Delta C}{\Delta Q} = \frac{dC}{dQ}. \qquad [22]$$

In other words, we have calculated the next-to-nothing value of delta Y/delta X. The arithmetical method is very cumbersome, even though the cost function is grossly simplified — and we can't rely on all cost functions being so helpful. We need, therefore, to find a means of deriving dy/dx for any function no matter how complicated it is. The Cognoscenti call this *differentiating* the function and, fortunately, there is an extremely simple and speedy method of doing this. Unfortunately, the exposition is neither.

Take the general form of the function used in the Brewer's case and carry out some simple arithmetic on it:

$$Y = x^2. \qquad [23]$$

What happens when the x variable gets a wee bit bigger? The y variable in consequence will also get a wee bit bigger, its growth depending upon the exact nature of the function [23] relating the two variables. We want to know by how much y changes for an infinitesimal change in x, or, in calculus notation, we want to find out the value of dy/dx.

If we let x grow by an infinitesimal amount, it becomes $x + dx$ (i.e., x plus a wee bit of itself) and this will make y grow to $y + dy$ (i.e., y plus a wee bit of itself). Equation [23] tells us that y changes for any growth in x by the square of x, which we write as

$$y + dy = (x + dx)^2 \qquad [24]$$

The growth in y *plus* y *is equal to the growth in* x *plus* x *all squared.*

The RHS $(x + dx)$ has to be squared (multiplied by itself) according to [24] and we oblige as follows:

$$\begin{array}{r} x + dx \\ \underline{x + dx} \\ x \cdot x + x \cdot dx + dx \cdot x + dx \cdot dx \end{array}$$

and by collecting similar terms:

$$x \cdot x = x^2$$
$$x \cdot dx + dx \cdot x = 2(x \cdot dx)$$
$$dx \cdot dx = (dx)^2.$$

Adding these together, we get

$$= x^2 + 2(x \cdot dx) + (dx)^2. \qquad [25]$$

Equation [24] becomes

$$y + dy = x^2 + 2x \cdot dx + (dx)^2. \qquad [26]$$

Looking at [26] closely, we remember from [23] that $y = x^2$ and any equation will remain in balance if we take the same number from each side (hence eliminating y and x^2):

$$dy = 2x \cdot dx + (dx)^2. \qquad [27]$$

The last term on the RHS, $(dx)^2$, is a really small number, bearing in mind that dx is next to nothing and squaring next to nothing

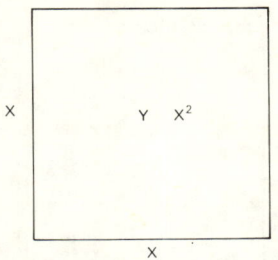

Figure 5.8

is still infinitesimal: a wee bit of x multiplied by itself is going to be extremely small. Thus, we treat $(dx)^2$ as so small that we can ignore it in [27] giving

$$dy = 2x \cdot dx. \qquad [28]$$

Dividing [28] by dx (treating each side the same) gives

$$\frac{dy}{dx} = 2x. \qquad [29]$$

The elimination of $(dx)^2$ is no sleight of hand; it follows from the nature of the term itself and can be illustrated by consulting Figure 5.8. Here we have a square of side x. The equation we have been discussing is $y = x^2$, which geometrically is simply the area of the square. If we increase the square in size by a wee bit of x, i.e., an infinitesimal amount, dx, we add to it two strips of dx width, as shown in Figure 5.9. This also

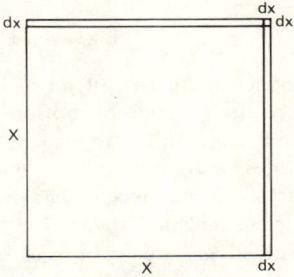

Figure 5.9

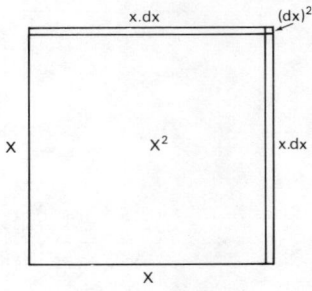

Figure 5.10

produces in the top right-hand corner of the square a small overlap, of sides dx by dx. Incidently, none of the Figures are drawn to scale — sizes as small as dx are extremely small; in fact, they are next to nothing. The area of the new square is found by multiplying its length by its breadth or, in other words, squaring $(x + dx)$. This operation is illustrated in Figure 5.10, and you will note that it follows the manipulation in equations [24] to [29].

The area of the original square of side x is $x \cdot x = x^2$. The area of the additional strips of dx width is plainly $x \cdot dx$, and we note that there are two of them. This leaves the area of the top right-hand overlap square, which has sides dx in length, and hence its area is $dx \cdot dx = dx^2$. Summing these areas together gives

$$x \cdot x = x^2$$
$$x \cdot dx + x \cdot dx = 2(x \cdot dx)$$
$$dx \cdot dx = (dx)^2$$
$$= x^2 + 2x \cdot dx + dx^2.$$

If you conceive the size of dx as being extremely small — next to nothing — and represented in graphical terms by the thinnest of lines (a fraction of the width of a pencil line), you will accept that the area dx is extremely small and that it can be safely ignored for all practical purposes. It is certainly extremely small compared with the area of the square x in Figure 5.10. For these reasons it is eliminated in calculus work.

Perhaps with $y = x^2$ we were just lucky! We check this out by trying some other functions, such as $y = x^3$ and $y = x^4$. The arithmetic is tedious but should present you with no problems. Let us take $y = x^3$ and multiply this out for an addition of a wee bit of x:

$$y = x^3 \qquad [30]$$
$$y + dy = (x + dx)^3. \qquad [31]$$

Expanding the RHS gives

$$\begin{array}{r} x + dx \\ \underline{x + dx} \\ x^2 + 2x \cdot dx + (dx)^2 \\ \underline{x + dx} \\ x^2 \cdot x + 2x^2 \cdot dx + x(dx)^2 \\ \underline{x^2 \cdot dx + 2x(dx)^2 + (dx)^3} \\ x^3 + 3x^2 \cdot dx + 3x(dx)^2 + (dx)^3 \end{array}.$$

[25]

[32]

We know that $y = x^3$ and therefore these are eliminated to give

$$dy = 3x^2 \cdot dx + 3x(dx)^2 + (dx)^3. \qquad [33]$$

Inspecting the RHS we note the last two terms dx^2 and dx^3. Both these terms must be extremely small, because dx itself is extremely small and multiplying a wee bit by another wee bit is bound to be almost insignificant. Hence they are deleted.

This leaves

$$dy = 3x^2 \cdot dx \qquad [34]$$

and dividing both sides by dx gives

$$\frac{dy}{dx} = 3x^2. \qquad [35]$$

Likewise with $y = x^4$:

$$y + dy = (x + dx)^4 \qquad [36]$$

and expanding the RHS gives

$$x^3 + 3x^2 \cdot dx + 3x(dx)^2 + (dx)^3$$

$$\frac{x+dx}{x^4+4x^3} \cdot dx + 6x^2(dx)^2 + 4x(dx)^3 + (dx)^4.$$

Because $y = x^4$ and the terms with $(dx)^2$, $(dx)^3$ and $(dx)^4$ in them are too insignificant we simplify this to

$$dy = 4x^3 dx \qquad [37]$$

and dividing both sides by dx gives

$$\frac{dy}{dx} = 4x^3. \qquad [38]$$

The cumbersome and boring arithmetic has been useful and necessary up to this point but has now served its purpose. We can set out the results and conclude that there is more than a lucky element in the relationship between a function and its *derivative* (i.e., the value found by differentiating the function):

Table 5.4   Values of Differentiated Functions

Function	$\frac{dy}{dx}$
$y = x^2$	$2x$
$y = x^3$	$3x^2$
$y = x^4$	$4x^3$
$y = x^5$	$5x^4$
$y = x^6$	$6x^5$
$y = x^7$	$7x^6$
$y = x^{100}$	$100x^{99}$

Differentiation appears to follow a regular pattern: *the power of the function is reduced by one and the original power entered as a multiplier of the variable.* Now you know how to differentiate! You must agree that it is extremely easy to go straight to the function and write down by inspection the differentiated terms called the *derivative* (by you-know-who).

The derivative of a cost function is its marginal cost and you now have a method of finding the marginal cost of additional output for any level of output: simply differentiate the cost function and enter in the relevant output level. Hence you could tell the Brewer that when his cost function is $C = Q^2$ his marginal cost is $2Q$, where Q is any output level he cares to ask about.

In general, the rule for differentiation of a function of the type $y =$ some power of x can be written as

if $\quad y = x^n$

then

$$\frac{dy}{dx} = nx^{n-1} \qquad [39]$$

To differentiate, reduce the power term by one and multiply the x term by the original number of the power.

The simplicity of differentiation does wonders for your confidence. You never need to pretend to anyone (with the possible exception of your clients) that calculus is difficult.

5.7   *For the Notebook*

Having ditched a lot of cumbersome arithmetical gear, you would deceive yourself if you believed that you could now climb without kit. We get rid of redundant baggage to make room for the special kit needed ahead. But no expedition would be complete without its porters, and there are plenty of them in these mountains ready to jog your memory when you are stuck with a problem. They have access to the Collective Memory of Mathematics and can deploy this on demand to those in difficulty (i.e., like the legendary St Bernard mountain dogs, take sustenance to those lost in blizzards).

Two of the rules you will need in the next climb can be stated with an economy of words, and you should note them down *now* and refer to them when you need to.

*What happens to constants in differentiation?

The short answer is: they are eliminated. Take a function like

$$y = x^2 + 2.$$

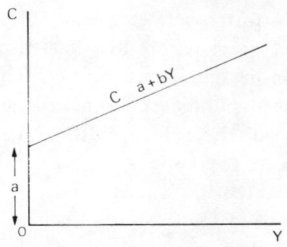

Figure 5.11

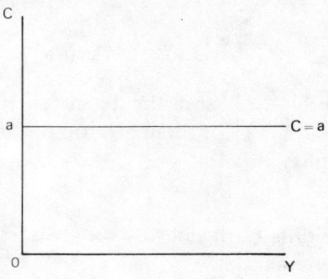

Figure 5.12

Differentiating gives

$$\frac{dy}{dx} = 2x.$$

Take another:

$$y = x^3 + x^2 + 3.$$

Differentiating gives

$$\frac{dy}{dx} = 3x^2 + 2x.$$

You can see why by looking at Figures 5.11 and 5.12. The first shows a linear consumption function $C = a + bY$. The derivative dC/dY gives the change in consumption for small changes in national income. When $Y = 0$ the constant a is positive (shown as the intercept) and as Y increases the constant a has no influence on the change in consumption because this is given entirely by the term bY. This is reinforced in Figure 5.12 where the constant a is drawn horizontally. No matter what value Y takes a remains the same (i.e., $da/dY = 0$) and clearly does not influence the change in consumption caused by changes in Y. Hence in differentiating the constant is eliminated.

*What happens to a variable multiplied by a constant?

Briefly: multiply the constant by the power term. Take a function like

$$y = 3x^2$$

and differentiate it:

$$\frac{dy}{dx} = 2(3)x$$

$$= 6x.$$

Or, again

$$y = 4x^3 + 2x^2 + x^{13}$$

$$\frac{dy}{dx} = 12x^2 + 4x + 13x^{12}.$$

There are several more rules for differentiation and some are covered in the next section, as they are needed, and are summarised in the notebook at the end of the chapter. The rules always look more fearsome than they are in practice. For our purposes they don't need to be learned (nor do their proofs) by rote — just turn to your notebook to follow a manipulation which uses them.

SIX

The Dance of the Derivatives

6.1 Introduction

Having struggled up from rock bottom to the brink of the calculus you are entitled to see some practical results from your exertions — and so you shall! But in contrast to the March of the Multipliers, this time you are required actively to participate. It isn't an onerous requirement, however — more like joining in a dance than being sentenced to a chain gang. In fact, the Dance of the Derivatives is among the most pleasant experiences of the mountains. It takes place off the beaten track, involving a few enthusiasts at a time. The mixture of thin mountain air, fantastic views, both to the plain below and to the higher ranges ahead, and large draughts of Practicality (from the Brewer you advised!) could create the kind of memorable encounter you will tell your grandchildren about (though some parts are forgettable).

All the themes of the dance come from intermediate microeconomics. In dancing with the derivatives you practise their application to familiar problems — and, perhaps, acquire some new insights into aspects of your economics.

6.2 Take your Partners

Derivatives have a repertoire of reels (pronounced' 'rules' by the Cognoscenti!) from a simple two-step to the whirling reels of the Highland Fling. Beginners are advised to dance slowly, concentrating on one step at a time; as you become an accomplished mover you can let yourself go with all the joyous abandon derivatives are famous for. Novices must learn to cope with the apparently endless variations on a theme, the rapid changes of partners (who join and leave the dance unannounced) and the complicated improvisations of the jiggers. Practice, however, is the *only* antidote for bafflement.

In these dances you will have a familiar partner, one you already know

$$\frac{dy}{dx}. \qquad [1]$$

Thus, in the case of marginal cost you would differentiate the total cost function and write

$$\frac{dC}{dQ}. \qquad [2]$$

Total cost is conceived as being a function of (or varying with) output (Q) which we write

$$C = f(Q) \qquad [3]$$

Cost depends upon output.

Whatever the functional relationship between cost and output, we enter the particular form in place of '$f(Q)$'.

The first dance is an elementary exercise illustrating the constant rule. The total costs of a neoclassical firm in the short run are composed of fixed costs (invariable with output) and variable costs (directly related to output). As output increases variable costs will increase, but fixed costs are spread across the output. The total cost function takes the form

$$C = f(Q) + FC \quad [5]$$

Costs are a function of quantity produced plus the fixed costs.

The change in total costs from producing extra output is not influenced by the amount of fixed costs. When [5] is differentiated the constant (FC) is eliminated by the rules of differentiation:

$$C = f(Q) + FC \quad [5]$$

$$\text{Marginal cost} = \frac{dC}{dQ} = f'(Q). \quad [6]$$

This agrees with your economics, because marginal costs are variable with output Q and fixed costs are not. (See *Notebook 6.12*)

6.3 The Power Reel

The Beginner's Power Reel is used to differentiate functions which are simple powers of a variable, such as x^2, or x^3. Suppose a brewery produces up to a 1,000 gallons of Practicality ('The New Stimulant for the Joyless') and its total cost function is given by

$$C = \frac{q^2}{1000} + 10 \quad [7]$$

Costs equal one thousandth of the square of the quantity plus ten.

There are three parts in the RHS: two constants, 1/1,000, and 10, and the variable (q). Differentiating [7] gives

$$\frac{dC}{dQ} = 2\frac{(1)}{1000}q^{2-1} \quad [8]$$

$$= \frac{2q}{1000}$$

$$= \frac{q}{500}. \quad [9]$$

Note, *en passant*, that $q^1 = q$.

Now try the basic steps yourself on the cost relationships in this example (go through the steps exceedingly slowly — at first!).

Suppose you want to find the total cost of producing 150 gallons of Practicality. You start by substituting 150 for q in [7]:

$$C = \frac{q^2}{1000} + 10$$

$$= \frac{150^2}{1000} + 10$$

$$= \frac{22500}{1000} + 10$$

$$= 22.5 + 10$$

$$= 32.5 \text{ (dollars)}.$$

Now tackle marginal cost using [9]:

$$\frac{dC}{dQ} = \frac{q}{500}.$$

What, for instance, is the marginal cost at 100 gallons output?

$$MC = \frac{100}{500}$$

$$= \$0.20.$$

For 50 gallons it is

$$MC = \frac{50}{500}$$

$$= \$0.10$$

and for 62.75 gallons

$$MC = \frac{62.75}{500}$$

$$= \$0.1255$$

and, lastly, for 750 gallons

$$MC = \frac{750}{500}$$

$$= \$1.50.$$

Have you ever done anything so simple? Providing you can translate your economics into a suitable form for calculus, you have some powerful tools for solving complicated problems.

6. The Dance of the Derivatives

We will now dance the Power Reel to a tune called Marginal Revenue. Total revenue (R) is the sum of the quantity (q) sold times the price (p) per unit it is sold at

$$R = pq. \qquad [10]$$

By definition, equation [10] can be used to find total revenue in all forms of markets. But there are distinctive steps to be taken when differentiating [10], according to the nature of the market. This point will be clarified to ensure that you follow what's going on. But don't become anxious; the mathematical problem has an economics slant with which you are most familiar.

Perfect and imperfect competition are the two basic market categories of microeconomics. At the industry level they have much in common — they both have downward-sloping *industry* demand curves. At the level of the *firm* significant differences exist. The following assumptions are made in respect of a firm in a perfectly competitive market:

1. The product is homogeneous
2. There is a large number of buyers and sellers
3. All firms are price-takers
4. There is free entry and exit to the industry
5. Firms have perfect information about the market
6. There is no collusion between firms.

Price is determined by the intersection of the market demand-and-supply curves (Figure 6.1) and this price is a *given* as far as the firms in the market are concerned (by a *given* we mean that no individual firm can influence the price of its product). The individual firm's demand curve is horizontal (Figure 6.1): it gets the same price no matter how much output it places in the market — its highest output being a very small fraction of the output of the industry. In [10] the RHS has two unknowns, p and q, and, in the case where price is both given *and* constant, it consists of a constant times a variable.

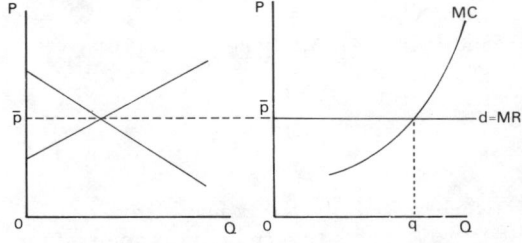

Figure 6.1

In the imperfectly competitive market the firm's demand curve is distinguished by its negative slope. Figure 6.2 shows the prices of various levels of output. Both price and quantity of output are variables and therefore, in [10], the RHS would consist of a variable multiplied by another variable.

At present you have been shown only how to differentiate a function which is confined to the products of constants and variables (the Power Reel); coping with functions which are products of variables is beyond you, at the moment.

You know the derivatives of terms such as x^2 or x^3 ($2x$ and $3x^2$, respectively) from the Power Reel, but what about a term like x or $3x$? The answer is simple: dy/dx of $x = 1$; and dy/dx of $3x = 3$. Remember $x^1 = x$ and by the rule of differentiation $dy/$

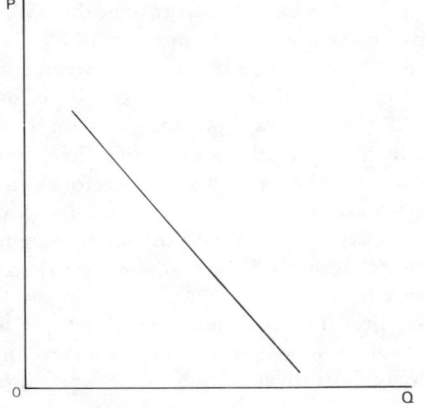

Figure 6.2

dx of $x^1 = 1x^{1-1} = 1x^0 = 1$ (because $x^0 = 1$ and $1 \times 1 = 1$). Applying this to [10] gives

$$R = pq$$

$$\frac{dR}{dq} = p \qquad [11]$$

where price is treated as a constant.

Any doubts (remember, St Thomas is the patron saint of students) you may have about the above can, let us hope, be assuaged by a dose of Practicality. Suppose the brewers of Practicality operate in a perfectly competitive market and can sell all their output at a price of $1.50 a gallon. What is the profit maximising output?

When price is set at $1.50 per gallon by the perfectly competitive market the total revenue function is given by

$$R = 1.5q \qquad [12]$$

and on differentiating this to find marginal revenue, we get

$$dR/dq = 1.5. \qquad [13]$$

The profit-maximising rule tells you to increase output as long as marginal revenue exceeds the marginal cost of producing it. Profit is maximised when marginal revenue (MR) equals marginal cost (MC) (i.e., where $MR = MC$). An increase in output beyond this point decreases profit (π: another Greek active in the notation business, read as 'pie'); given that π is the difference between total revenue (R) and total costs (C), it follows that if C increases more than R then π will fall. In the perfectly competitive firm, price is given by the market and therefore profit falls if output is increased beyond the point of equality of marginal cost with marginal revenue because of increasing marginal costs (Figure 6.1).

To find the profit-maximising output set marginal cost equal to marginal revenue; both are derivatives of their total functions:

$$MC = MR. \qquad [14]$$

In derivative form we write

$$\frac{dC}{dq} = \frac{dR}{dq}. \qquad [15]$$

We only need to enter into [15] the relevant details from [9] and [13]:

$$\frac{q}{500} = 1.5. \qquad [16]$$

This equation has a single unknown variable, quantity (q), and you know what to do when you see this — multiply both sides by 500 to get the unknown variable by itself and then trudge through the arithmetic:

$$q = 1.5(500)$$
$$= 750.$$

We conclude that when the output of the brewery is 750 gallons the plant is maximising its profit.

How much profit is it making at this output? A simple substitution using the relationship that profit is the difference between total revenue and total cost ($\pi = R - C$) will suffice:

$$\pi = R - C \qquad [17]$$

$$= 1.5q - \left[\frac{q^2}{1000} + 10\right]. \qquad [18]$$

When the brackets on the RHS are removed, the signs must change because everything in the brackets is being taken from $1.5q$:

$$\pi = 1.5(750) - \frac{750^2}{1000} - 10$$

$$= 1125 - \frac{562500}{1000} - 10$$

$$\pi = \$552.5.$$

In summary we conclude that at a price of $1.50 a gallon, the Brewer of Practicality will maximise profits of $552.50 at an output of 750 gallons per time period.

6.4 The Publisher's Tale

It is worthwhile practising the Power Reel on another example, this time from the world of publishing. Suppose you meet a publisher at a party (perhaps Mr Duckworth himself!) and being an aspiring economist, and brazen to boot, you ask about the economics of publishing (a wholly mysterious subject, much like the famous Schleswig-Holstein Question). Suppose further, and this is definitely in the realms of fantasy, the publisher wrote his total cost function on your business card and it read something like:

$$C = 20q + 0.001q^2. \qquad [19]$$

You can check the price of the book from one of the dust jackets lying about at the party (actual books are always scarce at these affairs); and, let us say, it is $45 retail. This means it is about $30 at the publisher's warehouse.

The question is: what print run should the publisher make in order to maximise his profits assuming that the book sells in a perfect market (i.e., the publisher can sell all the copies he produces and is only constrained by his cost function)? To find the maximum profit you must find the value of

$$\frac{dC}{dq} = \frac{dR}{dq}. \qquad [15]$$

You will need to differentiate the publisher's total cost and total revenue functions to solve [15]. Total cost is given in [19] and total revenue is price (to the publisher) times quantity sold (i.e., $R = 30q$). Differentiating these we get

$$C = 20q + 0.001q^2 \qquad [19]$$
$$dC/dq = 20 + 0.002q \qquad [20]$$
$$R = 30q \qquad [21]$$
$$dR/dq = 30 \qquad [22]$$

therefore

$$20 + 0.002q = 30.$$

The rest is pure arithmetic. Take 20 from both sides

$$0.002q = 30 - 20$$

and divide both sides by 0.002

$$q = \frac{10}{0.002}$$

$$q = 5,000.$$

To maximise his profit the publisher should produce 5,000 copies if he sells them at $30 each. But how much profit will he make on this book in these (laughably) hypothetical conditions? To answer this question you will have to find the value of [17]:

$$\pi = R - C. \qquad [17]$$

You will do this by substituting into the functions $q = 5000$ which you have calculated is the profit maximising print run:

$$= 30q - (20q + 0.001q^2)$$
$$= 30(5000) - [20(5000) + 0.001(5000)^2]$$
$$= 150,000 - 100,000 - \frac{25,000,000}{0.001}$$
$$= 50,000 - 25,000$$
$$\pi = \$25,000.$$

(Mr Duckworth insists that you are cautioned not to decide upon a career in publishing on the basis of these 'ridiculous' figures. 'Publishing remains more of a hobby for those bent on poverty than a meal ticket for the already penurious,' he insists.)

6.5 The Owner's Tale

Switching industries to one with more optimistic prospects — minicomputers — you can test your budding talents as a consultant on a problem bothering the technically-gifted owner of a small but growing operation. His plant produces 30 systems a day which are sold for $900 each through specialist computer magazines. The owner does not know whether he is maximising his profit or not and asks your advice. The second thing you do (the first being to agree the fee!) is ask for the total cost function of the operation. Assume that this is available and is in the form:

$$C = 50 + 28q^2. \qquad [23]$$

To find the current level of profits you subtitute the cost and revenue functions into

$$\begin{aligned}\pi &= R - C \\ &= 900q - (50 + 28q^2) \\ &= 900(30) - [50 + 28(30)^2] \\ &= 27{,}000 - (50 + 25{,}200) \\ &= 27{,}000 - 25{,}250 \\ \pi &= \$1750.\end{aligned}$$

The computer firm is making positive profits but could it do better and increase its daily profit?

Figure 6.3 shows profit levels for various outputs of a neoclassical firm. Up to some (low) level of output the firm makes losses (negative profits) — the costs of production exceed the revenue it earns from selling a small output. Beyond this point total revenue exceeds total costs and the firm makes positive profits, rising to a maximum at A and then diminishing through B to the horizontal, where it makes losses again. The computer company wants to know where it is on the profit curve: is it at A, the maximum profit level, or at a point such as B in Figure 6.3? If it is at B it could achieve this level of profit by reducing output to the quantity which earns the profit represented by point C (where $C = B$). Maximising output rather than profits is not an uncommon result of leaving production decisions to 'enthusiasts'. If you doubt this, consider what would happen in the book trade if it was the prerogative of authors to decide on the print run of their own books? Professional managers tend to take a more detached view of the commercial prospects of products than their creators!

The computer company operating at a profit level of B has asked you to find its profit-maximising output. You can do this in a trice by finding where

$$\frac{dC}{dq} = \frac{dR}{dq} \qquad [15]$$

Marginal cost equals marginal revenue.

Differentiating the total cost function $C = 50 + 28q^2$ and the total revenue function $R = 900q$ gives

$$56q = 900$$

$$q = \frac{900}{56}$$

$$q = 16.1.$$

The profit-maximising output of 16 systems a day is less than the current output of 30 systems, and therefore to maximise profits the computer company should reduce daily output by 14 systems (the odd 0.1 of a system is ignored because it is a result of the indivisibility mentioned earlier).

If the owner is dubious about your advice you can tell him exactly how much extra profit he will make if he follows it. Profit is given by: $\pi = R - C$ and agreeing to an out-

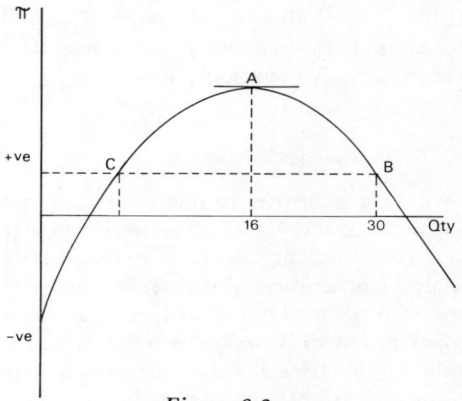

Figure 6.3

put of 16 gives

$$= 900(16) - [50 + 28(16^2)]$$
$$= 14{,}400 - (50 + 7168)$$
$$\pi = \$7182.$$

The decrease in output raises profit by $5432 a day, which even a 'non-commercial' computer enthusiast will find hard to resist, particularly if he can use the extra profit to finance the next generation of systems.

6.6 An Elastic Example

Another example from your economics which we can use to illustrate the use of calculus (and give you some practice in manipulation) can be taken from the concept of elasticity. Knowledge of the price elasticity of demand could be a great help to a firm in trying to decide on the effect of a price change on the demand for its product. Consider a firm in an imperfectly competitive market. It has a downward-sloping demand curve which takes the usual form

$$p = a - bq. \qquad [24]$$

If the demand curve was given by

$$p = 20 - 0.002q \qquad [25]$$

we could set about finding its point elasticity of demand in the following way. First, we have to rearrange [25] to express it in terms of the q variable:

$$0.002q = 20 - p. \qquad [26]$$

Therefore, dividing both sides by 0.002 will eliminate it on the LHS and take it over to the RHS:

$$q = \frac{20 - p}{0.002}. \qquad [27]$$

This enables us to find the derivative of q with respect to p which we need if we are going to find the coefficient of elasticity

given by

$$= \frac{dq}{dp} \cdot \frac{p}{q} \qquad [28]$$

(from the textbook definition of elasticity).

The RHS of [27] can be rewritten without altering its value as

$$q = \frac{20}{0.002} - \frac{p}{0.002}$$

$$= \frac{20}{0.002} - \frac{1}{0.002} \cdot p. \qquad [29]$$

This can be differentiated to give

$$\frac{dq}{dp} = -\frac{1}{0.002} \qquad [30]$$

because the first term on the RHS is a stand-alone constant (20/0.002) and these are eliminated on differentiation. The second terms on the RHS is differentiated using the standard form from your notebook:

$$y = ax^n$$

$$\frac{dy}{dx} = nax^{n-1}$$

which gives

$$1 \cdot \frac{1}{0.002} \cdot p^{1-1}$$

where $p^{1-1} = p^0 = 1$. This gives

$$= 1 \cdot \frac{1}{0.002} \cdot p^0$$

or

$$= \frac{1}{0.002}.$$

Taking [30] and returning to the expression for point elasticity of demand in [28] we can now write

$$= \frac{dq}{dp} \cdot \frac{p}{q} \qquad [28]$$

$$= \frac{1}{0.002} \cdot \frac{p}{q}. \qquad [31]$$

To find the elasticity at different prices and

Mathematics for Innumerate Economists

quantities the appropriate values for price and quantity can be inserted into [31].

6.7 Robinson's Reel

So far the derivatives of the functions we have been dancing with have confined themselves to a single circuit of the floor: the Cognoscenti call this 'finding the first derivative'. But there are other reels than are unconstrained in the number of circuits they attempt — in fact they dance until exhaustion has eliminated everything that can be differentiated. These are called, by you-know-who, Higher Order Derivatives. The sequence is, as always, very simple: *keep differentiating the derivatives*.

An example is called for. Take the function $y = x^3$ and find its first derivative:

$$\frac{dy}{dx} = 3x^2.$$

Now find its second derivative:

$$\frac{d^2 y}{dx^2} = 6x$$

and its third derivative:

$$\frac{d^3 y}{dx^3} = 6$$

and its fourth derivative:

$$\frac{d^4 y}{dx^4} = 0.$$

You will have noted that Mme. Notation has created an identifying style for the higher order derivatives. The Cognoscenti read these derivatives as: 'Dee Two Why Dee Ecks squared' and 'Dee Three Why Dee Ecks cubed' and so on.

But what does it all mean? First, consider a total revenue function in the form

$$R = 5{,}000q - 20q^2. \qquad [31]$$

To find the marginal revenue of this function you differentiate it:

$$MR = \frac{dR}{dq} = 5{,}000 - 40q. \qquad [32]$$

The first derivative tells you by how much *total* revenue changes for every increase in the quantity sold (assuming a downward-sloping demand curve). The second derivative is the rate of change of *marginal* revenue; i.e., by how much marginal revenue declines for every additional sale. Taking the second derivative of [32] we get

$$\frac{d^2 R}{dq^2} = -40. \qquad [33]$$

In economics: marginal revenue declines by $40 for every additional unit sold.

That marginal revenue declines faster than average revenue is one of the principles of microeconomics and has featured in examinations since Joan Robinson's classic work on imperfect competition [1933]. You can use your knowledge of higher order differentiation to establish the principle.

In Figure 6.4 the average and marginal revenue schedules for a firm have been drawn. If the demand curve is given by the equation of a straight line,

$$p = a - bq \qquad [25]$$

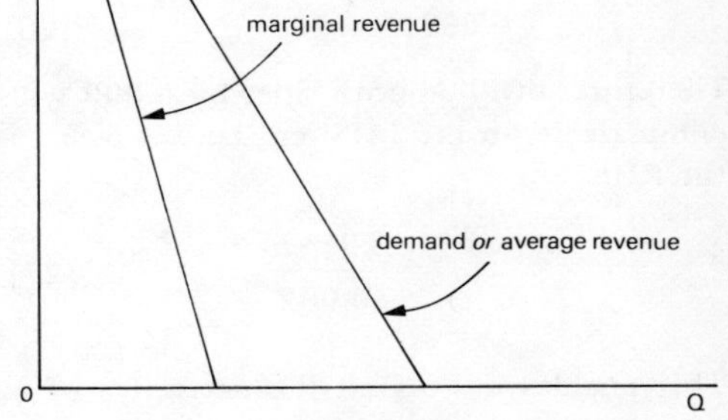

Figure 6.4

then total revenue can be found by multiplying [25] by q (remember that total revenue $= pq$):

$$R = aq - bq^2. \qquad [34]$$

Taking the first derivative we get

$$\frac{dR}{dq} = a - 2bq \qquad [35]$$

and the second derivative is

$$\frac{d^2R}{dq^2} = -2b. \qquad [36]$$

Inspecting [25] and [35], you will note that the slope constant (b) of the curves is $-b$ in the case of the demand curve and $-2b$ in the case of the marginal revenue curve. In other words, for a linear demand curve the marginal revenue curve has a slope *twice* as steep as the average revenue or demand curve. Mrs Robinson would be the last to claim that her result was of world-shattering importance — the neoclassical firm is a theoretical abstraction not a realistic description (and an abstraction which Joan Robinson explicitly repudiated in her later work [1962; 1978]) — but it is part of the body of doctrine your examiners expect you to know; so you may as well learn a handy proof using calculus.

However, it doesn't follow that Professor Peston [1969, p. vii] is correct in his dismissive comment about the 'discovery' of marginal revenue. 'These claims to originality being now seen to amount to the invention of the first derivative of a particular function, and therefore wholly laughable.' The debate at the time was more concerned with the acceptance of the idea of imperfect rather than of perfect competition as a model of the economy. Only if imperfect competition was accepted did the marginal revenue curve have any relevance, because in models of perfect competition the demand curve is horizontal and therefore average revenue coincides with marginal revenue. As is often the case in economics, the debate was about issues of greater substance to the profession, and *what it taught at the time*, than the surface quarrels suggest.

6.8 The Product Reel

The derivatives will demonstrate a higher-level dance known as the Product Reel which takes its name from the type of the functions it differentiates. A product function is one where the variables are multiplied together, such as in

$$Y = uv \qquad [37]$$

Y is equal to u, *multiplied by* v, *each representing some function of* x.

Total revenue is a multiple of two variables, price and quantity, and is an economic example of the product function:

$$R = pq. \qquad [10]$$

Earlier, we avoided the difficulties of differentiating [10] by confining the example to firms in perfect competition — thereby making the price term a constant by definition. But what happens when a cop-out is not available? To this end is danced the Product Reel.

The logical sequence of the steps is set out in 6.12, and you should check through them some time. However, stick for the moment with the finale and disregard the choreography:

$$\frac{dy}{dx} = u \cdot \frac{dv}{dx} + v \cdot \frac{du}{dx} \qquad [38]$$

To differentiate the product of two functions, multiply each function by the derivatives of the other and add the two products together.

In plain language you handle these functions by holding u constant while differentiating v, and v constant while differentiating u.

We shall use [10] to demonstrate the Product Reel. The firm's total revenue function R is the product of the quantity sold and its prices (pq):

$$R = pq. \qquad [10]$$

The marginal revenue function will be negative because it slopes downwards. To differentiate R we note that it is suitable for the application of the Product Reel: there are two variables multiplied together. First, we set the p variable equal to u and the q variable equal to v:

$$p = u \qquad [39]$$

$$q = v. \qquad [40]$$

Then we write out the Product Reel [38] (from our notebooks), it always being a sensible habit to write down standard formulae used in a **manipulation**:

$$\frac{dy}{dx} = u \cdot \frac{dv}{dx} + v \cdot \frac{du}{dx}. \qquad [38]$$

We are looking for the first derivative of R, (dR/dq), so we write it out, using [38] as the guide,

$$\frac{dR}{dq} = u \cdot \frac{dv}{dq} + v \cdot \frac{du}{dq}. \qquad [41]$$

and then we enter in the u and v variables:

$$\frac{dR}{dq} = p \cdot \frac{dq}{dq} + q \cdot \frac{dp}{dq}. \qquad [42]$$

There are two interesting features of [42]. You may have thought that there was a mistake in the derivative dq/dq but it follows from the substitution into [38] and as dq/dq is equal to 1 (a number divided by itself always equals unity) it follows that the p variable can stand on its own ($p \times 1 = p$). This gives

$$\frac{dR}{dq} = p + q \cdot \frac{dp}{dq}. \qquad [43]$$

Marginal revenue equals price plus quantity times the derivative of price.

The second point to note is the dp/dq term. This must be negative because price is falling along the negative sloped demand schedule and this makes the $q \cdot dp/dq$ term negative. However else [43] is interpreted, one thing is abundantly clear: marginal revenue is less than price (Figure 6.5) for the imperfectly competitive firm. The larger the negative second term on the RHS ($q \cdot dp/dq$) the greater the difference between price and marginal revenue; the greater the difference the more imperfectly competitive the firm.

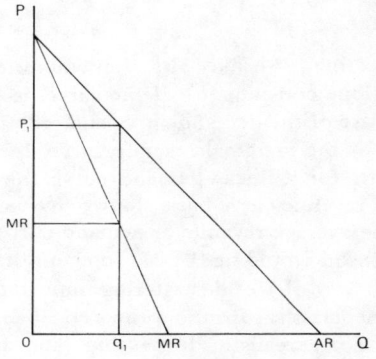

Figure 6.5

6.9 Another Elastic Example*

If you look closely at the second term in [43], you may think it looks familiar. Can I jog your memory by adding another variable to it? Taking

$$q \cdot \frac{dp}{dq} \qquad [44]$$

and inserting p, it becomes

$$\frac{q}{p} \cdot \frac{dp}{dq} \qquad [45]$$

which you will recognise as something like the measure of elasticity. The difference is that [45] is 'upside down'. Elasticity is measured by

$$\frac{dq}{dp} \cdot \frac{p}{q}. \qquad [28]$$

6. The Dance of the Derivatives

What follows is not very entertaining (every plot has some dull parts). We use several dodges, which, if not understood, can at least be admired — just as we can all admire the dance routines of Fred Astaire and Ginger Rogers even though we couldn't put two steps together ourselves. We want to find a relationship betwen marginal revenue and elasticity. You know there is a relationship because no intermediate course in microeconomics is complete without reference to it.

We start with [43]:

$$\frac{dR}{dq} = p + q \cdot \frac{dp}{dq} \qquad [43]$$

and want p in the RHS as divisor of q. To do this we multiply both terms by that most interesting of fellows, unity. This has the effect of 'opening up' the RHS without changing its value in any way because a term multiplied by 1 is itself. But the dodge is even cleverer than this: we put unity into the form p/p! (A number divided by itself is always 1):

$$= p \cdot \frac{p}{p} + q \cdot \frac{p}{p} \cdot \frac{dp}{dq}. \qquad [46]$$

To simplify this, without changing its meaning of course, we use brackets, on the principle that the brackets tell us to multiply everything inside them by the term outside them. The common term for [46] is the variable p, because this multiplies every term on the RHS. The first term is p times p/p or 1; hence we can write $(p \cdot 1)$. The second term is slightly less obvious until you note that $q \cdot p/p$ is the same as $p \cdot q/p$ and therefore reads p times q/p times dp/dq, which becomes $p(q/p \cdot dp/dq)$. Putting these together we get

$$= p\left[1 + \frac{q}{p} \cdot \frac{dp}{dq}\right]. \qquad [47]$$

This has brought p into the equation as divisor of q and we have got the second term in the RHS into the form we showed in [45]. However, we want to get it like [28]; that is, we want to *invert* it, or turn it upside down. The only way this can be done is to find its reciprocal, and we do this using the *inverse quadrille* which we will take time out to explain.

You know what dy/dx is and how it is found, but what does dx/dy mean and how is it related to dy/dx? Take the equation of the straight line $y = a + bx$ and find dy/dx:

$$y = a + bx \qquad [48]$$

$$\frac{dy}{dx} = b. \qquad [49]$$

(The constant a is eliminated in the differentiation and differentiating x $(=x^1)$ gives $x^{1-1} = x^0 = 1$.) If we want to find dx/dy we have to get equation [48] in terms of y:

$$y = a + bx. \qquad [48]$$

You know how to handle this kind of manipulation: take a from both sides and divide both sides by b:

$$\frac{y - a}{b} = \frac{a - a + bx}{b} \qquad [50]$$

giving

$$x = \frac{y}{b} - \frac{a}{b}. \qquad [51]$$

Differentiating [51] gives

$$\frac{dx}{dy} = \frac{1}{b} \qquad [52]$$

because a/b as constants are eliminated and differentiating y/b equals $(y \cdot 1/b)$ eliminates y.

Note that as dy/dx of the straight-line function equals b, dx/dy of the same function equals $1/b$, or its reciprocal. If the inverse of a derivative is ever required, you simply put it into its reciprocal. In this case because

$$\frac{dy}{dx} = b \qquad [49]$$

it follows that

$$\frac{dx}{dy} = \frac{1}{b}. \qquad [52]$$

The Inverse Quadrille is a useful dance, though you need't memorise it if you write it down in your notebook. Returning to [47] we can soon get the second term into the form we want by simply writing it in its inverse form. If

$$\frac{dR}{dq} = p\left[1 + \frac{q}{p} \cdot \frac{dp}{dq}\right] \qquad [47]$$

in inverse it becomes

$$\frac{dR}{dq} = p\left[1 + \frac{1}{\frac{p}{q} \cdot \frac{dq}{dp}}\right]. \qquad [53]$$

We can approach this step from another direction. Take the textbook definition of elasticity

$$\eta = \frac{dq}{dp} \cdot \frac{p}{q}.$$

The coefficient of elasticity is identified by a gift from the Greeks, η pronounced *eeta*. This can be rewritten in its inverse form as

$$\frac{1}{\eta} = \frac{dp}{dq} \cdot \frac{q}{p}. \qquad [54]$$

Returning to [53] you will note that the second term on the RHS can be substituted by

$$\frac{1}{\eta}$$

giving

$$\frac{dR}{dq} = p\left[1 + \frac{1}{\eta}\right] \qquad [55]$$

Marginal revenue equals price times 1 plus the reciprocal of the elasticity of demand.

The result in [55] has an intuitive appeal because it follows by inspection that the larger the coefficient of elasticity (the bit below the line on the RHS) the smaller the result of dividing it into the bit above the line and, therefore, remembering that this is a negative term, the smaller the amount to be taken away from price. This results in a small divergence of price from marginal revenue. On the other hand, if elasticity of demand is slight — going on inelastic — the result of dividing it into 1 will produce a larger number to be taken away from price, and this will create a larger divergence between price and marginal revenue.

From your literary economics you will know that the more price-elastic a firm's output the less influence it will have over its own price — the more it approaches the status of a price-taker. In this case the more its marginal revenue and price will approach identical values and in the limit — perfect competition — they will coincide. At the polar opposite — monopoly — the gap between price and marginal revenue is widened and the more he has control over his price. Indeed, the existence of such a gap is an indication of the extent of monopoly power. If elasticity is equal to 1, then marginal revenue will be zero; if it is greater than 1, marginal revenue will be positive, and if it is less than 1, marginal revenue will be negative. These relationships are shown in Figure 6.6.

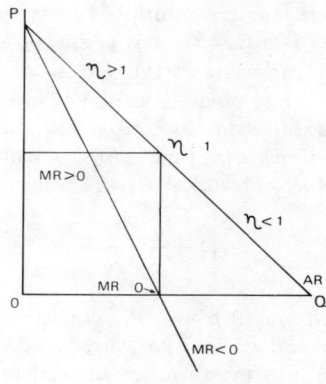

Figure 6.6

6.10 More Elasticity!

While we are on the topic of elasticity it might be appropriate to outline at this point another use for the calculus you have acquired so far. This concerns the special case of a unitary elasticity demand curve. From your textbook you know that a demand curve with the characteristic of constant elasticity is one where no matter what price/output combination is chosen the total revenue is the same. This amounts to saying that the total revenue at any price is the same because the area under the curve at any point is the same (Figure 6.7). To illustrate

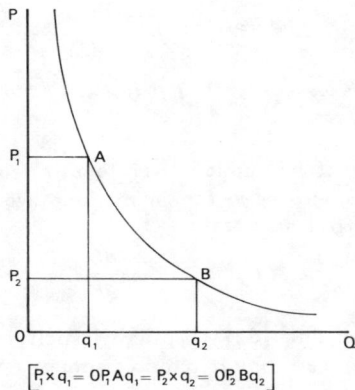

$$[P_1 \times q_1 = OP_1 A q_1 = P_2 \times q_2 = OP_2 B q_2]$$

Figure 6.7

this situation, consider a constant total revenue function such that

$$pq = \$8000. \qquad [56]$$

This means that

$$q = \frac{8000}{p}. \qquad [57]$$

To differentiate this type of function, we must put it into an equivalent form which uses the property that

$$\frac{1}{p} = p^{-1}.$$

Rewriting [57] we get

$$q = 8000 p^{-1}$$

and differentiating this we get

$$\frac{dq}{dp} = -1(8000)p^{-1-1}$$

$$= -\frac{8000}{p^2}. \qquad [58]$$

Elasticity is defined as

$$\eta = -\frac{dq}{dp} \cdot \frac{p}{q}. \qquad [28]$$

Substituting this into [58] (watching the signs!) gives

$$= \frac{8000}{p^2} \cdot \frac{p}{q} \qquad [59]$$

(If $dq/dp = -8000/p^2$, then $-dq/dp = 8000/p^2$).

The equation involves multiplying the top bit by p and dividing it by p^2, which is the same thing as dividing it once by p. This enables us to write [59] as

$$= \frac{8000}{pq} \qquad [60]$$

but $pq = 8000$ from [56] and [60] becomes

$$= \frac{8000}{8000}$$

$$\eta = 1.$$

Therefore the elasticity is constant and unitary along the demand curve. You will use this idea in several advanced applications of microeconomics.

6.11 The Trainer's Tale*

Suppose during the interval at the Dance of the Derivatives you get talking to the man next to you, who turns out to be in the business of selling training packages to top companies in Europe and North America. (You will often meet trainers at other people's performances looking for new ideas to sell to clients — under their own label of course — it's called 'creative plagiarism' in the trade!)

The Trainer's problem in this case is that he doesn't know what the demand curve for his services looks like, and without this information he can't operate a pricing policy based upon equating marginal cost with marginal revenue. The most common policy in his business is a 'mark up over costs' rule, though even here he still has to decide on the appropriate mark-up.

He could apply a fixed percentage of the costs to all quotations — the particular percentage having been chosen arbitrarily. Or, he could apply a varying percentage, depending on his reading of 'what the market will bear', which is surely a nod in the direction of the concept of price elasticity of demand? Market conditions will vary, so will the enthusiasm of clients for outhouse training packages. If the trainer is going to get anywhere near maximising his profits he will have to estimate 'what the market will bear' with consistent accuracy: if he over-prices, the client will look elsewhere or do without it, if he underestimates his prices, he will undertake business at lower profits than he could have made if he had got it right. The most successful training consultancies get it right more often than the competititon.

Now nothing you learn in an economics course will provide you with the magic codeword that will find a definite answer to the question 'What will this market bear at this moment?' If it did, you could set up in business as a consultant and make a small fortune. All your neoclassical economics teaches you is how to establish the profit-maximising price *if* the special conditions of the model are met. Real-world firms don't meet these conditions. Some Very Clever People have argued that if a real-world firm is maximising its profits (by guess or by God) it will be behaving *as if* it is meeting the neoclassical conditions. Some Less Clever but Practical People — the kind who have to meet a payroll once a week — have asked the Very Clever People if they could make their theory operational; i.e., tell them how to set about winning the prize rather than be awarded it if they find the answer themselves!

The Trainer you talked to in the interval may have described a particular sale he made last week (sales people tend to boast about the *alleged* deals they have made). Let us suppose that he charged his client a 10 per cent mark-up over marginal cost. This is equivalent to a pricing policy of charging 110 per cent of marginal cost. In symbols we could write this down on the back of the dance programme as

$$P = (1 + 0.10)\frac{dC}{dQ}. \qquad [61]$$

Price equals 110 per cent of marginal cost.

Indeed if he applied [61] to all pricing decisions, writing m for the mark-up, we could write [61] as

$$P = (1 + m)\frac{dC}{dQ}. \qquad [62]$$

Can we link [62] to price elasticity of demand? Yes, but it requires some extensive and dreary manipulation.

The first thing we do is get dC/dQ to the LHS on its own and this requires a reorganisation of [62]. An equation can always be adjusted as long as we treat both sides the same. In this case we simply divide both sides by $(1 + m)$:

$$\frac{P}{1+m} = \frac{(1+m)}{(1+m)}\frac{dC}{dQ}$$

getting

$$\frac{dC}{dQ} = \frac{P}{1+m}. \qquad [63]$$

(By convention we place the sought-for term on the LHS.)

The Trainer may flinch at the next step because it 'begs the question', but flushed with enthusiasm for neoclassical principles,

6. The Dance of the Derivatives

you brush aside his scepticism. The profit-maximising condition from your texbook is

$$MC = MR$$

Marginal cost equals marginal revenue

or

$$\frac{dC}{dQ} = \frac{dR}{dQ}.$$

If one thing is equal to another it can be substituted for it and you do this to the LHS of [63]:

$$\frac{dR}{dQ} = \frac{p}{1+m}. \qquad [64]$$

You do this again because from [55] you have an equivalent for marginal revenue and you substitute this for the LHS of [64]. Because

$$\frac{dR}{dQ} = p\left[1 + \frac{1}{\eta}\right] \qquad [55]$$

[64] can be written as

$$p\left[1 + \frac{1}{\eta}\right] = \frac{p}{1+m}. \qquad [65]$$

This rather awkward-looking equation gives us an expression for the mark-up in terms of something equivalent to marginal revenue. Both sides have the price variable in common and you use this to simplify the equation. If both sides are divided by p it will eliminate itself:

$$\frac{p}{p}\left[1 + \frac{1}{\eta}\right] = \frac{p}{p}\frac{1}{(1+m)}$$

giving

$$1 + \frac{1}{\eta} = \frac{1}{1+m}. \qquad [66]$$

Now follows some tortuous manipulation as we 'open up' [66]. You must write this down if the Trainer is to follow you and if you aren't to get lost yourself. We call up the dodge we used earlier by re-writing 1 in another form which doesn't change its value.

Let

$$\frac{\eta}{\eta} = 1.$$

Therefore the LHS can be written as

$$\frac{\eta}{\eta} + \frac{1}{\eta} = \frac{\eta+1}{\eta}$$

making [66]

$$\frac{\eta+1}{\eta} = \frac{1}{1+m}. \qquad [67]$$

If you multiply both sides by $(1+m)$ the equation will stay in balance:

$$(1+m)\frac{\eta+1}{\eta} = \frac{1}{1+m}(1+m)$$

giving

$$(1+m)\frac{\eta+1}{\eta} = 1. \qquad [68]$$

Next, multiply both sides by η, to get

$$(1+m)\left[\frac{\eta+1}{\eta}\right]\eta = 1 \cdot \eta$$

and simplifying and re-arranging to get

$$\eta = (\eta+1)(1+m). \qquad [69]$$

The RHS is now multiplied out, giving

$$1 + m$$
$$\frac{\eta+1}{\eta+1+m+m\cdot\eta}.$$

Inserting this in [69], gives

$$\eta = 1 + m + \eta + m\eta. \qquad [70]$$

Collect like terms to the LHS:

$$\eta - \eta - m\eta = 1 + m$$
$$-m\eta = 1 + m$$
$$-\eta = \frac{1+m}{m} \qquad [71]$$

Elasticity equals 1 plus the mark-up divided by the mark-up.

There is absolutely no way that such a result could be deduced by literary means, and it would also be very difficult to explain it without recourse to mathematics. It may be that the result isn't very important and is somewhat obscure in meaning, but the point is that it can be used to show a connection between the Trainer's view of price elasticity for his services and his mark-up rule. Though he doesn't know his marginal revenue curve nor his demand curve, he is still effectively looking for the point in Figure 6.8 where his

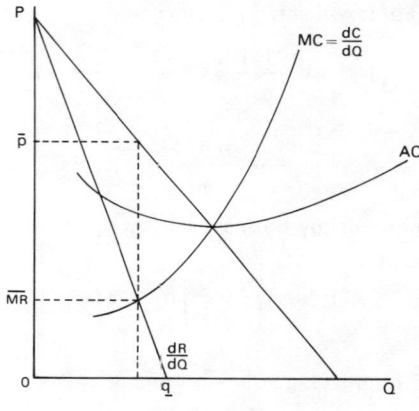

Figure 6.8

marginal cost and his unknown marginal revenue curves intersect — he is behaving, as the Very Clever People insist, *as if* he knew the exact shape of the relevant curves. You may not have convinced him, but you can be sure that you have entertained him and that he will file your manipulations just in case he is asked by a client to run a course in Mark-Up Economics at the local Hilton Hotel.

6.12 For the Notebook

The rules for differentiation need not be memorised as long as you know where to find them. Some of the ones from the dance are given here with some of the 'back-stage' workings. These may be ignored for all time if you only want to know were the light switch is.

*Addition rule: *Differentiate each function separately and add the result.*

Let $y = u + v$, where u and v are functions of x. When x increases by a wee bit it will become $x + dx$ and y will become $y + dy$. Thus, u becomes $u + du$ and v becomes $v + dv$:

$$y + dy = u + du + v + dv.$$

Taking y from the LHS and u and v from the RHS (because $y = u + v$ and taking the same from both sides leaves the equation in balance) we get

$$dy = du + dv.$$

To get dy/dx we divide through by dx to get

$$\frac{dy}{dx} = \frac{du}{dx} + \frac{dv}{dx}.$$

*Subtraction rule: *Differentiate each function separately and carry out the subtraction:*

Let $y = u - v$ where, again, u and v are both functions of x:

$$\frac{dy}{dx} = \frac{du}{dx} - \frac{dv}{dx}.$$

The back-stage working is the same as for the addition rule.

*Product rule: *Multiply each function by the derivative of the other and add the results.*

Let u and v be functions of x. If x grows by an infinitesimal amount it will become $x + dx$ and change y to $y + dy$. Thus u becomes $u + du$ and v becomes $v + dv$, and

$$y + dy = (u + du)(v + dv).$$

6. The Dance of the Derivatives

Multiplying out the RHS gives

$$u + du$$
$$\underline{v + dv}$$
$$uv + v \cdot du$$
$$\underline{ + u \cdot dv + du \cdot dv}$$
$$uv + v \cdot du + u \cdot dv + du \cdot dv.$$

The term $du \cdot dv$ is extremely minute and is disregarded ('next to nothing times next to nothing'). This gives

$$y + dy = uv + u \cdot dv + v \cdot du$$

and we know that the original function was $y = uv$ and therefore taking y from the LHS and uv from the RHS leaves the equation in balance, giving

$$dy = u \cdot dv + v \cdot du.$$

But we want dy/dx, so we divide through by dx (whatever we do to one side we do to the other) to get

$$\frac{dy}{dx} = u \cdot \frac{dv}{dx} + v \cdot \frac{du}{dx}.$$

Inverse function rule: to find dx/dy, put dy/dx as the denominator under 1 as the numerator.

$$\frac{dx}{dy} = \frac{1}{\frac{dy}{dx}}.$$

Summary of the rules for indices

* $x^n = n$ x's multiplied together

* $x^1 = x$

* $x^0 = 1$

* $x^{-n} = \dfrac{1}{x^n}$

* $x^{-n/m} = \dfrac{1}{m\sqrt{x^n}}$

* $x^{n/m} = m\sqrt{x^n}$

* $(x^n)(x^m) = x^{m+n}$

* $(x^n)(x^{-m}) = \dfrac{x^n}{x^m} = x^{n-m}$

* $x^{nm} = (x^n)^m$

*   *   *

There is an alternative notation to the dY/dX style which is well established in the literature, where typesetting costs are critical. The alternative notation is formally introduced here because you may be unable to follow what you have struggled to understand when the notation changes.

Equation [3], which is common to both notation systems, can be used to illustrate the new notation:

$$C = f(Q). \qquad [3]$$

Its derivative in Old Notation is written

$$\frac{dC}{dQ} \qquad [2]$$

but in new notation it is written

$$f'(Q) \qquad [6]$$

'E prime Q', or, *the first derivative with respect to Q*.

The difference is clearly a great economy in space and is thoroughly consistent (which always appeals to mathematicians). The second derivative is written $f''(Q)$, the third is written $f'''(Q)$ and so on.

SEVEN

Peaks, Valleys and Ledges

7.1 Introduction

The topography of a Mathematics Mountain depends on the relationship between y and x, but it isn't always obvious from the equation what the y value is for any given value of x. It is easy, therefore, to get lost. Apart from the perplexing terrain, there is always the prospect of a sudden mist closing in on the innocent. Learn some basic field craft and practise it regularly and you will cope with most emergencies. It is all very well being able to see the path ahead on a clear day, but in a mountain mist you will be lucky if you can see further than the RHS of an equation. If things are really bad you won't know whether you are at the top of a hill or at the bottom of a valley. In a mist, if you aren't where you think you are there could be a disaster. Try stepping upwards when you're on a peak and you will topple over; try stepping downwards when you're in a valley and you will stub your toe; try resting on a slope, believing it is a ledge, and you will slip and slide down. Consequently you must be able to find where you are, no matter how murky the mist around you.

The basic topgraphy of a Mathematics Mountain is shown in Figure 7.1. Starting at the trough of the valley floor, we have a Minimum Point — there is no point lower than where the sides of the adjacent slopes rise upwards. Occasionally ledges are crossed where, for an instant, there may be a flat bit which immediately breaks into another slope, or, sometimes, the slope changes from convex to concave without even a flat bit

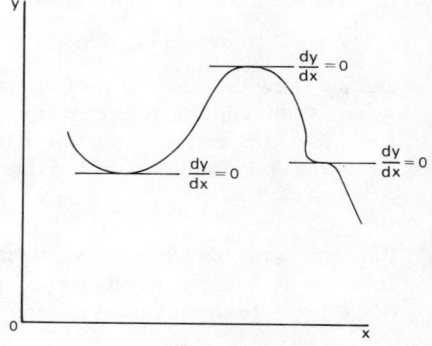

Figure 7.1

intervening. Among the more esoteric of the Cognoscenti these sudden slope changes are known as Points of Inflexion.

All peaks have a maximum point — there is no point higher than where the slopes of the adjacent sides fall downwards.

To survive in the mountains you must learn how to identify valleys, peaks and ledges in all weather conditions, which is precisely what you will cover in this chapter. It isn't just a question of knowing the topgraphy — you have to know where you are at any moment if your knowledge of the topography is going to be of any use.

7.2 Memory Joggers

Before setting off to explore new terrain you should check your equipment to ensure that only what is necessary stays in our backpack — what you keep, you carry. Fortunately some items from previous hikes have a use in this one and a brief survey of them may jog your memory sufficiently to put you in good heart for the climbs and descents ahead.

Let us revise what we already know about derivatives of functions and what they tell us when we read them.

The first derivative of the function $y = f(x)$ is written in old-style notation as dy/dx. If it is positive, we know that the tangent at the point is upward-sloping; i.e., rises upwards from left to right. For example, a supply curve is generally thought to be positively sloped. Conversely, if the derivative dy/dx is negative, we know that the tangent is downward-sloping; i.e., falls from left to right, such as in the case of a demand curve. The numerical size of the derivative tells us by how much the height (or, value of y) is increasing or decreasing at the point we are at. Thus, in general, the first derivative gives us information about the *direction* and *magnitude* of the change in height (or value of y) as x changes infinitesimally. If you like, it acts as a crude altimeter.

At any point on the mountain you can find out which way the slope is going — upwards or downwards — no matter what the conditions at the time, by examining the sign of the derivative and its magnitude. You know that a function can only increase if its rate of change is positive; i.e., for every step horizontally there is an increase in height, and therefore the curve of the mountain rises before you from left to right. Therefore for all values of x in which dy/dx is positive, you know that the function increases. Conversely, for all values of x in which dy/dx is negative you know that the function decreases as x increases, and therefore the curve of the slope falls before you from left to right. Even if you have completely lost your way in what you are doing and cannot see even the LHS of the equation, let alone the RHS, you can still recover your sense of direction by checking the sign of the derivative. You know this before you have attempted any of the work in this chapter!

We can add a third possibility to the two of positive or negative: that the derivative is neither. For our purposes if a derivative is neither positive nor negative, by the logic of elimination it must be equal to zero. If a slope is neither increasing nor decreasing it must be 'flat' — you are at the top of a peak or at the bottom of a valley or on the flat bit of a ledge (see Figure 7.1). The tangent touching the flat bit is parallel to the horizontal axis, which is the geometrical interpretation of the derivative being equal to zero.

The points where the derivative is equal to zero are called, by the Cognoscenti, Stationary Points. In a typical mathematics mountain range there will be a whole host of stationary points. They are distinguished from the adjacent points by being higher in the case of peaks and lower in the case of valleys. With ledges, the adjacent points will be lower on the left and higher on the right for upward-sloping curves, and higher on the left and lower on the right for downward-sloping curves (Figure 7.1).

7.3 A (Long) Tale of Two Averages

You don't get very far into a microeconomics course without being introduced to the 'average-marginal' relationship. It is used in the theory of costs of the firm and in the theory of production. Innumerate students are usually introduced to the relationship by analogous example — a line of soldiers standing shoulder to shoulder in ascending height order is one of the most commonly used in the classroom. The average height of the soldiers will continue to rise as long as the next soldier's height (the marginal change) is greater than the average height of the previous soldiers. If a soldier is the same height as the average height of the previous soldiers the average height will remain the same, and if the next soldier to join the line is smaller than the average height of those in the line, the average height of the line will fall.

Translating the analogy to economics, the

average-marginal relationship describes the behaviour of average and marginal cost and product curves. If the marginal change is greater than the average, the average curve is rising; if the marginal change is less than the average, the average curve is falling. At the point where the marginal and average curves are the same (intersect in a graph) the average is at a maximum or minimum. Figure 7.2 illustrates this familiar relationship using a graph of average and marginal product from microeconomics.

Can we use calculus to establish that the marginal product curve will intersect the average product curve at its maximum (peak) value? From your theory you know that this is an accepted result in economics and therefor the mathematical demonstration of the relationship involves you in no new conceptual effort. There is, however, a new mathematical tool required; namely, the Divider or, to Cognoscenti, the Quotient, Rule, which will be asserted rather than proved in what follows.

Consider what you already know about the theory of production. You know what a production function is, such as

$$TP = f(K, L) \qquad [1]$$

Total Product is a function of the inputs of capital and labour.

You know also that if one of the factors is held constant and varying amounts of the other factor increased, the amount of output will depend on the functional relationship between total physical product and the input. If capital input K is held constant, and labour input L varied, we can write the relationship as

$$P = f(L) \qquad [2]$$

Total product P is a function of the labour input.

The average product of the labour input is defined as the total product divided by the quantity of the input

$$AP = \frac{P}{L}. \qquad [3]$$

On the basis of these relations we can use some calculus to establish the average marginal relationship.

First, we substitute [2] into [3] to state the RHS in terms of labour only (because $P = f(L)$):

$$AP = \frac{f(L)}{L}. \qquad [4]$$

In Figure 7.2 the average product curve is shown. It is intersected at a maximum value by the marginal product curve which is downward-sloping to the right, conforming with the assumption that as more of an input is added to a fixed amount of another input the marginal product eventually diminishes. The marginal product is, of course, the first derivative of the *total* product curve and what we want to find at the moment is the first derivative of the *average* product curve:

$$\frac{d}{dL}\left[\frac{f(L)}{L}\right] \qquad [5]$$

First derivative of the average product curve.

The average product calculation requires a variable to be divided by another variable and to find the derivative of [5] we need to use the divider rule. This looks very fearsome — it has been known to give fainting

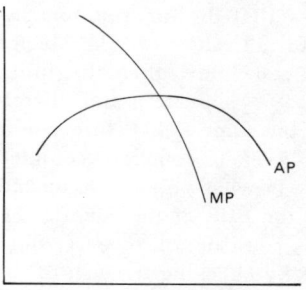

Figure 7.2

7. Peaks, Valleys and Ledges

shocks to students who, wandering innocently in the mountains, stumble across it for the first time. It looks like this:

$$\frac{dy}{dx} = \frac{v \cdot \frac{du}{dx} - u \cdot \frac{dv}{dx}}{v^2} \qquad [6]$$

The derivative of a divider function is found by multiplying the denominator by the derivative of the numerator, minus the numerator times the derivaive of the denominator and dividng the result by the denominator squared

when

$$y = \frac{u}{v}. \qquad [7]$$

This is a difficult idea to grasp in one, or even three, goes. Fortunately you don't need to in order to use the rule — remember the light switch! What you must do, is substitute into [6] in a careful way and follow the manipulation. This is *not* beyond you, especially as you know the answer already. To help your understanding, copy down the working rather than try to 'read' through it.

Average product is a division sum in the form of [7]:

$$y = \frac{u}{v} = \frac{f(L)}{L} \qquad [8]$$

and therefore qualifies for substitution into [6]. The best way is to take each term on its own and follow the manipulation in parts before assembling it together. We want to find how average product changes as labour inputs are increased, i.e., dAP/dL (using dAP to avoid confusion with marginal product). This gives the LHS of [6]. The v term is L and the derivative of u is the derivative of $f(L)$. Because $f(L)$ is an expression for total product P, it follows that the derivative of P with respect to L is dP/dL. We now have the first part of the numerator:

$$L \cdot \frac{dP}{dL}.$$

The second term is a little less obvious. The u term is $f(L)$ from [8]. The derivative of the v term (L) is the rate of change of L with dL (from the LHS: dAP/dL). This means finding dL/dL which is equal to 1 (the rate of change of a number with respect to the change in itself is itself, and a number divided by itself is unity). The term is written out as

$$f(L) \cdot 1$$

or $f(L)$. The numerator can be written as

$$L \cdot \frac{dP}{dL} - f(L).$$

The denominator is v, which from [8] is L, and therefore the whole equation is written as

$$\frac{dAP}{dL} = \frac{L \cdot \frac{dP}{dL} - f(L)}{L^2}. \qquad [9]$$

When average product is at a maximum its derivative must be equal to zero ($dAP/dL = 0$) and therefore [9] becomes

$$\frac{L \cdot \frac{dP}{dL} - f(L)}{L^2} = 0. \qquad [9']$$

To simplify [9'] we must eliminate the denominator. One way is to multiply both sides of [9'] by L^2. This eliminates L on the LHS (because a number multiplied and divided by the same number is itself) and on the RHS (because zero multipled by a number remains zero). This gives

$$\frac{L \cdot dP}{dL} - f(L) = 0. \qquad [10]$$

Now, if a number minus another number is equal to zero, the absolute value of the numbers are also equal to each other. Adding $f(L)$ to both sides gives

$$\frac{L \cdot dP}{dL} = f(L) \qquad [11]$$

and, dividing both sides by L, gives

$$\frac{dP}{dL} = \frac{f(L)}{L}. \qquad [12]$$

Examine [12] closely. You should recognise the terms. The LHS is the first derivative of the total product curve (dP/dL) and the RHS is the average product $[f(L)/L]$. Thus [12] tells you that when average product is at a maximum value it is equal to marginal product. In Figure 7.2 the marginal product curve intersects the average product curve at its maximum value.

Can we use this method to say anything about the relationship between average and marginal products at values other than the maximum average product? The answer, of course, is 'yes', providing some additional manipulation is carried out. We need to go back to [9]:

$$\frac{dAP}{dL} = \frac{L \cdot \frac{dP}{dL} - f(L)}{L^2} \qquad [9]$$

and, instead of setting this equal to zero for a maximum average product, we accept that the derivative is going to be positive for values up to the maximum average product (because average product is rising in this range). How then can we simplify [9] if the dodge of multiplying both sides by L is not available? Examine the first term in the numerator $L \cdot dP/dL$ and note that this is divided by L^2. To multiply by L and then divide by L^2 is the same as dividing by L and this can be written

$$\frac{\frac{dP}{dL}}{L}.$$

The second term is divided by L as well (because L^2 is the common denominator in [9]). This is the same as dividing the term by L and by L again. Thus it can be written as

$$\frac{\frac{f(L)}{L}}{L}.$$

Equation [9] is now rewritten as

$$\frac{dAP}{dL} = \frac{\frac{dP}{dL} - \frac{f(L)}{L}}{L} \qquad [13]$$

or

$$= \frac{1}{L}\left[\frac{dP}{dL} - \frac{f(L)}{L}\right]. \qquad [14]$$

You know that dP/dL is the marginal product of labour MP and that $f(L)/L$ is the average product of labour (AP). Equation [14] states that the derivative of average product (dAP/dL) is $1/L$ times marginal product minus $1/L$ times average product. Because average product is rising at values less than maximum average product it follows that the derivative of average product is positive. Thus

$$\frac{dAP}{dL} = \frac{1}{L}(MP - AP) > 0. \qquad [15]$$

The term $1/L$ can be ignored in what follows because by the laws of inequalities (see your notebook 3.8) the inequality remains (where $a > 0$) if the common multiplier is removed: if $ab - ad > 0$, then $b - d > 0$. [15] becomes

$$MP - AP > 0. \qquad [16]$$

If [16] is true then marginal product must be greater than average product, which is what is shown in Figure 7.2; for all values of average product less than its maximum while its function is increasing, marginal product is greater than average product.

When average product is declining, its derivative will be negative and [16] will become

$$MP - AP < 0. \qquad [17]$$

7. Peaks, Valleys and Ledges

Here marginal product is less than average product for all values of average product less than its maximum value when the function is declining or negatively sloped as shown in Figure 7.2.

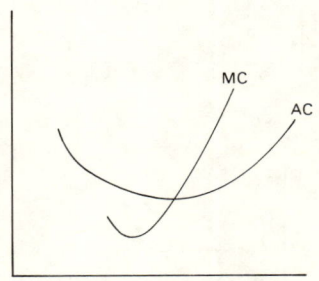

Figure 7.3

Applying the same method to the average marginal cost relationship should produce few problems for you if you take it slowly and follow through the working. The usual 'U'-shaped average cost curve is shown in Figure 7.3, with the marginal cost curve cutting through the average cost curve at its minimum point. Average cost is found by dividing the total cost of output by the quantity of output:

$$AC = \frac{C}{Q}. \qquad [18]$$

We want to find the derivative of the average cost curve, which involves finding

$$\frac{dAC}{dQ} = \frac{d}{dQ}\left(\frac{C}{Q}\right). \qquad [19]$$

This requires the divider rule:

$$\frac{dy}{dx} = \frac{v \cdot \frac{du}{dx} - u \cdot \frac{dv}{dx}}{v^2}. \qquad [6]$$

We substitute into [6] the appropriate values of v and u and their derivatives:

$$\frac{dAC}{dQ} = \frac{Q \cdot \frac{dC}{dQ} - C \cdot \frac{dQ}{dQ}}{Q^2} \qquad [20]$$

which, because $dQ/dQ = 1$, becomes

$$= \frac{Q \cdot \frac{dC}{dQ} - C}{Q^2}. \qquad [21]$$

Following the manipulations with the average product case we can immediately write [21] as

$$= \frac{\frac{dC}{dQ} - \frac{C}{Q}}{Q}$$

or

$$= \frac{1}{Q}\left[\frac{dC}{dQ} - \frac{C}{Q}\right]. \qquad [22]$$

We note that dC/dQ is marginal cost, or the first derivative of total cost, and that C/Q is average cost. Applying the rules of inequalities we can state the average-marginal cost relationships.

When the average cost curve is falling, the derivative of average cost will be negative and therefore

$$\frac{dAC}{dQ} = \frac{1}{Q}(MC - AC) < 0. \qquad [23]$$

This means that

$$MC - AC < 0$$

or

$$MC < AC \qquad [24]$$

Marginal cost is less than average cost.

When the average cost curve is at a minimum, the derivative will be equal to zero and therefore

$$\frac{dAC}{dQ} = \frac{1}{Q}(MC - AC) = 0 \qquad [25]$$

giving

$$MC - AC = 0$$

or

$$MC = AC \qquad [26]$$

Marginal cost equals average cost.

Finally, when the average cost curve is rising

the derivative of average cost will be positive and therefore

$$\frac{dAC}{dQ} = \frac{1}{Q}(MC - AC) > 0. \quad [27]$$

This means that

$$MC - AC > 0 \quad [28]$$

or

$$MC > AC \quad [29]$$

Marginal cost is greater than average cost.

7.4. Take Seconds

In the tale of two averages we already knew from economic theory whether we were dealing with a maximum or minimum value of the function. We can't always pick our examples so conveniently for our manipulations. If it isn't obvious from the function, or from our knowledge of theory, whether a point is a valley, a peak or a ledge, we have to find a way of determining what it is from the information given in the function itself. We know that for a point to be a valley, peak or ledge, the derivative of the function has to be equal to zero. Thus finding the zero values of the derivative will tell us that it is a stationary point of some kind, and we only have to decide which kind it is.

One fairly unwieldy way of finding whether a zero derivative is a valley, a peak or a ledge, is to find the number which makes the first derivative equal to zero, and then to enter numbers into the derivative a little smaller and then a little larger than the number giving a zero value and see if they work out positive or negative. If it is a valley, the value of the derivative to the left of the point where dy/dx is zero (X in Figure 7.4) will be negative, and to the right of X positive. If it is a peak, the value of the derivative to the left of the point where dy/dx is zero (X in Figure 7.5) will be positive and to the right negative.

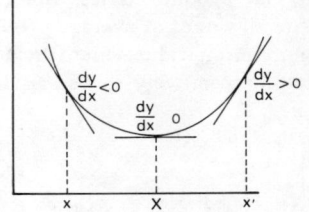

Figure 7.4

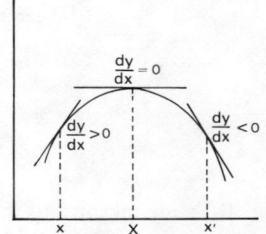

Figure 7.5

In the figures the slopes of the function are graphed. At X, dy/dx is equal to zero. If we try a number a little smaller than X, such as x, and enter it into the first derivative and find that it is negative, we know that its slope will be falling from left to right. If we repeat the exercise with a number a little larger than X, such as x', and find that the derivative is positive we know that the slope will be rising from left to right. Where the derivative dy/dx is negative, passes through zero and then increases, it means that X must be a minimum as in Figure 7.4 because the slope of the function, which the derivative describes, graphs as a valley. Similarly, if we try a number a little smaller than X and find that the derivative is positive and try a number a little larger than X and find the derivative is negative, we know that the graph of the slope of the function describes a maximum (or peak) as in Figure 7.5.

Suppose, the function is

$$y = 4x - x^2 \quad [30]$$

7. Peaks, Valleys and Ledges

then
$$\frac{dy}{dx} = 4 - 2x. \qquad [31]$$

If you put $x = 2$ into [31] the derivative will equal zero:
$$\frac{dy}{dx} = 4 - 2(2)$$
$$\frac{dy}{dx} = 0.$$

Is this a peak or a valley? Put $x = 1$ into [31]:
$$= 4 - 2(1)$$
$$\frac{dy}{dx} = 2.$$

This is a positive derivative, indicating that the slope is rising just before the zero point. Now put $x = 3$ into [31]:
$$= 4 - 2(3)$$
$$\frac{dy}{dx} = -2.$$

This is a negative derivative, indicating that the slope is falling just after the zero point. We conclude that this is a peak.

This is not the most elegant of methods and could involve considerable arithmetic. There is also a problem that the numbers chosen may 'hide' a shift in the slope between the number and the zero value — when you step off into the gap you find that there is a local shift in the slope not picked up by the numbers you have chosen. To obviate this effect you can choose numbers very close together, and the closer the numbers the less chance there is of missing a hidden change in the slope — but the more awkward the arithmetic. Naturally, the method we really want uses calculus 'next-to-nothing' values because then we are sure that there are no 'hidden' changes in slope. In practice too, we find that the arithmetic of calculus is paltry compared to the 'numbers-either-side' method.

You have already been introduced to higher order derivatives (the 'Dee Two Why Dee Ecks Squared' Dance), and you will be delighted to have them at your elbow at a time like this when you cannot see the slope of the mountain — it isn't always convenient to graph it to get a visual idea of the shape of the function, and anyway the idea is to cut down on the work, not increase it. You need to know exactly where the valleys, peaks and ledges are if you are to make sensible (neoclassical) decisions.

The second derivative d^2y/dx^2 [or, in new notation $f''(x)$ — read as 'eff double prime ecks'] measures the gradient or slope of the first derivative: it tells you the direction and magnitude of change of the first derivative as x changes (infinitesimally). You don't need to try numbers a step or so from you and then run through a trial test to find the direction of the slopes. All you need to do is to run the second derivative of the spot you are on, and in a split second you have the answer. It is better than radar, faster than sonar. The topography close to you is instantly revealed even when it is as black to the eye as a coal miner's teeshirt. You may proceed, with the greatest of confidence, up or down the function, as nimble as a mountain goat and sure-footed as a cat.

It is the peaks and the valleys, known respectively as the maximum and minimum values of the function, which are of most interest in neoclassical economics. You can test for these by finding the zero value of the first derivative and then applying the second derivative to test it for its sign: if the sign is negative you have a maximum value; if it is positive you have a minimum value. Thus you can see instantly whether the value of y in the function is a maximum or a minimum without the laborious arithmetic of taking numbers larger and smaller around X.

We can illustrate the economy of effort involved in taking seconds by looking back at the simple equation in [30] and using second derivatives to test if for a maximum or minimum point. If

$$y = 4x - x^2 \qquad [30]$$

$$\frac{dy}{dx} = 4 - 2x \qquad [31]$$

and if

$$\frac{dy}{dx} = 0$$

then

$$4 - 2x = 0$$
$$4 = 2x$$
$$x = 2.$$

This tells you that you will have a maximum or minimum point where x is equal to 2, and taking the second derivative of [31] we get

$$\frac{d^2y}{dx^2} = -2 \qquad [32]$$

which tells you that this is a maximum point because the second derivative is negative.

If you substitute $x = 2$ into [30] you will find what y equals:

$$y = 4x - x^2$$
$$= 4(2) - 2^2 \qquad [30]$$
$$= 8 - 4$$
$$y = 4.$$

The formal rules for finding maximum, minimum and inflexion points will be found in the notebook section at the end of this chapter. You should study them as you need them. Their relegation to the notebook doesn't mean that they are unimportant — far from it — but on your first read through I am trying to keep the work as informal as possible.

7.5 The Prophets' Trail

You are now ready to cross a rickety old bridge to the undulating and well-trod Trail of the Prophets. Everything is clear before us for the moment, but if the weather turns and things begin to get a little murky, we are now well prepared to handle the situation without panicking unduly. Remember your notebook and apply the rules and there is absolutely nothing to fear.

The Prophets' Trail takes you past some interesting examples of theoretical archeology. Alert students will find an early example in Karl Marx's *Capital* where he exclaims, in a rare moment of fun, 'Accumulate, Accumulate, that is the Moses and the Prophets!' The Old Spelling has been corrupted over the years and in modern textbooks you will find some structures, built in the neoclassical style of elegant simplicity, under 'Profit Maximisation'.

Profit maximisation is the sole goal ascribed to the neoclassical firm. Firms which aim to maximise profits, or minimise losses, are suitable for trying out your field craft for valleys, peaks and ledges. We assume that the firm's goal is to maximise the difference between its revenue (R) and its costs (C):

$$\pi = R - C. \qquad [33]$$

There are two particular structures we want to examine: a perfectly competitive firm, and a monopoly.

The perfectly competitive firm is graphed in Figures 7.6 (total revenue and cost functions) and 7.7 (average and marginal cost functions). Though it deals with finding one's way along a trail without a visual image of it, this chapter has more diagrams than most others — the diagrams are aids to the

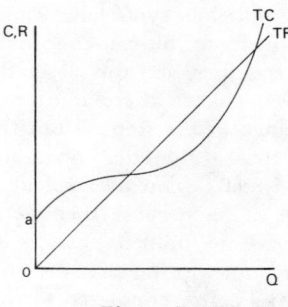

Figure 7.6

7. Peaks, Valleys and Ledges

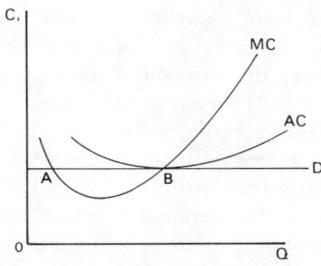

Figure 7.7

explanations and can be thought of as memory joggers for when you have to use your mind's eye to 'see' what can't, in the circumstances, or needn't, in the event, be seen.

A perfectly competitive firm is a price-taker. Its total revenue is found by multiplying the quantity sold by the price it is sold at:

$$R = pq. \qquad [34]$$

Its total costs (C) (as we saw in earlier work) are composed of a fixed cost (represented by the intercept constant a) and the variable cost arising from actually producing output. Variable cost depends upon output [$VC = f(q)$] and the cost function is written

$$C = a + f(q). \qquad [35]$$

Applying [33] as the objective we have

$$\pi = R - C$$

and substituting into [33] the equivalents from [34] and [35] (which leave the equation in balance), we get

$$\pi = pq - [a + f(q)]. \qquad [36]$$

To find the maximum profit position we put:

$$\frac{d\pi}{dq} = 0 \qquad [37]$$

The rate of change of profit with respect to output is zero.

If profit is neither increasing nor decreasing it must be either at a maximum position or a minimum position. To test for these we take first derivatives of the RHS of [36]:

$$\frac{d\pi}{dq} = p - f'(q). \qquad [38]$$

In [38], remember it is a perfectly competitive firm, and therefore price is constant not variable and is treated as such in differentiation. Also, when the brackets round the cost function were removed the sign in front of [$f(q)$] had to be changed to a negative. The constant a is eliminated by differentiation.

A maximum occurs where the first derivative [38] is equal to zero, i.e.

$$p - f'(q) = 0. \qquad [39]$$

Adding $f'(q)$ to both sides leaves the equation in balance:

$$p = f'(q) \qquad [40]$$

Price is equal to the first derivative of total cost; i.e., marginal cost.

This is precisely the profit-maximising rule for the perfectly competitive firm from your textbook.

But is it a maximum? It has fulfilled one of the conditions: the first derivative is equal to zero. In Figure 7.8 the profit function is shown below the total revenue and cost functions as the difference between them. Where $d\pi/dq$ is equal to zero you will note that it corresponds to the highest point of the profit curve — the tangent here is horizontal.

In Figure 7.8 there are two points where marginal revenue and marginal cost intersect. Marginal cost cuts the marginal revenue line from 'above' (at A) and from 'below' (at B). Only one of them is the profit-maximising intersection. This is the intersection on the right, where marginal cost cuts marginal revenue from below, because at points to the right of where marginal revenue is cut from above marginal revenue exceeds marginal

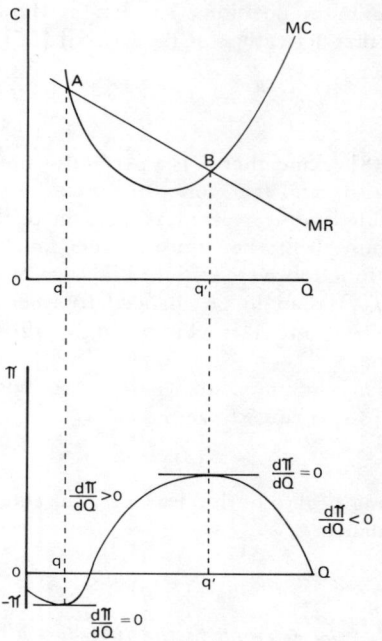

Figure 7.8

differentiation, leaving a negative term $[-f'(q)]$. Thus, we have the first derivative [38] equal to zero and a negative second derivative [42] which is a maximum point.

The imperfectly competitive firm operates in different market conditions. The monopolist has two choices: either to fix price and let the demand function decide the quantity of output, or to set output and then let the demand function determine price. The one thing he cannot do is to determine both.

If the monopolist chooses to fix his output (q) he must satisfy two conditions to maximise his profits:

$$1 \qquad \frac{dR}{dq} - \frac{dC}{dq} = 0 \qquad [43]$$

$$2 \qquad \frac{d^2R}{dq^2} - \frac{d^2C}{dq^2} < 0 \qquad [44]$$

i.e.

$$\frac{d^2R}{dq^2} < \frac{d^2C}{dq^2}. \qquad [46]$$

cost or, putting it in total terms, the contribution to total revenue from sales of additional output exceeds the increase in total costs from producing it. From the figure we know that when marginal cost rises its slope must be positive. This means that its second derivative (the measure of the slope of the first derivative) must be positive:

$$\frac{d^2C}{dq^2} > 0. \qquad [41]$$

If we take the second derivative of the profit function we find

$$\frac{d\pi}{dq} = p - f'(q) \qquad [38]$$

and

$$\frac{d^2\pi}{dq^2} = -f''(q). \qquad [42]$$

The constant p is now eliminated in the

You can think of [46] as being a comparison in the slopes of the marginal revenue and marginal cost functions: for profit maximisation marginal cost must be increasing faster than marginal revenue. This certainly occurs (see point B in Figure 7.8) when marginal revenue is declining and marginal cost is increasing. At A in Figure 7.8, marginal cost is falling faster than marginal revenue and this cannot be a maximum profit position because by adding to output, more is added to total revenue than is added to total costs. At B the marginal cost curve is now positive in a north-easterly direction $(d^2C/dq^2 > 0)$ and the marginal revenue curve is still declining $(d^2R/dq^2 < 0)$; this unambiguously means that the marginal cost curve is steeper and therefore we have a maximum profit position because more is added to total costs than is added to total revenue by increasing output.

7. Peaks, Valleys and Ledges

Figure 7.8 (lower segment of the diagram) shows the corresponding profit curve. Profit is at a maximum where marginal revenue is equal to marginal cost at B. Marginal revenue equals marginal cost is a *necessary* condition, which means that this condition must be met if the consequence associated with it is to follow, but the mere meeting of the necessary condition will not be *sufficient* to create the consequence, as is shown by point A where marginal revenue is also equal to marginal cost.

The relevance of necessary and sufficient conditions can be illustrated by the act of registering for a university degree which is normally a *necessary* condition for graduating at the end of the course. But the mere act of registration does not guarantee a degree: it is not *sufficient* — if it was, what would degrees be worth? (At a Faculty meeting during the days of 'Student Power' it was seriously proposed by student 'revolutionaries' that they should be awarded passes if they registered and 'tried-to-turn-up'; the 'reactionaries' *only just* got that amended to: 'turned-up-and-tried'!) If the *necessary* act of registration is completed, it is *sufficient* for the student to pass the examinations to be awarded a degree.

At output q the first derivatives of the cost and revenue curves are equal but this produces a negative profit (i.e., a loss). At output q' profit is at a maximum. The first derivative of the profit function is equal to zero:

$$\frac{d\pi}{dq} = 0 \qquad [47]$$

and the second derivative is negative:

$$\frac{d^2\pi}{dq^2} < 0. \qquad [48]$$

To the left of this maximum point the first derivative is positive because the profit function is increasing at outputs less than q'. At q' the first derivative is negative which means that profit falls as output is increased beyond q'.

Because profit is maximised at q' ($d\pi/dq = 0$) the second derivative is negative ($d^2\pi/dq^2 < 0$). We write

$$\frac{d^2\pi}{dq^2} = \frac{d^2R}{dq^2} - \frac{d^2C}{dq^2} < 0. \qquad [49]$$

For this to hold, it logically follows that

$$\frac{d^2R}{dq^2} < \frac{d^2C}{dq^2} \qquad [50]$$

because, in order to get a negative LHS equal to the difference between two terms on the RHS, the last term must be larger than the first. In mathematics [50] only tells you that the slope of the marginal cost curve must be greater than the slope of the marginal revenue curve (measured in an upward left-to-right direction) at the point of profit maximisation.

A couple of simple examples may assist your understanding of the general principles.

Suppose the demand function of a video cassette firm is given by

$$p = 20 - 0.001q \qquad [51]$$

where p is price and q is the quantity of cassettes sold per week. The total revenue R will be the number of cassettes sold times their price, which is found by multiplying [51] by q

$$R = 20q - 0.001q^2. \qquad [52]$$

If the total cost C is given by the function

$$C = 200 + 14q + 0.002q^2 \qquad [53]$$

we have sufficient information to find its profit-maximising output. Profit π is given by

$$\pi = R - C$$

and in this case this is

$$= (20q - 0.001q^2) - (200 + 14q + 0.002q^2)$$
$$= 6q - 0.003q^2 - 200. \qquad [54]$$

Equation [54] is the profit function and it is profit which the firm wishes to maximise. Differentiating [54] we get

$$\frac{d\pi}{dq} = 6 - 0.006q. \qquad [55]$$

For a maximum, or a minimum, the first derivative has to be equal to zero:

$$\frac{d\pi}{dq} = 0$$

which gives

$$0.006q = 6$$

$$q = \frac{6}{0.006}$$

$$= 1{,}000 \text{ per week.}$$

To test whether this is a profit-maximising or loss minimising output we take the second derivative of [55] and get

$$\frac{d^2\pi}{dq^2} = -0.006 \qquad [56]$$

which is negative, indicating that we have a maximum (because the profit function is declining after this point if the derivative is negative).

It may be of interest to find the price that must be charged to achieve this profit-maximising output, and this is easily done. The demand function is

$$p = 20 - 0.001q \qquad [51]$$

and the maximising quantity is 1,000. Substituting this into [51] gives

$$p = 20 - 0.001(1000)$$

$$= 20 - 1$$

$$= \$19.$$

The actual profit is found by putting $q = 1000$ into:

$$\pi = 6q - 0.003q^2 - 200 \qquad [54]$$

$$= 6(1000) - 0.003(1000)^2 - 200$$

$$= 6000 - 3000 - 200$$

$$= 6000 - 3200$$

$$\pi = \$2800.$$

A final brief example can be taken from the publisher's tale in the previous chapter. Here, you will recall, Mr Duckworth told you that his cost function was

$$C = 20q + 0.001q^2 \qquad [57]$$

and that the books at his warehouse were sold for $30. The profit was found by the difference between the revenue from sales and the cost of production; i.e.

$$\pi = R - C$$

which gives

$$= 30q - (20q + 0.001q^2)$$

$$= 10q - 0.001q^2.$$

The first derivative of the profit function is

$$\frac{d\pi}{dq} = 10 - 0.002q. \qquad [59]$$

For profit to be at a maximum (or minimum) the first derivative of the function must be equal to zero

$$\frac{d\pi}{dq} = 0$$

which gives

$$0.002q = 10$$

$$q = \frac{10}{0.002}$$

$$= 5000 \text{ copies.} \qquad [60]$$

To find the actual profit at this output substitute $q = 5000$ into:

$$\pi = 10q - 0.001(q)^2 \qquad [58]$$

$$= 10(5000) - 0.001(5000)^2$$

$$= 50000 - 25000$$

$$\pi = \$25000.$$

7. Peaks, Valleys and Ledges

This has been a rather long chapter because it is a critical one in your journey through the mountains. The importance of maximum and minimum concepts to neoclassical theory cannot be exaggerated and we have covered various topics with which you are expected by your examiners to be extremely familiar. To keep the expedition moving, the more formal rules that inevitably accompany this subject have been placed in the notebook which follows.

7.6 For the Notebook

The various formal rules for finding stationary points are summarised in this section. It is not necessary to learn them by rote — you only need to know where to find them when you need them.

In words the conclusions you draw from the second derivative for most occasions can be summarised neatly:

> *If you are standing on a spot where the first derivative is positive in sign and the second derivative also positive then the slope is increasing in steepness. You are standing on a spot similar to a in Figure 7.9.*

> *If you are standing on a spot where the first derivative is positive in sign and the second derivative negative, the slope is decreasing in steepness. You are standing on a spot similar to b in Figure 7.10.*

> *If you are standing on a spot where the first derivative is zero in sign and*

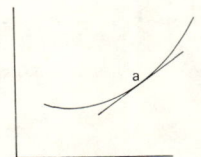

Figure 7.9

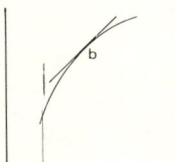

Figure 7.10

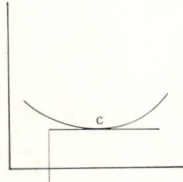

Figure 7.11

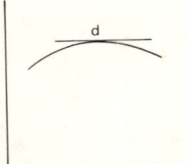

Figure 7.12

> *the second derivative positive, you are on a spot similar to c in Figure 7.11.*

> *If you are standing on a spot where the first derivative is zero and the second derivative negative, you are on a spot similar to d in Figure 7.12.*

> *If you are standing on a spot where the first derivative is negative in sign and the second derivative positive, you are on a spot similar to e in Figure 7.13.*

> *If you are standing on a spot where the first derivative is negative in sign and the second derivative negative then you are on a spot similar to f in Figure 7.14.*

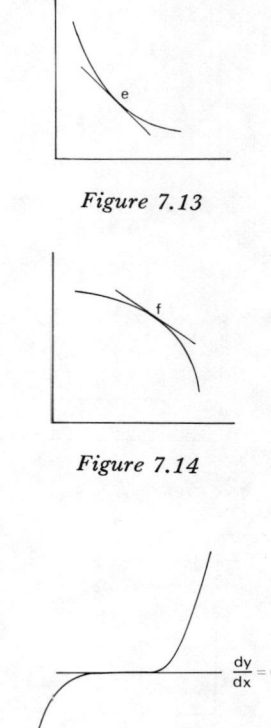

Figure 7.13

Figure 7.14

Figure 7.15

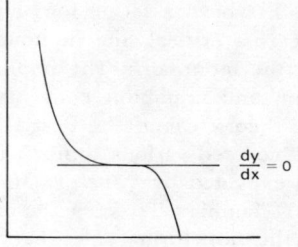

Figure 7.16

Figure 7.17

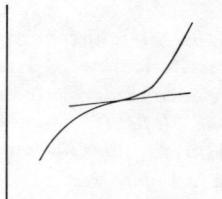

Figure 7.18

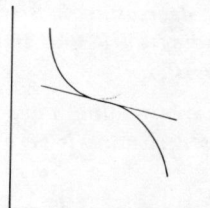

Figure 7.19

Figures 7.15–20 show Cognoscenti 'inflexions' and they are just as simple to calculate as maximum and minimum points. There are two change-in-bend-of-slope cases:

1. where the change passes through a flat bit (or ledge); (Figure 7.15 and 7.16)

and

2. where the change is continuous (no ledge) (Figure 7.17 to 7.20).

In case 1, the first derivative is equal to zero (the slope is not changing at the flat bit) and case 2 it is not equal to zero. *Both* cases have second derivatives equal to zero.

These cases have test rules which can also be summed up neatly (with a risk of overloading you with information):

7. Peaks, Valleys and Ledges 83

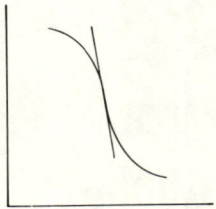

Figure 7.20

*If the second derivative is equal to zero there is a new bend (or Cognoscenti inflexion).

*If the first derivative is also equal to zero at this point, you can remain stationary *on the ledge* before climbing or descending (depending on the direction of the slope you are on).

*If the first derivative is non-zero at this point, you *cannot remain stationary* there but must keep moving either upwards or downwards, though the slope will alter its bend.

The main rules are summarised in the Table:

Table 7.1   Topography of the Maths Mountains

First Derivative	Second Derivative	You are	Maths Meaning
Zero	Negative	At a peak	Maximum
Zero	Positive	In a trough	Minimum
Zero	Zero	On a ledge	Stationary inflexion
Non-Zero	Zero	At a bend	Non-stationary inflexion

What could be simpler (or safer)? With Table 7.1 on your head-up display, you have a complete system for all-weather climbing in the Mathematics Mountains.

EIGHT

The Camp of the Curly Dees

8.1 Introduction

If you look back to where you were when the expedition began — way back, down there on the plain — you will be pleasantly impressed by the long distance you have travelled in the Mathematics Mountains. You really have come a long way since starting your climb in the foothills. The sights you have seen — some of them much too quickly on this occasion for you to take in fully their elegant splendours — will I hope have made an indelible impression.

You are now well into Calculus country, high-up off the plain. But the mountains soar yet higher and from where you are at this moment they stand like silent sentinels for uncounted leagues into the far distance. Nobody lives long enough to explore the enitre mountain range by themselves. Only in the collective mind of the Mathematicians' Union is there a more or less complete survey of the known territory, but tantalisingly this is not at our disposal; the imperative of scarcity intervenes even here to prevent our acquiring more than a minute fraction of what is available collectively. Lord Robbins [1932, p. 15] — one of the most talented economists of his generation — captured the essence of the prison of time in which we are forever incarcerated:

> ... When time and the means for acquiring ends are limited *and* capable of being distinguished in order of importance, then behaviour necessarily assumes the form of choice.

Through choice we enter the ambit of economics — the science of economising. Robbins also eloquently expressed the tyranny of choice (ibid.):

> If, in a limited lifetime, I would wish to be both a philosopher and a mathematician, but my rate of acquisition of knowledge is such that I cannot do both completely, then some part of my wish for philosophical or mathematical competence or both must be relinquished.

Such is the intricacy of philosophy and mathematics (and most other subjects) that even a lifetime of dedicated study by the world's most persistent individual, be she ever so brilliant, would not be enough to cover any subject in its entirety because the boundaries of knowledge move outwards in all directions at a rate which no individual could possibly match. Specialisation is one inevitable solution to this problem, carrying with it its own limitations: the hyper-specialist who knows more about less than anybody else working in the field — or, rather, furrow.

This should neither depress nor demoralise you. It is an imperative nobody can evade. On the contrary, it uplifts your spirits, because it relieves you of a tremendous burden: if it is impossible to learn *everything*, learning *something* is the measure of achievement!

Your next steps in the mountains are both an extension and a consolidation of what you have achieved to date. Completely new and exciting territory opens up, making accessible an enormous chunk of the body of economic doctrine. You will be able to get right into journal articles which until now, because of the mathematics in them, you have had to skip through. The inter-dependence of variables is incomparably more difficult to grasp by literary means than by the techniques of the following pages. This fact provoked Samuelson [1948, p. 6] to be uncommonly aggressive about literary exposition:

> The laborious literary working over of essentially simple mathematical concepts such as is characteristic of much of modern economic theory is not only unrewarding from the standpoint of advancing the science, but it involves as well mental gymnastics of a peculiarly depraved type. (!)

The territory just ahead is exhilarating. It is peopled by the Curly Dees, a most inventive and accomplished race of operators, as prolific as they are hard-working. And they enjoy their work! They like nothing better than tackling a function. They are trained to an exceptionally high pitch, each with a specified task, performing with Germanic efficiency. Working at such a rate, they need to relieve the pressures of their exertions, and they do this at their base camp by indulging in (private) carousing far from the eyes of the Mathematicians' Union (who would be horrified at what their most trusted servants got up to once their backs are turned). At these boisterous sessions the Curly Dees mimic their more memorable triumphs (all classics now in the literature) by teasing each other with charades — the first Curly Dee to guess correctly the operation they are miming gets, as a prize, a large draught of Complexity (the local ale!) A few hours of this behaviour and everybody is tired or emotional, and often both.

It is our privilege and, or course, pleasure to be able to join in the carousing at the Curly Dees' camp. We shall learn more under the influence of their pleasure-seeking than we will by watching them work. Early on in the party before the complexity competitions begin, we may be able to persuade some of them to perform replicas of what they do in economics but we won't be able to push them too hard, as their brisk and short performances will probably be accompanied by loud suggestions of whom else to talk to among the revellers — if we can find them — who allegedly can tell us more about the bit we are asking about (if they are still sober by the time we get to them). Visits to the camp of the Curly Dees are a case of pot luck — sometimes you come up trumps (so to speak) and you get a fantastic insight into their work; at other times it is difficult to learn anything worthwhile, and return visits are necessary. Let's find out whether our luck is holding this time.

8.2   *Down Memory Lane*

The best way to the camp of the Curly Dees is down Memory Lane, through the Permanent Exhibition of the Structure of Neoclassical Economics; it takes a little longer than the direct route but lets you see what the Curly Dees are *used* for, rather than how they mechanically do it.

Most lecturers in microeconomics usually wheel in exhibits of Subjectivist Utility Theory for the students to stare in awe at. Joan Robinson [1962] aptly described utility theory as being of impregnable circularity: the fact that goods have utility makes people demand them, and the fact that they are demanded proves they have utility!

In the early versions of the theory it was assumed that the utilities of individual goods were independent, measurable and additive. The utility from apples $[U_1(a)]$ could be added to the utility from pears $[U_2(p)]$ and both could be added to the utility from trousers $[U_3(t)]$. In sum they produce a total utility (TU) for that consumer:

$$TU = U_1(a) + U_2(p) + U_3(t). \quad [1]$$

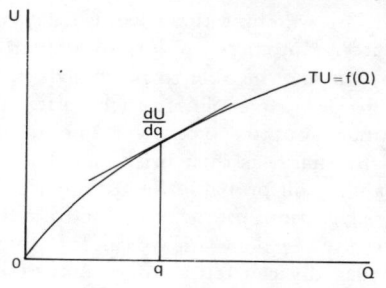

Figure 8.1

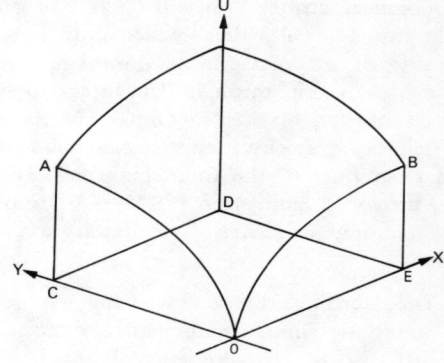

Figure 8.2

This, uncharitably, was eventually seen, especially in the case where a fictitious measure of utility (the *util*) was propagated, to be somewhat naive, and the additivity assumption was superseded. In Figure 8.1 total utility for a good (for a particular consumer) is graphed. The utility function rises as more of the good is consumed, but at a diminishing rate. The amount of marginal utility (the increase in total utility from consuming an extra unit of the good) can be measured by the slope of the tangent at the point on the utility curve perpendicular to the amount of the good on the horizontal axis. This, of course, is the first derivative of the total utility function:

$$\frac{dU}{dq}. \qquad [2]$$

Under the original version of the theory, a separate utility function would be graphed for every single good the individual consumed, but when additivity was dropped and utility became a function of the utilities of the several goods consumed together, the function was written

$$TU = U(a, p, t, \ldots n) \qquad [3]$$

and a different geometric construction was required. Instead of a myriad of two-dimensional slices as in Figure 8.1, a three-dimensional 'utility surface' was required as in Figure 8.2. Utility is measured vertically, with the line UD lying on the page and the measures of the quantities of goods X and Y coming out of the page. The utility surface, $OAUB$, 'bulges' out of the page too. The figure purports to give a geometric view of measurable but non-additive utility.

The sides OAC and OBE are similar to the slices of Figure 8.1 but they are at right angles to each other. As you move from O towards C or E, the slices intersect each other, much as cardboard in a wine case intersects to keep the bottles apart. This may be a little clearer in Figures 8.3 to 8.5 where the utility surface has been sliced through, first from O to E and then from O to C. In Figure 8.3, as the amount of Y is increased on slices that are further from the origin O, the amount of X is held constant. In Figure 8.4 the amount of X is increased and Y is held constant. Compare

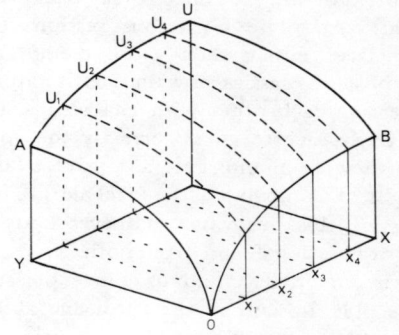

Figure 8.3

8. The Camp of the Curly Dees

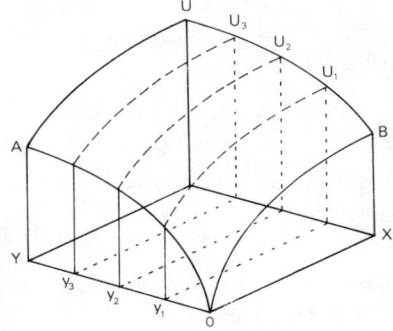

Figure 8.4

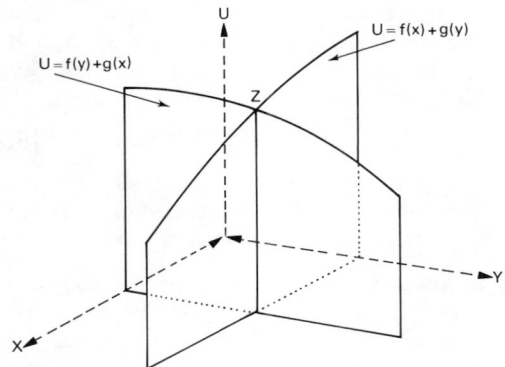

Figure 8.6

8.3 Bring on the Curly Dees!

In Figure 8.6 we have focused on one of the dots in the utility surface of Figure 8.5. The intersecting slices are shown in outline but the tangents touching the point have not been drawn to avoid cluttering up the diagram. The function of the X slope is given by

$$U = f(x) + g(y) \qquad [4]$$

Utility is a function of the varying amount of the X good plus the utility of the constant amount y of the Y good.

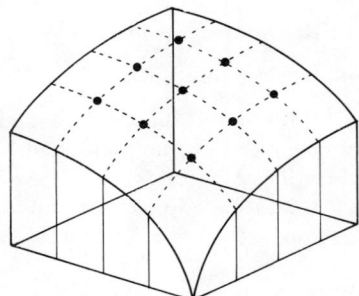

Figure 8.5

these circumstances with the dots on the utility surface in Figure 8.5: these represent combinations of X and Y.

Consider the meaning of these dots for a moment (stand back as you would in a gallery to study a painting). Each dot has two slices passing through it, one from the X axis and the other from the Y axis. If the function of the slice which the dot stands on is taken as being, say, the slice from the X axis, this is equivalent to holding X constant while you run up the Y function; if the slice is taken from the Y axis, this is equivalent to holding Y constant while you run up the X function. This is a conclusion of the greatest importance when we call upon the Curly Dees to do their stuff.

In plain language, [4] will provide a measure of the utility from consuming X according to how the utility of X varies for differing amounts for that consumer *plus* the utility from the constant amount of Y which that consumer has as well. The utility at the point Z will be given by the first derivative of [4] which is, of course, the marginal utility at that spot from an infinitesimal change in x:

$$MU = f'(x) \qquad [5]$$

Marginal utility is given by the first derivative of [4]. (Remember that the constant y in [4] is eliminated by differentation.)

Now, the spot identified as Z in Figure 8.6 also has the Y slice passing through it, and the function of the utility surface for this slice is given by

$$U = f(y) + g(x) \qquad [6]$$

Utility is given by the varying amount of the Y good plus the utility of the fixed amount x of the X good.

In plain language (analogous to [4]), the equation states that utility will depend upon how utility changes for varying amounts of the good Y for that consumer plus the utility from the constant amount of the good X the consumer has as well. Again the measure of marginal utility for that consumer at the point Z, using the Y function, will depend on the first derivative of the Y utility function:

$$MU = f'(y). \qquad [7]$$

The mathematics of this semi-geometric interpretation of the tangents at the spot Z can be summed up as follows: we are finding the first derivatives of the functions by holding one variable constant (and treating it as such in the differentiation) and differentiating the function of the other variable.

You know how to differentiate a function of one variable which has a constant in it: eliminate the constant if it is alone and multiply the constant by the power of the variable if it is associated with the variable. For example

$$\frac{d}{dx}(3x^2 + 8)$$
$$= 2 \cdot 3x$$
$$= 6x. \qquad [8]$$

(Remember, 8 is a constant and is eliminated).

There is absolutely no difference in the case of the spot Z if the function was

$$\frac{d}{dx}(3x^2 + 8y)$$
$$= 6x \qquad [9]$$

because we are treating $8y$ as a constant not a variable. Similarly, in differentiating the following function:

$$\frac{d}{dy}(3yx^2 + y^2 + 6x - 5y^6)$$

we treat x as the constant and differentiate y to get

$$3x^2 + 2y - 30y^5 \qquad [10]$$

because $d(3y)/dy = 3$ and therefore $d(3yx^2)/dy$ with x as a constant equals $3x^2$; $6x$ is a constant by itself and is eliminated and the other two terms follow standard differentiation rules.

When we treat y as the constant and differentiate with respect to x we get

$$6yx + 6 \qquad [11]$$

because $d(3yx^2)/dx$ when y is a constant requires the y term to be multiplied by the power of x, i.e. 2, and this gives $2 \cdot 3y \cdot x^{2-1} = 6yx$; y is an isolated constant and is eliminated along with $-5y^6$; and $d(6x)/dx$ equals 6.

In other words, the good news is that you already know how to handle differentiation involving more than one variable. There is hardly any difference between single-variable and multi-variable differentiation, except that the mathematical power of the latter is far greater than the former.

This is where the Curly Dees invite you to their party. You will recognise the Curly Dees from their widespread use in the literature (they are one of Mme. Notation's longest-running lines — 'a licence to increase the money supply', she once mused in a careless moment of 'Keynesian' frankness). They generally take the shape of

$$\partial$$

The standard Curly Dee model.

Cognoscenti call them 'partials' and the process of using them partial differentiation. they tell you that operations are under way in which some variables are being treated as constants.

8. The Camp of the Curly Dees

In examples [9] and [10] above we would write the operations out using Curly Dees as:

$$\frac{\partial}{\partial x}(3x^2 + 8y)$$

$$\frac{\partial U}{\partial x} = 6x \qquad [13]$$

and

$$\frac{\partial}{\partial x}(3yx^2 + y^2 + 6x - 5y^6)$$

$$\frac{\partial U}{\partial x} = 6yx + 6. \qquad [14]$$

$$\frac{\partial U}{\partial y} = 3x^2 + 2y - 30y^5 \qquad [15]$$

In economics you meet instantly recognisable Curly Dees such as the following:

Where $\quad U = f(q*, q')$

Utility is a function of the quantities consumed

$\dfrac{\partial U}{\partial q*}$ is the marginal utility of the good (*)

holding the amount of the other good constant. And

$\dfrac{\partial U}{\partial q'}$ is the marginal utility of the good ('),

holding the amount of the other good constant, and

where $\quad X = f(K, L)$

Output is a function of the quantities of two inputs

$\dfrac{\partial X}{\partial K}$ is the marginal product of capital

when the amount of labour input is held constant,

$\dfrac{\partial X}{\partial L}$ is the marginal product of labour

when the amount of capital input is held constant.

8.4 The Professors' Tale

The Theory of Production lies close to the heart of neoclassical economics. Whole areas of economics open up if you can get into the literature of this subject, from marginal productivity and the theory of distribution, through to general equilibrium theory. The key to the way in is through Curly Dees, because almost all of what is worthwhile in the literature is written with their aid.

The first glimmers of production theory are to be found in von Thunen (1783–1850) in his classic of 1826. (Von Thunen was the economist who was so pleased with his theory of the 'natural wage' that he had the mathematics of it engraved on his tombstone!) But real interest didn't develop until the 1890s when Wicksteed [1894] used the concept of a production function, followed by Wicksell [1901] who made it explicit. The theory of production in your textbook probably originated in Hicks's *Value and Capital* [1939]. But the history of the theory of production — often acrimonious, like that of marginalism generally — is sullied with the value judgments introduced into marginal productivity theory by John Bates Clark (1847–1938) in 1885 when he asserted that the theory of marginal productivity proved that the distribution of the product between wages and capital was 'fair'. This has given the theory a controversial image ever since: among radical economists, because they don't believe that any proof of fairness is acceptable, and among more conservative economists who think that ethical assertions are scientifically inappropriate. An excellent summary of the issues is provided in Blaug [1968, ch. 11: 'Marginal Productivity Theory of Distribution'] and at the end of this chapter you should be able to muddle through the mathematics he uses to explain the theories. (You should also try Heathfield [1971] — but slowly!)

Some Curly Dees are doing a turn on one of the wooden trestle tables over by the trees, and if we hurry we shall catch what they are saying. Apparently they were hired by a couple of American professors in the 1920s to perform some astonishing operations. It was the height of Prohibition at the time, and fouled-up operations involved high risks of acquiring cement overcoats and a swim in the Hudson River. Hence they undertook the assignment with some apprehension, which in the event was entirely unnecessary, as no kinder or more saintly an employer could be found to match the personality of Professor Douglas [see Samuelson, 1979].

Professor (sometime Senator) Douglas teamed up with Professor Cobb (a mathematician) to produce a production function which would (a) elucidate what others had been stumbling towards but couldn't formulate either empirically or theoretically, and (b) collect the empirical data necessary to 'prove' its existence in the form they claimed for it. Their results were first published in 1928 in the *American Economic Review*, and later Douglas published his *Theory of Wages* [1934]. You should also try his Presidential Address to the American Economic Association: 'Are there Laws of Production?' [1948].

One of the great debates among economists (then and now) is about the alleged constancy of the proportion (a) of total output (Y) that goes to wages (W), expressed in symbols by

$$W = aY. \quad [16]$$

From microeconomics you know that in the perfectly competitive firm the wages of labour are equal to the marginal product of labour. This means that the marginal product of labour is identified separately from the marginal product of any other input into production such as capital, which is another way of saying that the contribution of capital to total product is going to be held — conceptually — constant. Surely a job for the Curly Dees? Thus, the statement was written out as

$$w = \frac{\partial Y}{\partial L} \quad [17]$$

Wage rates are equal to the marginal product of labour, holding other factors constant.

If [16] has [17] substituted where $Lw = W$ we get

$$L \cdot \frac{\partial Y}{\partial L} = aY. \quad [18]$$

To derive this relationship mathematically, Cobb and Douglas had to find a function which would always produce a constant share of output for labour. Fortuitously, Douglas had amassed empirical data which tended to support the derivation they were looking for and, after some thought, the sought-for function emerged (though Wicksell almost had it in 1901).

If the following notation is used we can write out the Cobb-Douglas Production Function: $Y =$ output, $L =$ Labour inputs, $K =$ capital inputs, A is a constant, and α & β are (Greek) constants (read as 'alpha' and 'beeta'). Unfortunately, there is still no regulated market in notation for this function and you will find all kinds of symbols used, some of them from cowboy outfits which Mme. Notation considers bring discredit to the industry by confusing new users. The function reads

$$Y = AL^\alpha K^\beta \quad [19]$$

Output equals a constant times the factor input labour to a power alpha times the factor input capital to a power beeta.

The plain language meaning of [19] can best be brought out by examining an example, first in notation only, and then in numbers.

The Curly Dees (or partial derivatives) can quickly form themselves into expressions for this type of function:

$$\frac{\partial Y}{\partial L} = \text{marginal product of labour}$$

(holding capital constant)

and

$$\frac{\partial Y}{\partial K} = \text{marginal product of capital}$$

(holding labour constant).

Each partial gives the change in total product for a small change in one input, holding the other input constant. Working the differentiations out we remember that K is being treated as a constant and hence this isn't a case for the product rule: it is a simple case of a variable multiplied by some constants. We get

$$\frac{\partial Y}{\partial L} = \alpha A L^{\alpha-1} K^\beta. \qquad [20]$$

The term $L^{\alpha-1}$ is interesting, and if you check your notebook you will find it mentioned in the Laws of Indices:

$$x^{-1} = \frac{1}{x}$$

and

$$L^{\alpha-1} = \frac{L^\alpha}{L}$$

Putting this back into [20] gives

$$\frac{\partial Y}{\partial L} = \alpha A \frac{L^\alpha}{L} K^\beta$$

and this brings an expression equal to Y into [20]:

$$Y = AL^\alpha K^\beta$$

therefore we substitute Y for the expression to get

$$\frac{\partial Y}{\partial L} = \frac{Y}{L} \alpha \qquad [21]$$

The marginal product of labour under perfect competition equals a constant proportion, alpha, of the ratio of output to labour inputs.

It is well worth spending time going over this manipulation, because it is a vital part of the mathematics of the Cobb-Douglas production function.

The Curly Dees will now demonstrate the same operation for capital, holding L (labour inputs) constant:

$$\frac{\partial Y}{\partial K} = \beta A L^\alpha K^{\beta-1}. \qquad [22]$$

Again, from the laws of indices (in your notebook), we have

$$x^{-1} = \frac{1}{x}$$

therefore

$$K^{\beta-1} = \frac{K^\beta}{K}$$

and substituting this into [22] brings in an expression equal to Y:

$$\frac{\partial Y}{\partial K} = \beta A L^\alpha \frac{K^\beta}{K} \qquad [23]$$

but

$$Y = AL^\alpha K^\beta$$

and substituting Y for this in [23] gives

$$\frac{\partial Y}{\partial K} = \frac{Y}{K} \beta \qquad [24]$$

The marginal product of capital, under perfect competition is a constant proportion beeta of the average product of capital inputs.

The final reminiscence of the Curly Dees about their exploits for the two professors is both elegant and powerful. It follows from the above discussions, and shows that the relative shares of labour and capital in output are independent of the actual amounts of labour and capital used in an economy.

Again, assuming profit-maximisation and perfect competition in all markets, neo-classical firms hire factors until their marginal product equals their marginal cost. In this notation we would have

$$\frac{\partial Y}{\partial L} = w \qquad [25]$$

The wage rate (w) equals the marginal product of labour

and

$$\frac{\partial Y}{\partial K} = i \qquad [26]$$

The interest on capital (i) equals the marginal product of capital.

The sum of all wages (w) equals the aggregate wage (W) of the economy:

$$W = w \cdot L \qquad [27]$$

Aggregate wages equals the wage per unit of labour times the number of units employed.

and, likewise, for the sum of all interest paid on capital equals the aggregate return to capital in the economy:

$$I = i \cdot K \qquad [28]$$

Aggregate returns to capital equals the interest per unit of capital times the number of units employed.

Substituting [25] and [26] into [27] and [28] we get

$$W = \frac{\partial Y}{\partial L} \cdot L \qquad [29]$$

$$I = \frac{\partial Y}{\partial K} \cdot K. \qquad [30]$$

If we now call up the Curly Dees in [21] and [24] and substitute them into [29] and [30] we get

$$W = \frac{\alpha Y}{L} \cdot L$$

$$= \alpha Y \qquad [31]$$

and

$$I = \frac{\beta Y}{K} \cdot K$$

$$= \beta Y. \qquad [32]$$

Now put [31] and [32] in the form of a ratio:

$$\frac{W}{I} = \frac{\alpha Y}{\beta Y}$$

and because Y/Y equals unity we get

$$\frac{W}{I} = \frac{\alpha}{\beta} \qquad [33]$$

The relative shares of wages and interest on capital in an economy, assuming perfect competition, are equal to a constant ratio α/β.

8.5   Some Familiar Results

You may well be wondering what are the values of the constants alpha and beeta. Their real world values are found by econometric testing and most tests have found the equation works best when $\alpha + \beta$ are taken as equal to unity:

$$\alpha + \beta = 1$$

or

$$\beta = (1-\alpha). \qquad [34]$$

Suppose we accept [34] and try out an example. Let us assume that the Cobb-Douglas production function looks like

$$Y = 10L^{3/4} K^{1/4} \qquad [35]$$

noting that $A = 10$, $\alpha = 3/4$, $\beta = 1/4$, and $(3/4 + 1/4 = 1)$. The first thing we do is find the partial derivative of [35] with respect to labour (L), holding capital (K) constant:

$$\frac{\partial Y}{\partial L} = \frac{3}{4} \cdot 10L^{3/4-1} K^{1/4}$$

$$= \frac{3}{4} \cdot 10L^{-1/4} K^{1/4}. \qquad [36]$$

8. The Camp of the Curly Dees

(The expression is left as it stands, without calculating 3/4 of 10 etc, because we are going to use it in this form later on.)

Similarly, holding Labour (L) constant we find the partial derivative of [35] with respect to capital (K):

$$\frac{\partial Y}{\partial K} = \frac{1}{4} \cdot 10 L^{3/4} K^{1/4 - 1}$$

$$= \frac{1}{4} \cdot 10 L^{3/4} K^{-3/4}. \quad [37]$$

In both cases we have positive marginal products, which corresponds to our economic theory.

It is here that you make a wonderful discovery. The Curly Dees can also help you find other relationships well known to you in your economics. They can, for instance, derive an expression from a production function such as [35] to test for diminishing returns when one factor is increased and the other held still, with hardly any bother at all. Curly Dees are particularly suited to this kind of operation because by definition they hold one variable constant and vary the other!

To carry out this manipulation we have to find how the marginal product of labour is affected by additional inputs of labour, in other words, we must differentiate the marginal product of labour, which is the same as taking a second derivative of [36]:

$$\frac{\partial^2 Y}{\partial L^2} = \frac{\partial}{\partial L}\left[\frac{3}{4} \cdot 10 L^{-1/4} K^{1/4}\right] \quad [36]$$

$$= -\frac{1}{4} \cdot \frac{3}{4} \cdot 10 L^{-1/4 - 1} K^{1/4}$$

$$= -\frac{1}{4} \cdot \frac{3}{4} \cdot 10 L^{-5/4} K^{1/4}. \quad [38]$$

The important thing about this equation is the negative sign in front of it. The theory of diminishing returns says that though the marginal product of labour is positive, it diminishes as more labour is added to the constant amount of capital. In graphical terms the marginal product curve lies below the average product curve and is negatively sloped towards the horizontal axis.

For completeness, the same manipulation can be done to the marginal product of capital [37]:

$$\frac{\partial^2 Y}{\partial K^2} = \frac{\partial}{\partial K}\left[\frac{1}{4} \cdot 10 L^{3/4} K^{-3/4}\right] \quad [37]$$

$$= -\frac{3}{4} \cdot \frac{1}{4} \cdot 10 L^{3/4} K^{-3/4 - 1}$$

$$= -\frac{3}{4} \cdot \frac{1}{4} \cdot 10 L^{3/4} K^{-7/4} \quad [39]$$

which is, as expected, negative, indicating that diminishing returns occur when more capital is added to a constant amount of labour.

Two other relationships are of interest, namely, what happens to the marginal product of labour when there is an increment in the use of the other factor, capital and contrariwise, what happens to the marginal product of capital when there is an increment in the use of labour? The Curly Dees can handle even this complicated relationship.

The answer involves us taking second derivatives of [36] and [37], or differentiating the marginal product of labour with respect to a change in capital and differentiating the marginal product of capital with respect to a change in labour:

$$\frac{\partial^2 Y}{\partial K \partial L} = \frac{\partial}{\partial K}\frac{3}{4}\left[10 L^{-1/4} K^{1/4}\right] \quad [36]$$

$$= \frac{1}{4} \cdot \frac{3}{4} \cdot 10 L^{-1/4} K^{-1/4 - 1}$$

$$= \frac{1}{4} \cdot \frac{3}{4} \cdot 10 L^{-1/4} K^{-3/4} \quad [40]$$

and

$$\frac{\partial^2 Y}{\partial L \partial K} = \frac{\partial}{\partial L} \frac{1}{4} \left[10 L^{3/4} K^{-3/4} \right] \quad [37]$$

$$= \frac{3}{4} \cdot \frac{1}{4} \cdot 10 L^{3/4-1} K^{-3/4}$$

$$= \frac{3}{4} \cdot \frac{1}{4} \cdot 10 L^{-1/4} K^{-3/4}. \quad [41]$$

In both cases, the answer is identical and the sign is positive, indicating that the marginal product of labour increases if more capital is added and that the marginal product of capital increases if more labour is added.

If we return to the example in the previous section which showed that the relative shares of wages and capital in the economy, assuming perfect competition and a Cobb/Douglas type production function were equal to a constant ratio α/β, we can re-run the example using the shares that alpha = 3/4 and beeta = 1/4. Thus we would write

$$Y = AL^{3/4} K^{1/4}. \quad [42]$$

Then

$$\frac{\partial Y}{\partial L} = \frac{3}{4} \cdot AL^{3/4-1} K^{1/4}$$

$$= \frac{3}{4} \cdot AL^{3/4} \frac{1}{L} \cdot K^{1/4}. \quad [43]$$

Substituting Y from [42] into [43] in place of $AL^{3/4} K^{1/4}$ gives

$$\frac{\partial Y}{\partial L} = \frac{3}{4} \cdot \frac{Y}{L} \quad [44]$$

The marginal product of labour is equal to 3/4 of the average product of labour.

The total income accruing to labour will be the wage rate times the number of units of labour, and under perfect competition the wage rate is equal to the marginal product of labour. The amount of labour is given by L and we get this over the the LHS by the usual expedient of multiplying both sides by L, giving

$$L \frac{\partial Y}{\partial L} = 3/4 Y \quad [45]$$

Wages account for 3/4 of national output.

Manipulating the partial derivative with respect to capital the same way produces

$$Y = AL^{3/4} K^{1/4} \quad [42]$$

$$\frac{\partial Y}{\partial K} = \frac{1}{4} \cdot AL^{3/4} K^{1/4-1}$$

$$= \frac{1}{4} \cdot AL^{3/4} K^{1/4} \cdot \frac{1}{K}. \quad [46]$$

Substituting Y from [42] into [46] in place of $AL^{3/4} K^{1/4}$ gives

$$= \frac{1}{4} \cdot \frac{Y}{K}. \quad [47]$$

The total income accruing to owners of capital will be the interest rate times the number of units of capital, and under perfect competition the interest rate is equal to the marginal product of capital. The amount of capital is given by K, and we can get this over the LHS by multiplying both sides of [47] by K, giving

$$K \frac{\partial Y}{\partial K} = \frac{1}{4} \cdot Y \quad [48]$$

Profits account for 1/4 of national output.

We can now write the expression showing that the total product is exhausted by the shares going to wages and to profits (the interest on capital):

$$L \cdot \frac{\partial Y}{\partial L} + K \cdot \frac{\partial Y}{\partial K} = \frac{3}{4} \cdot Y + \frac{1}{4} \cdot Y$$

$$= Y. \quad [49]$$

8. The Camp of the Curly Dees

In general we can write the shares as

$$Y_K = \beta Y \qquad [50]$$

and

$$Y_L = \alpha Y. \qquad [51]$$

The share of total product going to each factor is found by writing out the value of Y on the RHS from [19] and taking the output going to labour as a proportion of total output (Y_L/Y). This is the same as giving [51] the denominator Y. Thus

$$\frac{Y_L}{Y} = \alpha \frac{AL^\alpha K^\beta}{AL^\alpha K^\beta}$$

$$= \alpha \frac{Y}{Y}$$

$$= \alpha. \qquad [52]$$

The same manipulation on capital's share gives

$$\frac{Y_K}{Y} = \beta \frac{AL^\alpha K^\beta}{AL^\alpha K^\beta}$$

$$= \beta \frac{Y}{Y}$$

$$= \beta. \qquad [53]$$

Factor shares depend only upon the coefficients, alpha and beeta, and are not influenced by the size of the stock of capital or the numbers in the workforce (assuming all the conditions of the model of perfect competition are operating and that there is something meaningful about an aggregate production function — which many economists have grave reservations about: see Harcourt [1972]).

8.6 Badges of Rank*

The Curly Dees cavorting round the camp look the same at a distance, but the closer you get the more you can distinguish the various Badges of Rank attached to their uniform. In fact, Cognoscenti point out that there are six different ranks among the Curly Dees, and to make things really confusing they can change their uniforms without notice. You have already been introduced informally to two of the ranks in the Cobb/Douglas demonstration. After their hard work those particular Curly Dees have gone off for a well-deserved draught of Complexity and a new group have assembled their props for the next act.

Marshallian demand theory involves the relationship between price and quantity only, other influences on demand being held constant. Economics has gotten a great deal of mileage out of this highly restrictive model, not least in the theory of market equilibrium. But every economist accepts that there are other influences on demand. For instance, there is the price of other goods (particularly close substitutes), the tastes of the consumer (including fashions induced by other consumers — the proverbial 'Jones's), the wealth of the consumer, the rate of taxation, the time period and the income of the consumer. Suppose we include in our analysis one of these other influences such as income. The function would become:

$$Q = f(p, y)$$

Quantity demanded is a function of the price of the good and the income of the consumer.

where p is the price of the good and y is the income of the consumer.

Let us also suppose that the demand function takes the form:

$$q = 9y^2 + 4y^4 p^{-3} - 3p^2. \qquad [54]$$

The Curly Dees can handle this type of equation by differentiating one variable while the other is treated as a constant. Taking the price variable and holding income constant, we ask what happens to demand if price changes:

$$\frac{\partial q}{\partial p} = -12y^4 p^{-4} - 6p \qquad [55]$$

The effect of a price increase on quantity is to reduce the quantity demanded at a constant income level by the expression on the RHS.

Remember that the isolated constant $(9y^2)$ is eliminated in the differentiation; also the rule for differentiating a negative indice (ax^{-n}) is given by $-nax^{-n-1}$ and thus the yp term becomes $-3 \cdot 4y^4 \cdot p^{-4}$. Now let us see what happens when income changes and price is held constant:

$$\frac{\partial q}{\partial y} = 18y + 16y^3 p^{-3} \qquad [56]$$

The effect on the quantity demanded when income is increased and price held constant is to increase the amount demanded by the expression on the RHS.

Both these partials correspond with economic theory: demand is negatively related to price and positively related to income (for normal goods).

These partials are known as the first order partials — they are the assault troops of the Curly Dees and are always first under fire. The second order partials go into action behind the first order partials, though their courage is just as great.

They would answer, in the case we are discussing, questions about the effect of a change in price for a given change in income (how sensitive is $\partial q/\partial p$ to changes in the level of income?) and the effect of a change in income for a given change in price (how sensitive is $\partial q/\partial y$ to changes in the price level?).

To answer these kind of questions we must take second order partials, or second derivatives.

Taking [55] we differentiate it again with respect to y and write

$$\frac{\partial}{\partial y}(-12y^4 p^{-4} - 6p)$$

$$= -4 \cdot 12 y^{4-1} p^{-4}.$$

(Remember the constant $-6p$ is eliminated.) This gives

$$= -48 y^3 p^{-4}.$$

This is normally written, using the inverse of the negative index, p^{-4} as

$$= -\frac{48 y^3}{p^4}. \qquad [57]$$

This is a negative expression. If income rises, demand becomes more sensitive to price changes.

What is the effect on the response of quantity to income when price changes? This requires that we differentiate [56]:

$$\frac{\partial}{\partial p}(18y + 16y^3 p^{-3}) \qquad [56]$$

$$= -3 \cdot 16 y^3 p^{-3-1}$$

(remembering that the constant $18y$ is eliminated), which gives

$$= -48 y^3 p^{-4}$$

and in inverse form is written as

$$= -\frac{48 y^3}{p^4}. \qquad [58]$$

This too is negative and therefore the responsiveness of quantity to a change in income declines as price changes.

You will immediately note that the Curly Dees have produced the same result as in [57] and you may care to note that this is one of the standard rules of second order partials:

$$\frac{\partial^2 q}{\partial p \partial y} = \frac{\partial^2 q}{\partial y \partial p}$$

Once you have worked out one, you can immediately write down the other.

Another interesting question in this exercise is: what is the effect on $\partial q/\partial p$ of a change in price; i.e., does the level of price affect the change in demand following a price increase? This requires that we differentiate the partial derivative with respect to price again:

$$\frac{\partial}{\partial p}(-12y^4 p^{-4} - 6p). \qquad [55]$$

Differentiating it, with respect to p, we get

$$= -4 \cdot -12y^4 p^{-4-1} - 6$$

$$= 48y^4 p^{-5} - 6$$

$$= \frac{48y^4}{p^5} - 6. \qquad [59]$$

The sensitivity of demand to changes in price will depend entirely upon the values of the terms in [59]; at some price–income combinations the response will be greater than at others (price elasticity changes along the demand curve and will be different for different income levels — the rich respond to a price change differently from the poor).

What is the sensitivity of quantity demanded to a change in income if income is also changing? We must take the second derivative of quantity to income, holding price constant:

$$\frac{\partial}{\partial y}(18y + 16y^3 p^{-3}). \qquad [56]$$

Differentiating [56] with respect to y, we get

$$= 18 + 48y^2 p^{-3}$$

$$= 18 + \frac{48y^2}{p^3}. \qquad [60]$$

This is positive and tells you that the quantity demanded as a result of a change in income increases in sensitivity as income increases.

At this point the Curly Dees call off the serious work — they have much playing to do, having worked hard all day before being called out to perform hectic demonstrations for you in unpaid overtime.

8.7 For the Notebook

There is another form of notation on the market which is used to indicate that a second-order differentiation is in progress. This places a scrolled 'f' in front of the variables being partialled instead of the traditional Curly Dee. They are illustrated here just in case you are confused by new style Curly Dees and wonder what is going on.

$$\frac{\partial z}{\partial x} = fx$$

$$\frac{\partial z}{\partial y} = fy$$

$$\frac{\partial^2 z}{\partial x \partial y} = fxy$$

$$\frac{\partial^2 z}{\partial y \partial x} = fyx$$

$$\frac{\partial^2 z}{\partial x \partial x} = fxx$$

$$\frac{\partial^2 z}{\partial y \partial y} = fyy$$

NINE

Climbs of the Curly Dees

9.1 Introduction

The camp of the Curly Dees is strategically placed close to some high passes in the Mathematics Mountains. A group of peaks, high valleys and plateaux lie a short but stiff climb above the camp. There are a number of routes up to this particular group, and we will follow the Curly Dees as they make their way up some of these trails. The trails don't go straight up a perpendicular set neatly at right angles to the axes — which is what, fortunately, we have been confined to so far — but can follow a contour round a mountain or take off diagonally to the axes. This means we must learn how to handle some new kit — Total Diffs and Total Dees — in case the weather closes in and we aren't sure where we are.

9.2 Paths and Contours

To illustrate the nature of the terrain above the camp of the Curly Dees we have a highly simplified sketch of a mountain we shall soon be climbing (Figure 9.1). From the work you have done, you know how to find your way along a perpendicular function such as LD or KA. If you begin at the origin (O) and walk directly to the point L, you can join the path to D by walking up the function LD, which consists of a fixed or constant amount of L (in economics this could be units of labour) and varying amounts of K (such as units of capital).

The surface shape of the mountain depends on how K changes as you climb towards D. In other words it is given by the function relating the height of the surface to the increasing distance of the K units from the perpendicular through L. Analogously, starting from a point K you know how to climb towards A. You also know how to check whether it is a maximum or a minimum point, or, where the maximum and minimum points are, by using second derivatives, and how to find even more complex slopes through the second order partials.

Suppose that at D you find a path that runs along the surface of the mountain towards A such that every point on the path is exactly the same height above the plain. If that path is projected 'inside' the mountain on to the plain below it produces a dotted line like the one in Figure 9.2. A series of these dotted lines could be drawn from similar paths of equal height running along

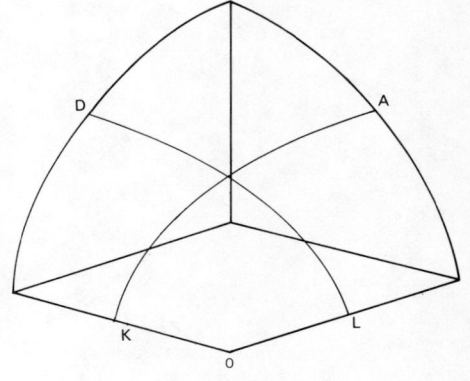

Figure 9.1

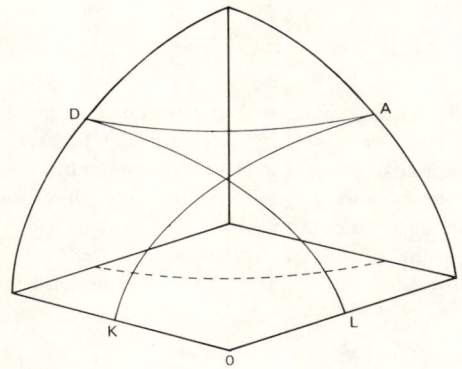

Figure 9.2

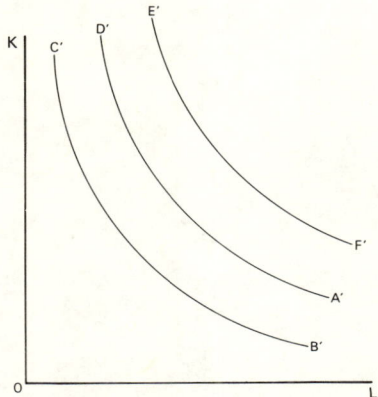

Figure 9.4

the surface of the mountain producing a set of lines looking like Figure 9.3. Each line represents points on the surface of exactly the same height. They are like contours on a map. If you think of the moutain as being an output surface, from economics, with each point on the surface representing the output that would be produced if labour and capital were used in combination, the dotted lines on the plain representing equal outputs become the isoquants (equal-quantities) from your production theory. Projected to the axes on the plain (Figure 9.4), each point shows the combination of capital and labour needed to produce a constant output. As the combinations of inputs of K and L are varied the relationship between them will either

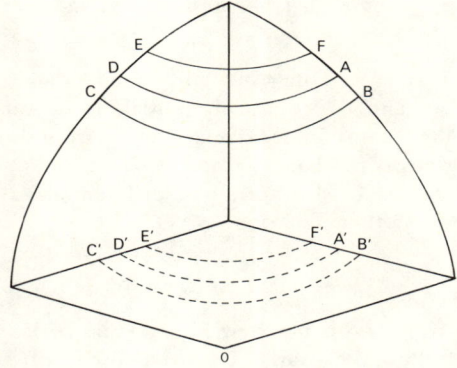

Figure 9.3

produce a constant output (the isoquants establish the quantities of each necessary to achieve this) or a varying output (the adjacent isoquants will establish the quantities of each necessary to change total output; i.e., move up or down the output surface).

The change in output is dependent upon the change in both capital (K) and labour (L) *at the same time* because the shape of the output surface is a product of both inputs in combination. Up to now we have assumed that when one input is held constant, the change in the other is independent of the constant. In other words, we considered functions which had independent variables but now we are moving on to interdependent variables.

These new functions may be clearer when you study Figure 9.5, which shows diagonal climbs up the moutain from points L and K. As you climb up the surface both K and L are changing at every point. In combination the change in inputs determines the height of the surface at each point. Projected on to the plain this appears as a straight line cutting across the isoquants.

Any movement you make on the surface of the mountain will bring into play two effects. There is the influence on the height of the surface of the change in distance

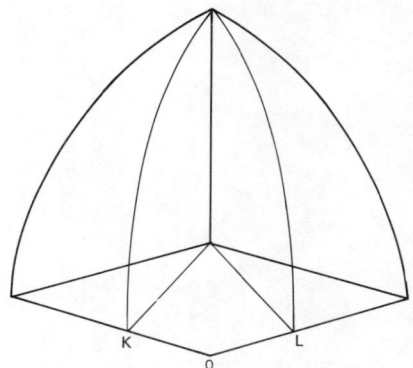

Figure 9.5

along one perpendicular and also the influence of the change in distance along the other perpendicular. Both these influences when added together fully describe the change in the height of the surface. Finding a mathematical form for this combined influence is the subject of the next section.

9.3 Total Diffs

We begin a brief recapitulation of partial differentiation of a function with independent variables such as

$$z = f(x,y). \qquad [1]$$

In this function z changes when x changes (y remaining constant) by the Curly Dee partial

$$\frac{\partial z}{\partial x}$$

and changes when y changes (x remaining constant) by

$$\frac{\partial z}{\partial y}.$$

Hence if Δz represents the increment in z consequent upon an arbitrary small increment in x, of Δx, then (approximately)

$$\Delta z = \frac{\partial z}{\partial x} \cdot \Delta x \qquad [2]$$

and

$$\Delta z = \frac{\partial z}{\partial y} \cdot \Delta y. \qquad [3]$$

The change in z for independent changes in x and y is given by [2] and [3] but what happens when the two independent variables x and y vary at the same time and change z in combination?

The answer is remarkably simple: just add the changes together! In this case we get

$$\Delta z = \frac{\partial z}{\partial x} \cdot \Delta x + \frac{\partial z}{\partial y} \cdot \Delta y \qquad [4]$$

The increment in z when x varies alone is given approximately by the first term on the RHS, and the increment in z when y varies alone is given by the second term on the RHS, but when both vary together the increment in z is given by the sum of the two increments.

Putting this into its limiting values we get

$$dz = \frac{\partial z}{\partial x} \cdot dx + \frac{\partial z}{\partial y} \cdot dy \qquad [5]$$

The change in z is equal to the rate of change in z with respect to x, y being held constant, multiplied by the infinitesimal change occurring in x plus the rate of change in z with respect to y, x being held constant, multiplied by the infinitesimal change occurring in y.

This is a 'Total Diff' or, among the Cognoscenti, a Total Differential. It measures the sum of the changes in z from both sources of change, x and y. The best way to appreciate the notion of differentials is to watch them working.

9.4 Three Swift Climbs

Armed with our new kit of Total Diffs, we follow the Curly Dees up three of the nearest peaks. Starting with Mount Utility,

9. Climbs of the Curly Dees

we can use differentials to establish familiar features from your textbook. Suppose the utility function is given by

$$U = f(x, y) \qquad [6]$$

Total utility is a function of the amount of utility provided by consuming quantities of goods x and y.

The Total Diff can immediately be written down because the change in utility will equal the rate of change of utility contributed by the goods (the other good being held constant) multiplied by the small changes in the amounts of the goods. This gives

$$dU = \frac{\partial U}{\partial x} \cdot dx + \frac{\partial U}{\partial y} \cdot dy. \qquad [7]$$

If you are walking round a path on Mount Utility in such a way that the height never changes (Figure 9.3), it follows that the change in total utility at every point on the path is equal to zero:

$$dU = 0. \qquad [8]$$

Where this is true, the dotted line projected from the path to the plain beneath the mountain produces a contour which corresponds in your economics to an indifference curve (Fig. 9.4, with re-labelled axes). The power of the differential is such that you can escape from two-dimensional geometric representations of the relationship between variables to more 'solid' three-dimensional models.

If we put [7] equal to zero we get

$$dU = \frac{\partial U}{\partial x} \cdot dx + \frac{\partial U}{\partial y} \cdot dy = 0. \qquad [9]$$

This must be the equation of an indifference curve. You know its meaning in economics, and you should have a *notion* of its mathematical meaning as well:

$$\frac{\partial U}{\partial x} \cdot dx + \frac{\partial U}{\partial y} \cdot dy = 0. \qquad [10]$$

If one term added to another equals zero, they must be equal in the absolute sense, but have different signs. This gives

$$\frac{\partial U}{\partial x} \cdot dx = -\frac{\partial U}{\partial y} \cdot dy. \qquad [11]$$

If we divide both sides by $\partial U/\partial x$ we get

$$\frac{\dfrac{\partial U}{\partial x} \cdot dx}{\dfrac{\partial U}{\partial x}} = - \frac{\dfrac{\partial U}{\partial y} \cdot dy}{\dfrac{\partial U}{\partial x}}$$

which cancels out on the LHS. Now divide both sides by dy to get

$$\frac{dx}{dy} = - \frac{\dfrac{\partial U}{\partial y}}{\dfrac{\partial U}{\partial x}} \cdot \frac{dy}{dy}$$

which cancels out on the RHS to give

$$\frac{dx}{dy} = - \frac{\partial U/\partial y}{\partial U/\partial x} \qquad [12]$$

The slope of the indifference curve is equal to the negative ratio of the Curly Dees (partial derivatives) of the utility function.

The partial derivatives in [12] are in fact the marginal utilities of the goods, measuring the contribution to total utility of an increment in one good and the corresponding reduction in total utility caused by a decrement in the other good (total utility remains constant along the indifference curve). Thus [12] tells you that the slope of the indifference curve is equal to the (negative) ratio of the marginal utilities of the two goods.

Not all mountain paths run along indifference curves. While we are ascending or descending Mount Utility our utility isn't constant; it is changing as both y and x are changing. The extent of the change will depend on the utility function of the particular mountain we are on. We can use the Total Diff to measure the change in total utility caused by a simultaneous change in the consumption of two goods. Suppose the utility function of Professor Douglas was given by

$$U = f(x, y) \qquad [13]$$
$$= 15x + 30y - x^2 - y^2 + 4xy.$$

The Total Diff is immediately written down — that's how easy it is! —

$$dU = \frac{\partial U}{\partial x} \cdot dx + \frac{\partial U}{\partial y} \cdot dy \qquad [14]$$

and differentiating [13] by partials, first with respect to x and next with respect to y, we get

$$dU = (15 - 2x + 4y)dx$$
$$+ (30 - 2y + 4x)dy. \qquad [15]$$

The increment in Professor Douglas's total utility is given by dU as expressed in equation [15].

The Curly Dees are soon off on a second climb, this time up Mount Savings. The slope of the mountain is given by the saving function:

$$S = f(Y, i) \qquad [16]$$

Savings are some function of the national income and the rate of interest.

The partial derivative of [16] with respect to national income measures the rate of change of savings for changes in national income, or, the marginal propensity to save:

$$\frac{\partial S}{\partial Y} = \text{MPS}. \qquad [17]$$

Any change in savings due to arbitrary small changes in national income can be represented by

$$\frac{\partial S}{\partial Y} \cdot dY. \qquad [18]$$

Similarly, the partial derivative of [16] with respect to interest rates is

$$\frac{\partial S}{\partial i} \qquad [19]$$

and any change in savings due to arbitrary small changes in the rate of interest can be represented by

$$\frac{\partial S}{\partial i} \cdot di. \qquad [20]$$

The total change in savings due to changes in both national income and interest rates is given by the total dee as

$$dS = \frac{\partial S}{\partial Y} \cdot dY + \frac{\partial S}{\partial i} \cdot di \qquad [21]$$

The change in savings is equal to the rate of change of savings with respect to national income multiplied by the infinitesimal change in national income plus the rate of change of savings with respect to the rate of interest multiplied by the infinitesimal change in the rate of interest.

Equation [21] illustrates the power of a mathematical formulation of a relationship. Even if it was impossible to 'fill-in' specific values for Y and i, it would still be of tremendous value to an analyst to have available a clear statement of the relationship between the variables, as set out in [21]. To attempt a purely literary statement of the relationship would be very difficult.

The last climb is similar in scope to the mountain we went up first — in fact, one of the beauties of mathematical economics is the extent to which a common core is applicable to a number of concepts in the neoclassical system. This economises on new work; once the results in one piece of the structure are understood, they can be applied to others. You can compare, for instance, the analysis using indifference curves in demand theory with the analysis of isoquants in production theory, or the equimarginal

9. Climbs of the Curly Dees

principle applied to consumer demand with the theory of the firm.

Suppose we have a production function:

$$x = f(a, b) \quad [22]$$

Output is a function of inputs a *and* b.

In the case where we are dealing with equal output levels — isoquants — we have the function $f(a, b)$ as a constant. The marginal products of the inputs are given by

$$\frac{\partial x}{\partial a} \quad [23]$$

and

$$\frac{\partial x}{\partial b} \cdot \quad [24]$$

Because [22] is equal to a constant we can write

$$\frac{\partial x}{\partial a} \cdot da + \frac{\partial x}{\partial b} \cdot db = 0 \quad [25]$$

which is the relationship between the increments da and db in the inputs along the constant output curve or isoquant.

Re-arranging [25] we write

$$\frac{\partial x}{\partial a} \cdot da = -\frac{\partial x}{\partial b} \cdot db$$

and dividing simultaneously by $\partial x/\partial a$ and db we get

$$\frac{da}{db} = -\frac{\frac{\partial x}{\partial b}}{\frac{\partial x}{\partial a}} \quad [26]$$

which is negative in sign, indicating that the curve slopes downward towards the right. Equation [26] is actually the marginal rate of substitution (see Hicks [1939], chs. 6 to 8) of input b for factor a. The equation [26] will tell you how much a must be increased to leave the output constant when a small reduction in b occurs. With diminishing marginal product [26] must increase in value as the amount of b decreases and a increases. This expresses the increasing marginal rate of substitution that is required as it becomes more awkward to replace the decreasing b factor with an increase in the a factor.

9.5 Total Dees

Total Diffs, or total differentials, lead on nicely to a related but more complex topic, namely, Total Dees, or total derivatives. The Total Diff covered cases where the variables x and y in a function such as

$$z = f(x, y) \quad [27]$$

were in some way dependent upon each other. In this section we ask what happens when z, x and y are also related to some other variable, such as t? For these climbs we need to add total dees to our kit.

Advanced mathematical texts provide exhaustive (and exhausting!) derivations of Total Dees, but our approach is less theoretical. First we take a look at a typical terrain to grasp what is involved, and secondly we follow the Curly Dees up some familiar slopes in economics.

In Figure 9.6 we have a typical mountain slope in three dimensions. The x and y axes are at right angles to each other and form

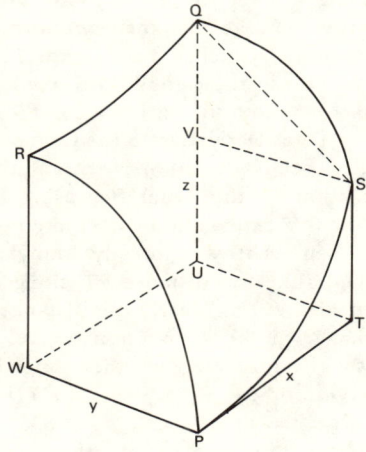

Figure 9.6

the plain on which the mountain stands. The mountain rises above the plain and its height is measured up the z axis. Traversing the mountain slope in any direction alters our height above the plain. The particular surface illustrated in Figure 9.6 is shown as *PRQS*. If we climb parallel to the *x* axis from any point on the *y* axis, we alter our position in respect of *z*. If the slopes in a *PR* and *SQ* direction are different (mountain slopes are rarely symmetrical), moving parallel to the *x* axis from different points on the *y* axis is also bound to result in a different *z* position, depending on the relative difficulty of the climb (how *z* changes along particular coordinates drawn from the *y* and *x* axes). Moving diagonally up the mountain side will compound the relative difficulties of various routes.

If climbs are relatively more or less difficult given by the shape of the surface, it follows that the *z* position for any particular lapse in time will also be different, depending on how the surface changes in one direction of the axis relative to the change in surface along the other axis. The rate of change of *z* relative to time *t* will vary as *x* and *y* varies with time *t*. For example, climbing directly up a vertical slope may be easier, and therefore faster, than diagonally traversing a steep slope with one leg continuously bent at the knee and the other continuously stretched full length. To find how *z* varies in these conditions requires the use of a new item of kit known as the Total Dee, or Total Derivative to the Cognoscenti.

Let us see if we can arrive at an intuitive explanation of the Total Dee using Figure 9.6. For this explanation we require nothing other than what you already know about calculus. Take the distance *PT* along the *x* axis in Figure 9.6. Clearly this distance gives the change in the *x* direction or Δx. Likewise the distance *TU* gives the change in the *y* direction or Δy. From the figure *TU* is the same distance as *SV* (i.e., $TU = SV = \Delta y$). The change in height *z* up the mountain from *P* to *Q* is the height of *Q* above the plain *PTUW* or Δz. Looking at the various distances involved in the figure we can write

$$\Delta z = UQ$$
$$= UV + VQ$$
$$= TS + VQ. \qquad [28]$$

We want to find alternative expressions for these distances. First we find an expression for the distance *TS* by noting that *TS* is the opposite side of a triangle *PTS*. A straight line drawn from *P* to *S* will have a slope *b*, and we know that the distance *PT* is Δx; so we can write the height *TS* as

$$TS = b\Delta x. \qquad [29]$$

Similarly we can find an expression for the height *VQ* by noting that *SVQ* forms a triangle with the straight line *SQ* acting as a chord to the curve through *S* and *Q*. The chord will have a slope *d*, and we can write the distance *VQ* as

$$VQ = d\Delta y. \qquad [30]$$

The change in height of *z* from *P* to *Q* ($= UQ$) is the combined change in *z* due to the changes in *x* and *y*. This is written as

$$\Delta z = b\Delta x + d\Delta y. \qquad [31]$$

But the rate of change of *x* and *y* depends on how they change through time *t*, and consequently the rate of change of height *z* is also a function of how *x* and *y* change through time *t*. The average rate of change of *z* through time *t* is given by dividing [31] by the change in *t*. This gives

$$\frac{\Delta z}{\Delta t} = b \cdot \frac{\Delta x}{\Delta t} + d \cdot \frac{\Delta y}{\Delta t}. \qquad [32]$$

If the distances *PT* and *TU* are next-to-nothing [32] takes the limiting value

$$\frac{dz}{dt} = b \cdot \frac{dx}{dt} + d \cdot \frac{dy}{dt}. \qquad [33]$$

Also, in the case where we are measuring the

slopes of the straight lines between PT and SQ we are taking partial derivatives, because in each case we hold one variable constant and differentiate the other. This means we can interpret the slopes b and d as partial derivatives and write [33] as

$$\frac{dz}{dt} = \frac{\partial z}{\partial x} \cdot \frac{dx}{dt} + \frac{\partial z}{\partial y} \cdot \frac{dy}{dt} \qquad [34]$$

The rate of change of height z through time is equal to the partial derivative of z with respect to changes in x when y is held constant times the small change of x through time, plus the partial derivative of z with respect to changes in y when x is held constant times the small change of y through time.

This is the Total Dee. It is total because the changes in z through time t take account of the simultaneous partial changes in z caused by the changes in the other variables through time t.

To illustrate the Total Dee we can watch the Curly Dees at work on production functions such as

$$Z = f(K, L) \qquad [35]$$

where capital and labour inputs change through time. The Curly Dees write out the change in output per unit of time using the Total Dee and get

$$\frac{dZ}{dt} = \frac{\partial Z}{\partial K} \cdot \frac{dK}{dt} + \frac{\partial Z}{\partial L} \cdot \frac{dL}{dt} \qquad [36]$$

The rate of change of output with respect to time depends on the rate of change of output with respect to changes in capital inputs times the rate of change of capital with respect to time plus the rate of change of output with respect to labour inputs times the rate of change of labour inputs with respect to time.

You should now be able to understand the meaning of a relationship written in total derivative form, which means in effect that you will soon be able to climb slopes as fast as the experienced Curly Dees.

Consider next a Total Dee involving the varying combinations of capital and labour which keep output at a constant level. This is the familiar constant output or isoquant diagram. Output Z is a function of the inputs K and L which are not perfect substitutes for each other (hence the isoquant is convex to the origin instead of a straight-line). This also ensures that the variables are not independent of each other because as less capital is used more labour has to be substituted for it. The rate at which capital is substituted for labour depends on how much labour is already being utilised if a constant output is to be maintained.

The production function can be written

$$Z = f(K, L). \qquad [34]$$

To find how output changes for changes in the labour input L we must take account of the effect of changes on output of diminishing amounts of the capital input K and how the amount of K changes with respect to L. We also need to know, of course, how output changes with changes in the amount of L it self. To this end we write the total dee as

$$\frac{dZ}{dL} = \frac{\partial f(K, L)}{\partial K} \cdot \frac{dK}{dL} + \frac{\partial f(K, L)}{\partial L} \cdot \frac{dL}{dL}.$$

[37]

The numerator has been written here with the term $f(K, L)$ in place of Z in order to emphasise how Z is a function of the two inputs. Also, the last term on the RHS, dL/dL, is included to remind you that when we write a Total Dee in terms of one of the variables of the function there is bound to be a term equal to unity ($dL/dL = 1$). This obviously can be dropped because a number multiplied by unity is itself. Presentations of the Total Dee in the literature automatically exclude this term and you may not be aware why unless it is explained at least once for you.

Taking account of these points we can write [37] as

$$\frac{dZ}{dL} = \frac{\partial Z}{\partial K} \cdot \frac{dK}{dL} + \frac{\partial Z}{\partial L}. \qquad [38]$$

By definition on an isoquant there is equal output for all combinations of capital and labour inputs. Therefore [38] becomes

$$\frac{dZ}{dL} = \frac{\partial Z}{\partial K} \cdot \frac{dK}{dL} + \frac{\partial Z}{\partial L} = 0 \qquad [39]$$

and, as usual, when two terms added together are equal to zero they must be equal to each other but have different signs:

$$-\frac{\partial Z}{\partial K} \cdot \frac{dK}{dL} = \frac{\partial Z}{\partial L}. \qquad [40]$$

It follows by maninpulation that

$$-\frac{dK}{dL} = \frac{\dfrac{\partial Z}{\partial L}}{\dfrac{\partial Z}{\partial K}}. \qquad [41]$$

The LHS of [41] is the slope of the negatively sloped isoquant, and from your economics you know it as the Marginal Rate of Technical Substitution ($MRTS$). The RHS consists of the partial derivatives of output with respect to labour (the marginal product of labour) and to capital (the marginal product of capital). Interestingly we have the familiar proposition that the $MRTS$ is equal to the ratio of the marginal product of labour and capital, or, more generally, the marginal rate of technical substitution of one factor for another on an isoquant is equal to the ratio of their marginal products.

It would not be very difficult on the basis of the above to derive the proposition from consumer theory that the marginal rate of substitution of one good for another is equal to the ratio of the marginal utilities of the goods. However, this would delay the expedition. The Curly Dees are eager to get on with the work and show you some interesting climbs on more difficult slopes, where they have to operate under constraints.

9.6 Curly Dee Meets Leaning Lambda*

In Figure 9.7a U is the highest point or peak of the mountain. Compare U with a point such as V, the highest point on a slice through the mountain (shaded in the figure). This corresponds to the idea of a *constrained maximum*. Given an unconstrained choice you would go for the U, the peak, but 'Nature is niggardly', writes Robbins, and so we are often constrained to points below the summit. We must aim for V instead. Looking at the mountain from above, as in Figure 9.7b, the point V is on the line AB drawn across the contours which represent various height levels. Any point on the line AB is attainable, but only V maximises our opportunity given the constraining line. V is a constrained maximum because, though it is the maximum point on the line across the contours, it is below the peak of the mountain. If you were compelled to remain on the left-hand side of the line AB — perhaps some bandit Curly Dees had seized the territory on the right-hand side of the line — then V is the highest point you would be able to reach on the mountain.

The tyranny of choice under the constraint of scarcity is an inescapable imperative of the way we live. The fact that we have a choice is probably the only bright

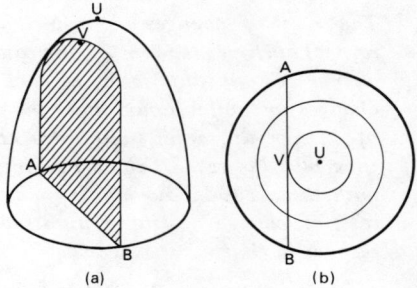

Figure 9.7

side of the otherwise dark shadow we live under. It depends on how you look at it. The cry of despair 'Make me a slave so that I may be free' is one way of eluding choice — let somebody else make the choice for you.

Most people are certainly not indifferent to the outcome. Given an unconstrained choice we should probably choose the maximum rather than the minimum of pleasure and the minimum rather than the maximum of pain. But life is nowhere near so generous. We have to choose between outcomes which are short of the maximum, or greater than the minimum, because we are *constrained* by scarcity of the means to achieve our many ends.

Those who seek perfection find themselves wanting. They are forced to do without. While there is something admirable in striving for perfection, there is something really tiresome in those who continuously expect to achieve it. There are some heights we cannot expect to scale — although hope knows no boundaries.

In previous sections we have outlined methods for finding maximum or minimum points on mountains or in valleys. The computational problem that faces you now is how to maximise (or minimise) a variable when it is subject to constraints — how do you go about finding a point such as V?

The French mathematician Joseph Lagrange (1736–1813) developed a special technique for handling equation systems involving constraints. It is known today among the Cognoscenti as the 'Lagrange undetermined multiplier' method, and once again the best way to see the power of a technique is to watch it at work. Why the method works will not be explained — we are just looking for the light switch!

In the high country we are now walking through there lives a tribe of operators who work in tandem with the Curly Dees, much like the Sherpas who serve climbers in the Himalayas. They are rather a shy tribe and their mountain life has imposed upon them the hereditary feature that they tend to lean over to the left on flat ground because their legs are really designed for walking on the mountain side — one leg is shorter than the other. Hence they are known as the Leaning Lambda Tribe. They can always be recognised in the following form:

$$\lambda$$

Lambda.

The Lambda have an important role in mathematical economics because of their help in solving problems of maximisation under constraints.

The tactical task we have to accomplish in order to find V is to convert it into the same kind of problem as maximising U. This means converting the function for U into a constrained maximising function for V, in such a way that if the constraint is met we automatically reach V when we maximise for U. This boils down essentially to maximising each of the variables subject to the constraint and maximising the constraint subject to the variables. Apart from writing the special Lagrangean function, the only computational task is to solve simple simultaneous equations from school algebra.

Figure 9.8 redrafts Figure 9.7b into a familiar diagram from economics. In this case we interpret it as an isoquant/isocost diagram from production theory.

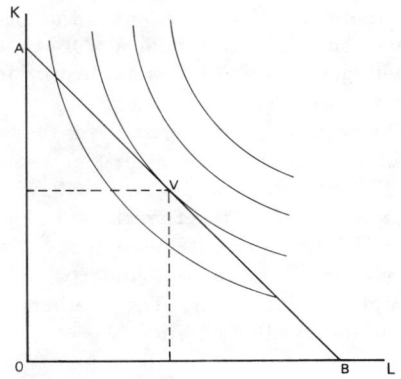

Figure 9.8

The neoclassical firm aims to maximise profits. It can do this by producing a given output at a minimum cost. The profit maximising output will be given by the tangency of the isocost line with the isoquant. Suppose the firm's production function is given by

$$Z = f(K, L) \qquad [34]$$

where Z, K, and L are output, capital input and labour input respectively. We already know that the slope of the isoquant will be equal to the ratio of the marginal products of the inputs capital and labour

$$\frac{dK}{dL} = -\frac{\frac{\partial Z}{\partial L}}{\frac{\partial Z}{\partial K}}. \qquad [41]$$

Assuming perfect competition, to produce a given output Z the firm will aim to minimise its costs of production, which are given by the wage rate of labour w times the quantity of labour hired L, and the interest rate on capital i times the quantity of capital borrowed K. This requires the firm to minimise its costs C which consist of

$$C = wL + iK. \qquad [42]$$

Alternatively the firm can maximise its output Z given by [34], subject to its cost constraint, which is equivalent to finding the highest output a given budget will produce. It will get exactly the same answer from both approaches.

The isocost line in Figure 9.8 is the locus of all combinations of capital and labour which, given their prices, will exhaust the available budget. Therefore, if we take the cost of labour and capital used in any combination away from the total budget there will be nothing left over. The mathematical presentation of this situation is

$$C - wL - iK = 0. \qquad [43]$$

If the LHS of [43] is multiplied by a constant it will not alter its equality with zero. In the Lagrange method the constraint is multiplied by an unspecified constant lambda λ.

The value of lambda is not specified and as we shall see it does not need to be. Students should put this curiosity down to an aspect of M. Lagrange's personality. From what we know of him, he probably invented the undetermined multiplier to tease some of his wayward students. One of the them reported (long after he had established his own reputation as a mathematician) that Professor Lagrange often contributed to mathematical seminars by saying 'There are a lot of important things to be said on this subject, but I shall not say them'! With a style like that, is it any wonder his multipliers remain undetermined (at least in this part of the mountains)?

Multiplying [43] by lambda gives

$$\lambda(C - wL - iK) = 0. \qquad [44]$$

The next step is to add the constraint to the function to be maximised, in this case $Z = f(K, L)$, giving a new Lagrangean function

$$V = f(K, L) + \lambda(C - wL - iK). \qquad [45]$$

If the constraint is equal to zero, and hence satisfied, V is maximised in the same way as U, because V is expressed in terms which include the constraint.

How can we both include the constraint multiplied by lambda and eliminate it at the same time? The answer is devilishly cunning. Simply treat lambda as another variable and partially differentiate it along with the other variables. This will produce equations suitable for simultaneous solution.

The Curly Dees can be written out for [45] without any trouble as

$$\frac{\partial V}{\partial K} = \frac{\partial Z}{\partial K} - \lambda i. \qquad [46]$$

Partially differentiating V with respect to capital eliminates the stand-alone constants; i.e., L in the production function and C and

9. Climbs of the Curly Dees

L in the constraint. The term λi keeps the constraint in the partial itself. As [46] is a general function for which we are seeking a general solution, the production function is not specified and the partial derivative of Z with respect to K is left formally stated on the RHS. Differentiating V with respect to L gives

$$\frac{\partial V}{\partial L} = \frac{\partial Z}{\partial L} - \lambda w. \qquad [47]$$

Again the stand-alone constants are eliminated and lambda remains in the partial. The last term to be partially differentiated is lambda itself, and this eliminates the production function (there being no lambda terms in it) and leaves the constraint as the partial because it is a constant times the lambda variable

$$\frac{\partial V}{\partial \lambda} = C - wL - iK. \qquad [48]$$

To find the values of the derivatives that satisfy the tangency of the isocost line with the isoquant curve, we set the derivatives equal to zero and get

$$\frac{\partial Z}{\partial K} - \lambda i = 0 \qquad [49]$$

$$\frac{\partial Z}{\partial L} - \lambda w = 0 \qquad [50]$$

$$C - wL - iK = 0 \qquad [51]$$

which gives

$$\frac{\partial Z}{\partial K} = \lambda i \qquad [52]$$

$$\frac{\partial Z}{\partial L} = \lambda w. \qquad [53]$$

$$C = wL + iK. \qquad [54]$$

If [51] and [52] are formed into a ratio we get

$$\frac{\frac{\partial Z}{\partial K}}{\frac{\partial Z}{\partial L}} = \frac{\lambda i}{\lambda w}. \qquad [55]$$

Lambda is eliminated by the ratio (to multiply and divide the RHS by the same number does not alter the RHS).

The economic interpretation of [55] should be familiar to you. The LHS is the ratio of the marginal products of capital and labour and the RHS is the ratio of their prices. The conclusion is to hire factors such that

$$\frac{\frac{\partial Z}{\partial K}}{i} = \frac{\frac{\partial Z}{\partial L}}{w} \qquad [56]$$

Capital and labour should be hired in quantities that equalise the ratio of their marginal products to their prices.

This is, of course, the same maximising rule for arriving at a point like U and the obvious question is: how does achieving [56] ensure arriving at a constrained position such as V when U is not attainable? The answer is equally obvious: don't forget equation [54]! The firm is required to satisfy the constraint

$$C = wL + iK \qquad [54]$$

Costs must not exceed the sum of the wage rate (proportionate to marginal product from [55]) times the quantity of labour and the interest rate (proportionate to marginal product from [55]) times the quantity of capital.

By meeting both conditions in [56] and [54] the firm will arrive at a maximum position V given its constraints. The lambdas have done their work magnificently. They have allowed you to find the constrained maximum without intruding too much into the picture, and they have gone as quickly as they arrived with the self-effacement they are famous for (in the manner of the personality of their originator M. Lagrange!).

The indefatigable Curly Dees are off on a climb up a likely looking mountain in the utility group and we must hurry on if we are to observe them and the leaning lambdas at work on another familiar problem from economics.

Suppose a consumer's utility depends on her consumption of two goods, X and Y and her utility function is given by

$$U = x \cdot y \qquad [57]$$

where x is the amount of good X consumed and y is the amount of good Y consumed. If she was unconstrained in her consumption she would consume the goods until the marginal utility from consumption was equal to zero, which would correspond to a maximum utility position or the peak of the utility mountain. However, she is constrained (inevitably) by her budget and the respective prices of X and Y. If her budget is $48 and X costs $2 and Y costs $3 her budget constraint can be written

$$B = 48 = 2x + 3y. \qquad [58]$$

To maximise her utility subject to the constraint, she must reach V, the highest point on the utility mountain available to her, given her constraint line AB in Figure 9.8 (with the axes appropriately relabelled).

Using the leaning lambdas we write out the Lagrangean function

$$V = (x \cdot y) + \lambda(48 - 2x - 3y). \quad [59]$$

This is partially differentiated with Curly Dees, and each derivative is set equal to zero, giving

$$\frac{\partial V}{\partial x} = y - 2\lambda \quad = 0 \qquad [60]$$

$$\frac{\partial V}{\partial y} = x - 3\lambda \quad = 0 \qquad [61]$$

$$\frac{\partial V}{\partial \lambda} = 48 - 2x - 3y = 0. \qquad [62]$$

To find the quantities of X and Y which maximise her utility subject to her budget constraint we must solve the equations simultaneously; i.e., find values for x and y which meet the conditions of each equation at the same time. We do this by inspecting the equations and finding a multiple of one of them so that it makes one of the variables the same in two of the equations. For example, if [60] is multiplied by 3 it gives

$$(y - \lambda 2)3 = 3y - 6\lambda = 0 \qquad [63]$$

and [61] multiplied by 2 gives

$$(x - \lambda 3)2 = 2x - 6\lambda = 0. \qquad [64]$$

Neither equation has been altered by the multiplication because they are still equal to zero, but they both now contain the same lambda term. If [64] is subtracted from [63] we get

$$3y - 6\lambda - 2x + 6\lambda = 3y - 2x = 0 \qquad [65]$$

which eliminates the lambdas. Inspecting [62] we note that it has a term $-3y$ and [65] has a term $+3y$. Thus if we add [62] to [65] we will eliminate the y term and keep the equation in balance with zero:

giving
$$48 - 2x - 3y + 3y - 2x = 0$$
$$48 - 4x = 0. \qquad [66]$$

The elimination of lambda and y leaves an expression for x only which we can solve easily to find the value of x. If a number minus another number is equal to zero then the numbers must be equal to each other:

$$48 = 4x$$
$$\frac{48}{4} = x$$
$$12 = x. \qquad [67]$$

To find the value of y we simply insert the value for x which we have just found into [62]

$$48 - 2(12) - 3y = 0$$
$$48 - 24 - 3y = 0$$
$$24 - 3y = 0.$$

Again we have an equation for one of the

variables, both x and lambda being eliminated, and we can soon solve for y by

$$24 = 3y$$

$$\frac{24}{3} = y$$

$$8 = y. \qquad [68]$$

We now have $x = 12$ and $y = 8$ and we can check that this meets the constraint by inserting into [62] the x and y values:

$$\$48 - 12(\$2) - 8(\$3) = 0$$

$$\$48 - \$24 - \$24 = 0.$$

The consumer will maximise her utility given her budget and the prices of X and Y by purchasing 12 of good X and 8 of good Y.

9.7 For the Notebook

Some technical rules are summarised in this section for you to use when and if you need them, either in your own work or because they appear in somebody else's work without explanation. The first rule is the so-called Chain Rule and it is very similar to some of the work in this chapter. It comes from the rules for differentiating functions of functions.

Given a function

$$y = f(z)$$

and

$$z = g(x)$$

how do we find

$$\frac{dy}{dx}?$$

If y depends on z and z depends on x then a change in x influences changes in y by the extent to which x influences z and z influences y. The total change must be the product of the changes (think of gear ratios in an engine). We can write out the derivative for functions of a function as

$$\frac{dy}{dx} = \frac{dy}{dz} \cdot \frac{dz}{dx}.$$

The chain rule is applicable for functions of functions, such as

$$y = f(u)$$
$$u = g(v)$$
$$v = h(w)$$
$$w = i(x)$$
$$x = j(z)$$

giving

$$\frac{dy}{dz} = \frac{dy}{du} \cdot \frac{du}{dv} \cdot \frac{dv}{dw} \cdot \frac{dw}{dx} \cdot \frac{dx}{dz}.$$

Total derivatives deal with composite functions. The three most common types are

1. $$z = f(x, y)$$
$$y = g(x).$$

The derivative dz/dx gives the rate of change of z for infinitesimal changes in x. The total derivative gives the direct effect on z of a change in x plus the indirect effect on z of a change in x through the other variable y. The total derivative is written as

$$\frac{dz}{dx} = \frac{\partial z}{\partial x} + \frac{\partial z}{\partial y} \cdot \frac{dy}{dx}.$$

2. $$z = f(x, y)$$
$$x = g(w)$$
$$y = h(w).$$

The total derivative measures the effect on z of changes in x and y caused by changes in w. The total derivative is written as

$$\frac{dz}{dw} = \frac{\partial z}{\partial x} \cdot \frac{dx}{dw} + \frac{\partial z}{\partial y} \cdot \frac{dy}{dw}.$$

3. $z = f(x, y)$

    $x = g(u, v)$

    $y = h(u, v)$.

With two variables influencing the variables in the main function we have to write the total derivative in partial form — one for each variable — differentiating z with respect to both u and v. If we tried to differentiate z with respect to u alone we would be trying to pick up the changes on z from u through x and y when x and y were also being influenced by u and v. This requires the writing of two total derivatives:

$$\frac{\partial z}{\partial u} = \frac{\partial z}{\partial x} \cdot \frac{\partial x}{\partial u} + \frac{\partial z}{\partial y} \cdot \frac{\partial y}{\partial u}$$

and

$$\frac{\partial z}{\partial v} = \frac{\partial z}{\partial x} \cdot \frac{\partial x}{\partial v} + \frac{\partial z}{\partial y} \cdot \frac{\partial y}{\partial v}.$$

The similarity between these total derivatives and the chain rule is not accidental — they are in fact extensions of it.

TEN

From Scenes Like These

10.1 Introduction

The expedition is almost over. You have climbed to considerable heights. You have already achieved much, and from where you are standing in the Mathematics Mountains you can see the Promised Land. Some of you may be tempted to consider signing up for another, longer, expedition to this land, which is within your grasp but, for the moment, just beyond your reach. Others of you, who have seen, for the moment, as much of the Mathematics Mountains as you need, may be under pressure to return to the plain to attend to other pressing business (such as preparing for Finals).

However, one of the delights of climbing is the opportunity it affords for spectacular views (providing the weather permits, which isn't always the case, so don't fret if there is still a deal of fog about). It would be a pity to waste an opportunity to admire the view of the terrain you have crossed, even if much of it remains in a stubborn mountain mist on this occasion. It wouldn't be correct to regard this as a summary of everything you have done. Most of the panorama concentrates on the views of the Calculus group of mountains, because most of the early material lies below the tree-line and is as difficult to see from above as it is from the plain below.

If you stand on a mountain, or even a hill, your eye tends to rove as far as you can see. There is something wonderfully relaxing about a spectacular view over a great distance. Behind my house stand the Braid Hills, from which, on a clear Edinburgh day, it is possible to see across the Firth of Forth to Fife and its hills, or along the southern shore towards North Berwick in East Lothian (though the most prominent feature on this coast is the huge power station at Cockenzie, about twelve miles away). So looking to the far distance is the first and natural thing to do. For that reason we will begin with the earlier work in calculus and the next-to-nothing first derivatives of two-dimensional space.

10.2 Hunting for Zeros

Even when confined to two dimensions, the power of calculus extends to whole areas of economics. Truly you could spend much time exploring that territory without really retracing your steps, and you would get a great deal of mileage out of your computations. But remember, it is only possible to make use of calculus notions in your economics because assumptions have been made about the relationships between economic variables. It is assumed that these relationships are *continuous* and *smooth*, and because of this the functions representing the relationships have a derivative and at every point the curve of the function has a tangent. If discontinuities existed — if the surface were more like the steps of a staircase than the side of a mountain — calculus would be inappropriate and indeed irrelevant.

The first derivative of a function is found by the rules of differentiation (the 'Dance of the Derivatives'). You have been introduced to some of these rules. If you undertook a more detailed exploration of the early slopes of the calculus group you would require to learn, or know where to find, some of the other rules. But you know how to find the value of dy/dx, which has a long and honourable history in mathematics, sometimes known as the 'Leibniz Notation', after Gottfried Wilhelm Leibniz (1646–1716), a co-inventor, with Isaac Newton, of the Calculus — though each spent a lifetime denouncing the claims of the other!

The really interesting work in microeconomics is concentrated on finding 'turning points' in the slopes. Neoclassical economics is about equating marginal values and maximising or minimising key variables such as profits, costs, revenue, sales and so on. This means finding the points similar to those marked in Figure 10.1.

Point A is to remind you of the relationship between the tangent at the point, and the derivative as the limit value, of the incremental ratio of the two variables. As the incremental distance diminishes, the chord approaches the value of the tangent at the point.

At B there is a maximum. You are standing on the summit of a hill. It isn't necessarily the highest hill in the group — there could be other higher hills elsewhere (e.g., Z) — but it is the highest point compared with all the points immediately adjacent to it. Among the Cognoscenti this is known as a 'local' maximum. The first derivative is equal to zero, because there is no change taking place in the slope of the function at this point. This could be a point of maximum profit, as in Figure 10.2 from Baumol's sales maximisation hypothesis [1967]. For a maximum it is *necessary* that the derivative be equal to zero. It is not *sufficient* that it be zero. To test for a maximum you must take the second derivative. If the second derivative is negative then it is a maximum.

At point C there is a minimum. You are standing at the floor of a valley. It isn't necessarily the lowest point in the group, but it is the lowest point compared with all the points immediately adjacent to it. It could be a point of minimum production and selling costs, such as Q in Figure 10.3 from Chamberlin's theory of monopolistic competition [1933, 7th ed., ch. 6, p. 148]. To test for a minimum, having discovered

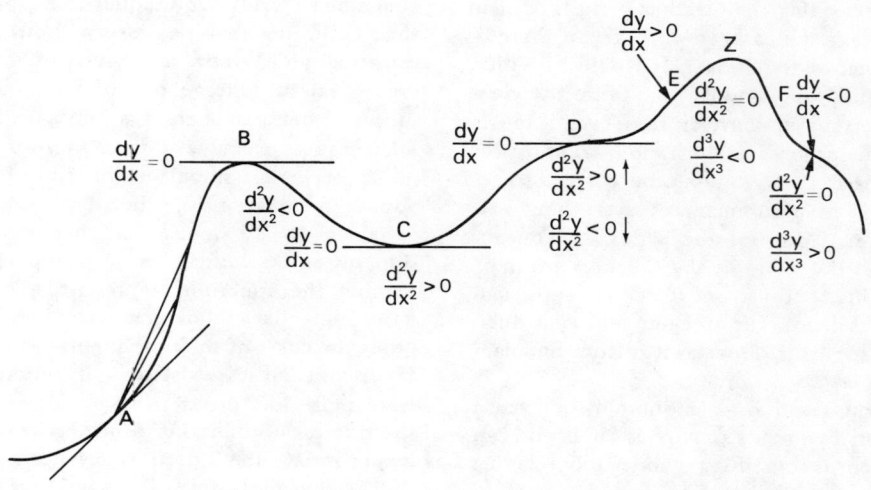

Figure 10.1

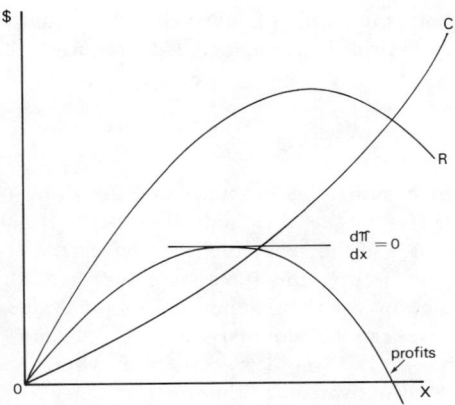

Figure 10.2

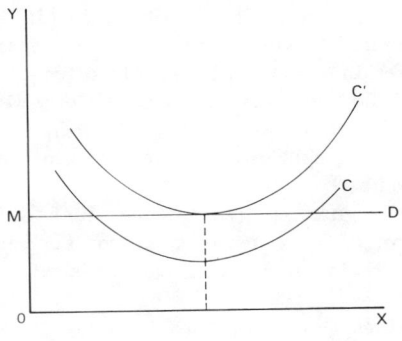

Figure 10.3

that the first derivative is equal to zero (the necessary condition for a minimum), you must take the second derivative. If the second derivative is positive, it is a minimum.

Point D is a point of inflexion — a ledge — and it is one of those inflexion points where the first derivative is equal to zero. A point of inflexion is a change in the direction of curvature of the hill or mountain side, and in economics it is a feature of total cost, revenue and product curves. The second derivative has to be equal to zero if the necessary and sufficient conditions for this type of inflexion are to be met. However, this doesn't exhaust the possibilities for finding points of inflexion.

It is possible that the first derivative isn't equal to zero but that the second derivative is. If the second derivative is equal to zero, it is a point of inflexion, but a different type to point D. It is like point E or F. At E the curves switch from convex from below (think of the outline of the lower half of an orange on a table) to concave from below (the opposite or top half). This can be tested for by taking the third derivative (d^3y/dx^3). For this type of point of inflexion the third derivative would be negative. The other kind (point F) is the exact opposite. The curves run from concave to convex from below and the third derivative would be positive.

Remembering all the cases for maximum, minimum and inflexion points is no easy task and is best avoided. Write them into a notebook and look them up as the need arises. This is even truer when you consider the multitude of possible cases in constrained maximisation using Curly Dees.

The literature on the theory of the firm using calculus is now open to you. Most textbooks will use calculus to illustrate optimisation, profit maximisation, elasticity and marginal revenue concepts. You could try Tangri [1966], 'Omissions in the Treatment of the Law of Variable Proportions', which uses dY/dX in the course of the argument, to get some confidence in handling the notation. You can also cope with most of chapters 3, 4 and 5 of Naylor & Vernon's otherwise difficult mathematical presentation of the theory of the firm [1969].

10.3 Summits, Valleys and Passes

It is not possible to travel very far into the Mathematics Mountains without switching from two to three dimensions. For one thing, to stay in two dimensions limits your itinerary, and for another the novelty of always climbing the same peaks wears off eventually. Once you can handle Curly Dees a considerable amount of the literature becomes accessible, with a consequent boost to your understanding of economics. For example, chapters 4 and 5 of Wildsmith [1973], 'Revenue Maximisation' and 'Managerial Discretion', have much more to offer if you can follow the mathematics of Curly Dees (the Appendix to chapter 3, 'Profit Maximising Equilibrium', is well within your scope now).

In Figure 10.4 the three dimensional section of a mountain is shown. There are three basic climbs you can undertake on these kinds of slopes. You can go up route M, which starts at a constant value for one of the variables and then adjusts as the function of the other variable wraps itself along the surface. Another route (N) has the same characteristics; one variable is held constant and the other adjusts according to the nature of the function. These routes are followed in production theory when one factor is increased while the other is held constant. They are represented by Curly Dee notation:

$$\frac{\partial z}{\partial x} \text{ (holding } y \text{ constant)}$$

and

$$\frac{\partial z}{\partial y} \text{ (holding } x \text{ constant)}.$$

The third route (P) goes up the slope with both variables changing together, such as when the scale of operation of a multi-input firm is changing. This requires the total dee

$$dz = \frac{\partial z}{\partial x} \cdot dx + \frac{\partial z}{\partial y} \cdot dy$$

which sums the influence on the slope of changes in the x variable (the x-effect) and changes in the y-variable (the y-effect).

As before, the interesting points in the functions are the maxima and minima values. These can be summarised (for your notebook). The simplest cases are where the partial derivatives of the function $z = f(x, y)$ are either positive or negative. The Curly Dees

$$\frac{\partial z}{\partial x}, \quad \frac{\partial z}{\partial y}$$

measure the slope of the gradient at the point. If the Curly Dee is positive, the slope rises from left to right (Q); if it is negative, the slope falls from left to right (R) (Figure 10.5).

The meaning of the second derivative can be seen from Figure 10.5. The second derivative measures the rate of change of the first derivative. In the case of a positive $\partial z/\partial x$, the second derivative, $\partial^2 z/\partial x^2$, tells you how z increases while y remains constant. If the second derivative is positive at the point (S) the slope is becoming steeper; if $\partial^2 z/\partial x^2$ is negative, the surface is becoming flatter (T).

When the cases are reversed you get the opposite effect: a negative $\partial z/\partial x$ with a negative second derivative is becoming steeper in a downwards direction (U); a positive $\partial^2 z/\partial x^2$ is becoming flatter in a downward direction (V).

The meaning of the Cross Partial $\partial^2 z/\partial x \partial y$ is a little obscure but can be grasped if you imagine you are standing on a mountainside which slopes in two directions: first, it slopes directly up in the direction you are facing towards the summit; and secondly, it slopes in a different direction parallel to your

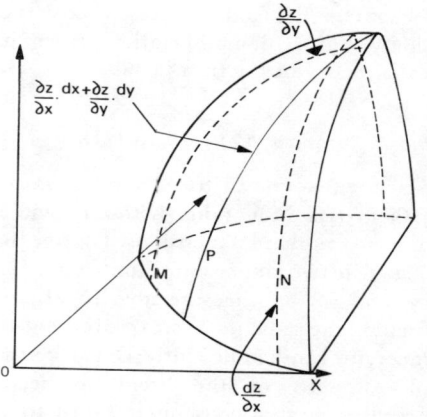

Figure 10.4

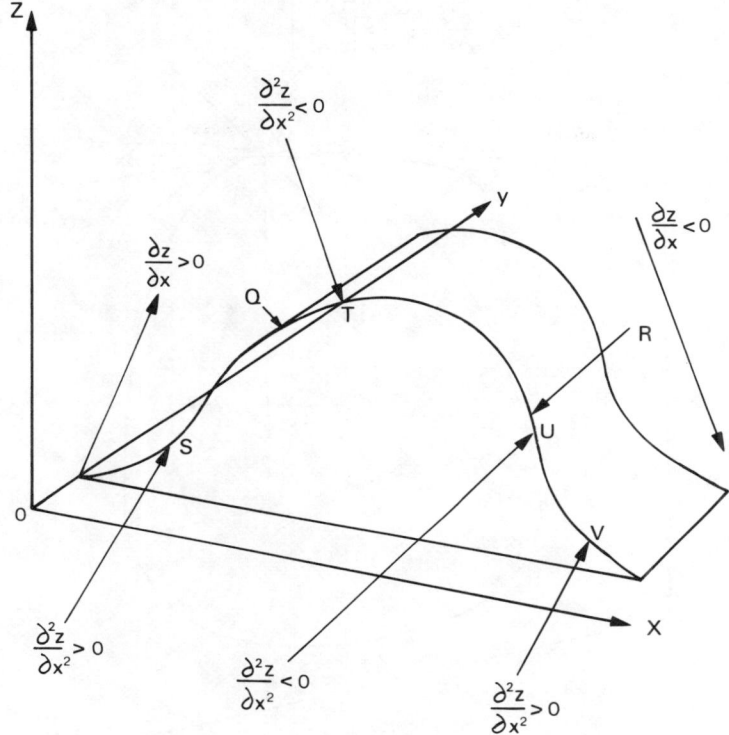

Figure 10.5

shoulders. Remember, the cross Curly Dee measures the rate of change of $\partial z/\partial x$ as y increases (x constant) *and* the rate of change of $\partial z/\partial y$ as x increases (y constant). As you move up the mountain, the slope parallel to your shoulders and the slope of the mountain changes.

If the cross Curly Dee is positive, the slope parallel to your shoulders is becoming steeper as you move up the function and the slope of the function is also becoming steeper as you move sideways. If it is negative, the inclines of the slopes are reversed: moving up the mountain the slope parallel to the shoulders becomes flatter and the slope ahead falls as you move sideways.

So much for clambering along the slopes of the mountain; how are the maximum and minimum points found? By finding the points where the derivative is equal to zero and then testing the second derivative. If the first derivative is equal to zero and the second derivative is negative, the point is a maximum (point W in Figure 10.6). If the second derivative is positive, it is a minimum (point Z in Figure 10.7). The Curly Dees must meet these conditions along both routes $\partial z/\partial x$ and $\partial z/\partial y$. If they don't then it isn't a summit maximum.

Strictly, the second derivatives should be taken for more than two directions to make sure that it is a true summit, but generally it is assumed that if it is a summit, or trough, for two directions it is likely to be so for them all.

One way to make sure that it is a true

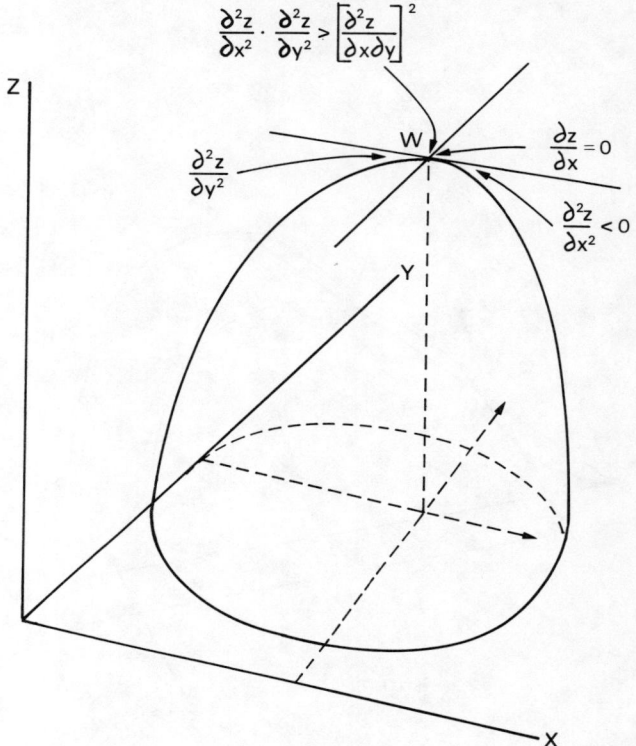

Figure 10.6

summit or trough is to use a specially designed criterion (for which no proof will be given!). This states that, if the second derivatives are multiplied together and they are greater than the square of the cross Curly Dee, the summit or trough condition is fully defined. In notation this becomes:

When $\dfrac{\partial z}{\partial x} = \dfrac{\partial z}{\partial y} = 0$

and

$$\dfrac{\partial^2 z}{\partial x^2} < 0; \quad \dfrac{\partial^2 z}{\partial y^2} < 0$$

then, if

$$\dfrac{\partial^2 z}{\partial x^2} \cdot \dfrac{\partial^2 z}{\partial y^2} > \left[\dfrac{\partial^2 z}{\partial x \partial y}\right]^2$$

the point is a maximum. Conversely, if the second derivatives are positive

$$\dfrac{\partial^2 z}{\partial x^2} > 0; \quad \dfrac{\partial^2 z}{\partial y^2} > 0$$

and

$$\dfrac{\partial^2 z}{\partial x^2} \cdot \dfrac{\partial^2 z}{\partial y^2} > \left[\dfrac{\partial^2 z}{\partial x \partial y}\right]^2$$

the point is a minimum.

What happens if the product of the second derivatives is less than the squared cross partial when the second derivatives are positive or negative

$$\dfrac{\partial^2 z}{\partial x^2} \cdot \dfrac{\partial^2 z}{\partial y^2} < \left[\dfrac{\partial^2 z}{\partial x \partial y}\right]^2 \quad ?$$

This is an interesting surface illustrated in Figure 10.8. It corresponds to a mountain pass: as you climb through the pass you rise to a maximum height and then descend on

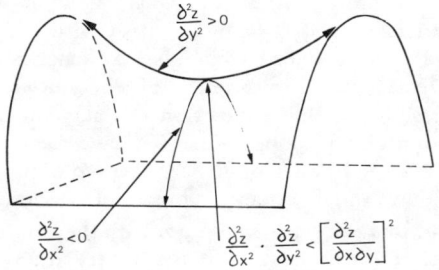

Figure 10.8

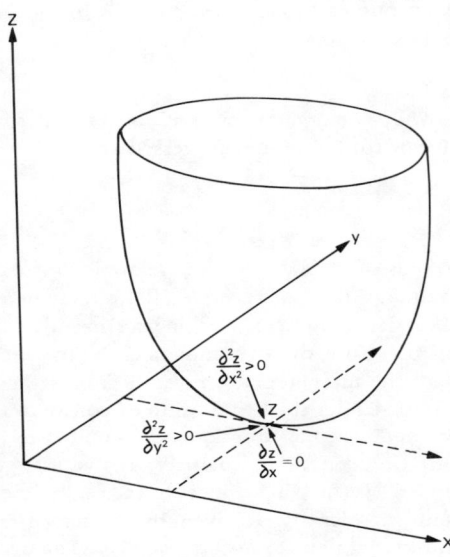

Figure 10.7

the other side; the slopes of the mountains on either side rise on both sides of the pass to their summits. Hence, in one direction, through the pass, we have a maximum and in the other direction, perpendicular to the pass, we have a minimum. This surface, from its appearance, is sometimes called a Saddle, and the point at which it is a maximum in one direction and a minimum in another is known as the Saddle Point (they feature a great deal in Game Theory).

A pass or saddle point is bound to appear when the second derivatives of the right-angled slopes are considered. The line through the pass is bound to have a negative second derivative, because it is a Maximum, and the line at right angles from summit to summit of the mountains is bound to be positive, because it is a minimum; a negative multiplied by a positive gives a negative product.

As was emphasised in the last chapter, the maxima and minima points of the mountains are likely to be unattainable. We are confined in the real world to maximisation under constraints and for this reason the mathematics of constrained maximisation have been introduced in the discussion of Lagrangean undetermined multipliers.

Before we discuss some of the literature that you may find useful we can use the time it takes to get you back to the plain with a brief (and I mean brief!) look at an important topic in calculus, namely Integration.

10.4 A Brief Encounter with the Summing Sids*

It is time to return to the plain. Getting up a mountain is only half the work; getting down is the other half (and it is sometimes just as hazardous). On the way up we haven't paid too much attention to our bearings, distracted as we were with the joys of discovery. Rather than return directly, those who want to can spend a short time in a minor detour, the benefits of which are out of all proportion to the time it takes. (Those who prefer not to take in the Integral Calculus on this trip can pass on to the next section — you can always come back and tackle this section another time.)

The Curly Dees, which have been a magnificent help in the climb, are less useful in the descent. Where they excel in dividing a function into its infinitesimal pieces, they have all the dexterity of the king's horses and the king's men in putting it back together again. Fortunately help is at hand. Unfortunately the helpers are not the easiest of companions, either to work with or to understand, at first; but contact with them, even for a short while, has a remarkable effect. Only the briefest of encounters is possible on this expedition. To stay on the mountain any longer than we have spent on this expedition would endanger your motivation and, perhaps, your understanding, and therefore our encounter with these hardy and faithful helpers must be regarded as purely introductory and by no means comprehensive. It has been included only to give the reader a 'feel' for the Integral Calculus and to remove some of the inexplicable terrors that accompany the appearance of integral notation.

Figure 10.9 shows an average revenue curve and the related marginal revenue curve. We want to make some elementary remarks about the relationships of the curve to total revenue. You know that average revenue AR is related to total revenue R by

$$AR = \frac{R}{q}$$

where q is quantity sold, or

$$R = AR \cdot q.$$

In graphical terms this gives total revenue for an output of T as an area, shown in Figure 10.9 as the area

$$R = OPRT.$$

What is marginal revenue? It is the derivative of total revenue, expressed as

$$MR = \frac{dR}{dq}.$$

How is marginal revenue related to total revenue? Marginal revenue is the increment in total revenue from selling an extra unit, and therefore total revenue must be the sum of all the increments in revenue from selling q units. Under the assumption of continuous cost and revenue functions, the number of q units (increments in quantity) is a very large number. In fact in calculus terms each increment in quantity is given by a change in quantity of next-to-nothing size dq. The perpendicular from the marginal revenue curve of width dq gives the increase in total revenue from selling that extra (very small) amount. The total revenue at any point on the average revenue curve is the area under the marginal revenue curve. In Figure 10.9 this is the area $OQST$.

If total revenue is average revenue times quantity, or, the sum of the marginal revenue of each unit sold, it follows that in area terms we can write

$$AR \cdot q = \text{area } OPRT = R$$

and

$$\sum MR \cdot q = \text{area } OQST = R.$$

This amounts to saying that the area under the average revenue curve at output T is equal to the area under the marginal revenue curve at output T.

Finding total revenue from the average revenue curve is not difficult — almost everybody understands how to find the areas of rectangles (just multiply one side by the other). But finding the area under the marginal revenue curve looks a trifle more fearsome. Conceptually, however, it oughtn't to prove difficult to grasp. We have stated that total revenue is composed of all the

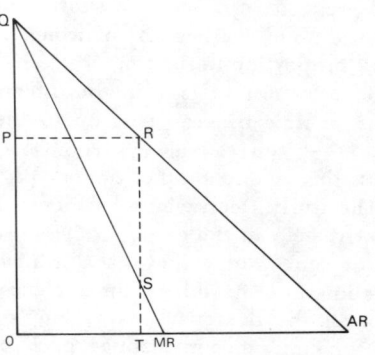

Figure 10.9

marginal revenue perpendiculars of width dq under the marginal revenue curve. Therefore to find the area simply sum all the perpendiculars! We could write this out as

> Find the sum of individual marginal revenues (dR) for all the quantity changes (dq) from zero to quantity T.

In symbols this could be written as

Sum $(MR \cdot dq)$ from 0 to T.

Have a look now at Figure 10.10, which is a stylised cost curve graph from neoclassical economics. The marginal cost curve is below the average cost curve and then rises to cut it at the point of minimum average cost. You know that average cost is related to total cost by the following expressions

$$AC = \frac{TC}{q}$$

or

$$TC = AC \cdot q.$$

In graphical terms total cost of producing output T is the area $OPRT$ in Figure 10.10.

How does marginal cost fit into this relationship? Marginal cost is the increment in total cost for each unit increase in quantity, and in the calculus presentation the increase in quantity is a size that is next-to-nothing, or dQ. Analogously to the revenue case, the total cost of an output of, say, OT is the sum of all the increments in total cost for each output change from zero to T. Each output change of dq in size has a corresponding contribution to total cost of the perpendicular under the marginal cost curve of width dq. The sum of all these additions to total cost is the area under the marginal cost curve of $OQST$.

Finding total cost from the average cost curve is not difficult $(AC \cdot q)$. But what of the marginal cost curve? Again the conceptual issue ought not to be difficult. Simply add all the marginal costs of each dq. In words we could write

> Find the sum of all the marginal costs (dC) for all the quantity changes (dq) from zero to T.

In symbols this could be written

Sum $(MC \cdot dq)$ from 0 to T.

In both cases we have an instruction to sum a derivative over a finite distance (from 0 to T) to get an area under the curve. You have to know how many marginal changes there are in that distance and you know from calculus that there is a lot of them of dq width. You now have all the information needed to write out a calculus expression for the area under the curve!

The operating instruction is to *sum* all of the derivatives of dq width between zero and quantity T. The Greek symbol for summing anything is sigma, Σ, but in a rare example of the triumph of the Anglo-Saxons in the notation business, the old English elongated S has managed to hold its position with a tenacity which defies explanation — none the less welcome for that — and convention decrees that the mathematician's symbol for the operation of summing in the calculus shall be

In these parts the locals call the enlongated S's, the Summing Sids (after a tribe of

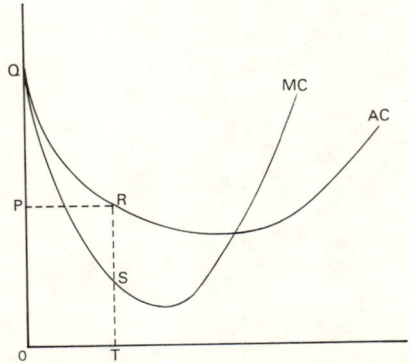

Figure 10.10

Saxons who escaped integration under the Norman occupation and survived in rural Cambridgeshire until around Isaac Newton's time), because they were noted for their constructive efforts to put back together what the more boisterous Franco-Normans were wont to break-up (much in the manner of their descendants, the Curly Dees) in their cavorting about the English countryside.

In the above examples, the instructions for finding the area are written

$$\int_0^T MR \cdot dQ$$

(where the sub- and superscripts alongside the S tell you the range along the horizontal to be summed) and

$$\int_0^T MC \cdot dQ.$$

Understanding the conceptual issues is an important part of the calculus of integration, but it is only a part. We ought now to try to get a firmer idea of what is involved.

The best way to approach integration is in stages. If you accept that total revenue or total cost can be calculated by finding the area under the marginal revenue or marginal cost curve, you ought to accept that finding the change in revenue or cost between two discreet outputs is simply a matter of calculating the difference between two areas.

Suppose you wanted to find the change in total cost between S and T in the total cost curve graphed in Figure 10.11. If you know the function of the cost curve, all you need to do is to substitute values for T and S to give the total cost at output T and the total cost at output S. Taking S from T, leaves the gap UW as the change in total costs. Now suppose you don't know the total cost function but only have its derivative, marginal cost. How would you set about finding the change in total cost over a (relatively) large finite distance? This is where the Summing Sids come into their own. They enable you to integrate what the derivative has *dis*-integrated; they enable you

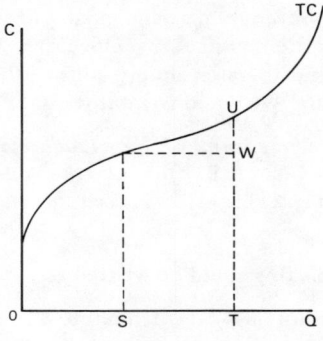

Figure 10.11

to put back together what has been separated into wee bits by the process of differentiation. If dy/dx is the limiting value of a wee change in x, $\int dx$ is the summing together of all the wee changes.

In Figure 10.12 the function $C = f(q)$ has been graphed (its exact form is not relevant to this part of the discussion) and the derivative has been exaggerated in size for illustrative purposes. The distance horizontally is given by dq and the distance vertically is given by dC. The rate of change of costs to output at any point will be given by the derivative of the function and the value of q at that point. The derivative we know is

$$\frac{dC}{dq}.$$

If the function was given by

$$C = \frac{q^2}{1000}$$

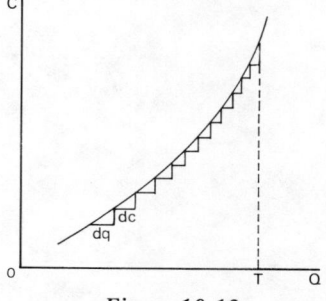

Figure 10.12

the derivative would be

$$\frac{dC}{dq} = \frac{q}{500}.$$

The rate of change of costs at 100 gallons of output of the local ale, Practicality, would be found by substituting 100 for q (i.e., $100/500 = 0.20$ cents per gallon). Similarly for other output levels.

To find the total cost for any output level, say, T, we have to sum all the little dC's up to the output level T. We could write this as

$$\int dC.$$

But for every dC there is a dq, and summing all the dC's is the same as summing all the dq's times the derivative, because all the changes in output are given by the derivative of the function times the changes in output between zero and T. Thus we can write

$$\int_0^T dC = \int_0^T \frac{dC}{dq} \cdot dq = \int_0^T \frac{q}{500} \cdot dq.$$

To get further with this expression we must find the function for which it is the derivative. If differentiating $C = f(q)$ gave the derivative dC/dq, it follows that integrating dC/dq will give us the original function. In this case we already know that the function is

$$C = \frac{q^2}{1000}$$

and this will help us to put back together what the derivatives have taken apart.

The process of differentiating a function such as

$$y = ax^n$$

involves calculating

$$y = nax^{n-1}.$$

Integrating involves getting back to the original function:

$$y = \int nax^{n-1} \cdot dx$$
$$= ax^n.$$

The rule we use to integrate x^n is written as

$$\frac{1}{n+1} \cdot x^{n+1} + C.$$

To integrate add one to the power and divide the derivative by 1 plus the power.

Applying this to the derivative of total cost we get

$$\frac{dC}{dq} = \frac{q}{500}$$

and

$$\int \frac{q}{500} \cdot dq = \frac{\frac{1}{500} \cdot q^{1+1}}{1+1} + C$$
$$= \frac{q^2}{1000} + C.$$

The first thing to clear up is the meaning of the term C. This must be included in the integration, because when a function is differentiated any stand-alone constants in the function are eliminated and won't appear in the derivative. Hence, when putting the derivatives back together, we have to indicate the possibility that the original function contained a constant, and we do this by writing C into the function. The value of C is not specified — it is left indefinite. This type of integration is known among the Cognoscenti as *indefinite* integration.

If we go back to the function $q^2/1000$ and its derivative $q/500$ we can illustrate the use of the Summing Sids in a simple exercise. Suppose we want to find out the change in costs of increasing output of Practicality from 100 to 150 gallons when we are given the derivative. How do we set about it?

First, we have to set out the problem in mathematical form. The integral can be written down using a Summing Sid as

$$\text{Find: } \int_{100}^{150} \frac{q}{500} \cdot dx$$

$$= \frac{1}{500} \int_{100}^{150} \frac{q^{1+1}}{2} + C$$

$$= \frac{q^2}{1000} + C$$

$$= \frac{150^2}{1000} + C - \left[\frac{100^2}{1000} + C\right]$$

(the indefinite constant C is eliminated)

$$= \frac{22500}{1000} - \frac{10000}{1000}$$

$$= 22.5 - 10$$

$$= \$12.5.$$

Be quite clear that you have followed this calculation. Using the derivative, the function is found by integration and the output levels are entered into the function to find the change in costs as output is increased from 100 to 150 gallons (see Figure 10.13). Once the integration is completed, the problem resolves itself into an ordinary question of changes in costs for a change in output for a given cost function; i.e., finding total costs at one output and the total costs at another output and subtracting the smaller from the larger to find the change in output.

To reinforce this point we will work through another simple example. This time the marginal cost to the firm is given by the derivative

$$125 + 8q.$$

What is the increase in cost when output rises from 6 to 12 units? The answer will be the difference in total cost at 12 units compared with the total cost at 6 units, and therefore we must find the total cost function. Once again the Summing Sids are used to state the problem. We must find the function for total cost from the integral of the derivative; i.e., find

$$\int_6^{12} (125 + 8q) \cdot dq.$$

The Summing Sid tells us to find the function which has the above for a derivative. Using the rule to find the second term we must apply

$$8\left[\frac{1}{1+1} \cdot q^{1+1}\right]$$

to get

$$125q + \frac{8}{2} \cdot q^2$$

$$f(C) = 125q + 4q^2.$$

The change in cost will be given by the total cost when the function is at 12 units minus the total cost when the function is at 6 units. This gives

$$C = f(12) - f(6)$$

$$= 125(12) + 4(12)^2 - [125(6) + 4(6)^2]$$

$$= 1500 + 576 - (750 + 144)$$

$$= 2076 - 894$$

$$= \$1,182.$$

Well, that is the end of our brief encounter with the Summing Sids. I hope you have acquired some idea of what the integral calculus is about and have at least learned not to panic at the sight of a page of Summing Sids when you flick through the latest

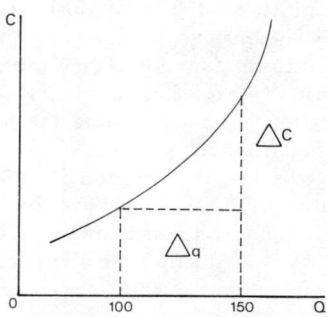

Figure 10.13

journal. Many articles that use mathematics use Summing Sid notation, and while what we have covered is only the smallest fraction of what the integral calculus has to offer, the ice should have been broken with this outline sketch.

10.5 The Way Ahead

Hard as the expedition has been, you know that you have only scratched the surface of the Mathematics Mountains. I say this not to demoralise you but to entice you to extend and deepen your mathematical experience. The highly selective and spartan additional economics reading mentioned below is one way ahead. You will soon appreciate how many opportunities for practising your mathematics there are in the literature and you will inevitably gain some experience in your studies of economics beyond intermediate level. You are bound to come across a lot of mathematics which is totally unfamiliar to you, and this will demand attention at an early opportunity if your mathematical momentum is to be kept going. If you continue with economics you have considerable incentive to keep your mathematics in tune with developments, particularly in axiomatic set-theory.

Enough has been said to give you an idea of what is going on when the authors set out optimising equations and identities. You have an idea of what some of the terrain looks like, at least from a distance, and ought to be able to find your way, though slowly at first, through the mountains you are expected to be familiar with in your elementary economics. But there is no substitute for experience. Armchair mountaineering is not the same as working your way up or across a slope. You have to get out of the armchair and on to the slopes to experience the subtleties of the techniques, as well as their uses and limitations. Between those who damn and those who idealise mathematics there is a middle way. You now have some ability to find out for yourself on which extreme, or neither (the saddle point perhaps?), you are going to pitch your tent. The best way is to try to read the literature.

10.6 Selected Ideas on Further Reading

Among the material available to you if you can handle simple differentiation are some quite advanced contributions to mainstream economics. J. Kregel, *The Theory of Economic Growth* [1972] will give you an introduction and survey of growth theory which you can read in a few hours, and uses nothing more difficult than differentiation and some delta ratios. You can also read Olson's classic contribution to the theory of public goods [1971] (ch. 1, 'Small Groups').

Why not try Samuelson's 'The Simple Mathematics of Income Determination' [1948]? You know the economics and have been exposed to the mathematics. Of course, what is 'simple' to a leading economist like Samuelson (author of the seminal mathematical economics classic *Foundations of Economic Analysis* [1949]) may appear a trifle more daunting to you when you first attempt it; but remember, Samuelson is also one of the world's foremost teachers of economics to first-year students and his basic textbook [1948 and eleven editions to 1980] has been a major influence in universities across the world. You can step up a level of difficulty by trying Ball and Bodkin [1963], 'Income, the Price Level and Generalised Multipliers in Keynesian Economics', but don't expect too much on a first reading. You can also usefully try C. Kennedy & A.P. Thirlwall, 'Import Penetration, Export Performance and Harrod's Trade Multiplier' [1979].

You will certainly profit from reading S.K. Nath, *A Reappraisal of Welfare Economics* [1969], which sets out the Paretian rules using Curly Dee notation. A feature of Nath's book is the verbal statements of the mathematical equations (most of them stating the equilibrium conditions). This is very useful, because you can check that you are reading the mathematics correctly. Mishan's *Introduction to Normative Economics* [1981] is bound to become a classic text in this field, and with Nath's book will give you all the welfare economics you need.

It is a good idea to try more difficult texts, such as Peacock and Shaw *The Economic Theory of Fiscal Policy* [1971]. The 'March of the Multipliers', supplemented by differentiation and Total Diffs and Dees should help in the early chapters. The mathematics of dynamics and matrix algebra in the later chapters hasn't been covered in this text; but persevere, because there are 'islands' of topics using the mathematics you have been exposed to — in mathematics, and economics, it is worth looking for the odd nugget and not being intimidated by pages of what look to you at this moment like sand.

In this spirit try the 'Mathematical Development of the Model' in Blinder & Solow [1974]. Their article 'The Analytical Foundations of Fiscal Policy' is a classic exposition of public finance.

Parts I and II of David Simpson, *General Equilibrium Analysis* [1975], may be within your grasp, if you take them slowly; and they will also contribute a great deal to your understanding of General Equilibrium Theory, which is a feature of most Honours courses. Try Walsh's new text (with Gram), *Classical and Neoclassical Theories of General Equilibrium* [1980]. It is difficult but revealing.

Harry G. Johnson, *International Trade and Economic Growth: studies in pure theory* [1967] contains several articles all within your grasp — or, at the least, more within your grasp than they were before you read this book! Try Johnson's 'An Economic Theory of Protectionism, Tariff Bargaining, and the Formation of Customs Unions' [1965], where the calculus is in footnotes and not beyond you. In international trade theory you should have no trouble with I.F. Pearce, *International Trade* [1970], Book I. It uses the Edgeworth-Bowley Box diagram *with* elementary calculus throughout, and an astonishing amount of ground is covered thereby. (For Book II it is necessary to acquire some knowledge of Determinants.)

One of the most useful ways to practise mathematics is to observe them at work, and I know of no better text with which to introduce beginners to the application of mathematics than Irma Adelman, *Theories of Economic Growth and Development* [1961], which covers the work of Adam Smith, Ricardo, Karl Marx and Schumpeter, and concludes with a neo-Keynesian model. Adelman outlines each contribution using a common production function and comparing how the competing theories cope with the interesting questions that a growth model must answer. The notation is entirely in Curly Dees (with a few Total Dees popping up) and your confidence will be boosted as you find you are able to follow what is going on both in the economics and the mathematics. (You may have to search in the library for a copy as it is probably out of print.)

On the fringe of difficulty for the beginner is Williamson's classic *The Economics of Discretionary Behaviour: managerial objectives in a theory of the firm* [1967]. (Once again matrix algebra raises its elegant head; but much of the calculus will make sense and as it is also a basic text in the intermediate theory of the firm it is often presented in a literary format.) You could also try Williamson's 'Peak Load Pricing and Optimal Capacity under Indivisibility Constraints' [1966], which uses Lagrangean multipliers.

Current concerns suggest that you should tackle Friedman's 'The Quantity Theory of Money: a Restatement' [1956] and Samuelson's 'What Classical and Neoclassical Monetary Theory Really was' [1968], followed by Johnson's *Macroeconomics and Monetary Theory* [1978]. You may find the economics more difficult than the mathematics!

In the same category is Harcout's *Some Cambridge Controversies in the Theory of Capital* [1972]. The content is very esoteric even for the queen of subjects (monetary theory being the king), but if you are specialising in this field this is one text you must struggle through by literary means if you cannot handle the mathematics. You will enjoy working through Jones' *An Introduction to Modern Theories of Economic Growth* [1975]. He covers all the growth theory you need and uses the mathematics you now have.

In labour economics you can cope with Becker, 'A Theory of the Allocation of Time' [1965]. You should also read N. Kaldor, 'Alternative Theories of Distribution' [1955–6] (reprinted by Mr Duckworth in Kaldor's *Essays on Value and Distribution*, being vol. 1 of Lord Kaldor's eight volumes of collected economic essay); but don't miss Solow, 'A Skeptical Note on the Constancy of Relative Shares' [1958]. This will set you up for Hahn's *The Share of Wages in the National Income: an enquiry into the theory of distribution* [1972], which uses mathematics in the main within your grasp. It is also an important area in this topic of theory.

An elementary theory text which uses the mathematics developed in this book is Ralph W. Pfouts, *Elementary Economics: a mathematical approach* [1972]. Most of the theory is explained using partial differentiation (there is some integration, but you can skip it without real loss). The book is recommended because it never leaves the reader behind. Professor Pfout keeps his main objective of presenting economic theory for students who have differential calculus — it is a book about economic theory not mathematics.

Anna Koutsoyiannis, *Modern Microeconomics* [1975] is among the intermediate microeconomics texts which you may care to read over again having completed this book. You should be able to cope with almost all the mathematical exposition she uses and, at the same time, thoroughly revise your oligopoly theory. In the same vein you can easily read Duncan Reekies, *Managerial Economics* [1975]. You can also gain confidence in the use of mathematical ideas by reading Bacharach's *Economics and the Theory of Games* [1976]. For a look across the boundary of your mathematical understanding, you can pick your way through selected parts only of Henderson & Quandt's long-running classic *Microeconomic Theory: a mathematical approach* [3rd edition 1980]. (It is always a good idea to stretch yourself a little beyond your present ability — the challenge does wonders for your motivation.) Everything in Harry Townsend's *Price Theory: selected readings* [1980] should be within your scope now.

10.7 Mathematics for Numerates?

Turning to textbooks in mathematics there are a number of excellent ones on the market making the more traditional approach to the subject. Archibald & Lipsey, *An Introduction to a Mathematical Treatment of Economics* [3rd edition 1977] is among the best available. However it suffers from one defect as far as innumerates are concerned: each edition is becoming more *rigorous*, and therefore more difficult, for genuine beginners and those working on their own. You may be better advised to go into the second-hand market and get the first edition if you can. S.G.B. Henry, *Elementary Mathematical Economics* [1969] is good value, even at 111 small pages. So is Dowling's *Mathematics for Economists* [1980] which is comprehensive and has 1,752 worked examples!

The classic text is undoubtedly R.G.D. Allen, *Mathematical Analysis for Economists*, first published in 1938. It is a rigorous but surprisingly readable text which it would pay you to dip into. Recent editions have appeared in paperback, and it is well worth buying even though much of it will be beyond you for the moment. When you can read Allen you are no longer innumerate.

Another text, much praised by economists, is A.C. Chiang, *Fundamental Methods in Mathematical Economics* [1967]. Like the others in the genre it is very comprehensive and looks far more forbidding than in fact it is. You could work through Chiang on a teach-yourself basis. It is used a great deal in University mathematical economics courses.

The text by J. Parry Lewis, *An Introduction to Mathematics for Students of Economics* [1959] is a straightforward mathematics textbook, fully comprehensive in its coverage but not intimately concerned with economics. It is a handy reference work and well worth working through, especially the chapters on calculus.

A straight mathematics text of justifiably great renown among generations of beginners is Silvanus P. Thompson, *Calculus Made Easy*, first published in 1910 and still going strong in reprints of its third edition [1946].

There are several other books on the market. Among the most useful for beginners are R.W. Quincey & F. Neal, *Using Mathematics in Economics* [1973], L.W.T. Stafford, *Mathematics for Economists* [1971], R. Morley, *Mathematics for Modern Economics* [1972], D.E. James & C.D. Throsby, *Introduction to Quantitative Methods in Economics* [1973] and J. Colin Glass, *An Introduction to Mathematical Methods in Economics* [1980]. William Baumol, *Economic Theory and Operations Analysis* [3rd edition 1972] introduces linear programming in a readable style and is very popular among students.

Most conventional texts cover matrix algebra, but Maurice Peston, *Elementary Matrices for Economics* [1969] (read in conjunction with Archibald & Lipsey or Chiang) may help you to get started.

An introduction to modern axiomatic economics using elementary set theory and topology is provided by Robert Russell and Maurice Wilkinson in *Microeconomics: a synthesis of modern and neoclassical theory* [1979]. It will also help your calculus.

This is the end of our expedition. As an innumerate, you have at least laid to rest some of the terrors of the Mathematics Mountains. Perhaps we will meet again at the Camp of the Curly Dees, or on a stroll with the Summing Sids? If you make yourself known to me, I will be delighted to share a litre or so of Practicality and perhaps, if we are in funds, some Complexity as well!

References

Adelman, Irma: *Theories of Economic Growth and Development*, 1961

Allen, R.G.D.: 'The Concept of Arc Elasticity of Demand', *Review of Economic Studies*, vol. 1, June, pp. 236–9, 1934

——: *Mathematical Analysis for Economists*, Macmillan Student Editions, 1969 [1938]

Archibald, G.C. & Lipsey, R.G.: *An Introduction to a Mathematical Treatment of Economics*, 3rd edition, 1977

Bacharach, Michael: *Economics and the Theory of Games*, 1976

Ball, R.J. & Bodkin, R.G.: 'Income, the Price Level and General Multipliers in Keynesian Economics', *Metroeconomica*, vol. 15, pp. 59–81, 1963

Baumol, W.J.: *Business Behaviour, Value and Growth*, 1959

——: *Economic Theory and Operations Analysis*, 3rd edition, 1972

Black, R.D., Coates, A.W. & Goodwin, C.D.W.: *The Marginal Revolution in Economics*, 1973

Blaug, M.: *Economic Theory in Retrospect*, 2nd edition, 1968

Blinder, A.S. & Solow, R.M.: 'Analytical Foundations of Fiscal Policy' in (ed.): *The Economics of Public Finance*, Brookings Studies in Government Finance, 1974

Chiang, A.C.: *Fundamental Methods of Mathematical Economics*, International Student Edition, 1969

Clark, J.B.: *The Philosophy of Wealth*, 1895

Cobb, C.W. & Douglas, P.H.: 'A theory of production', *American Economic Review*, supp. vol. 18, 1928

Cournot, A.: *Researches into the Mathematical Principles of the Theory of Wealth* (translated by N.T. Bacon) [1838] [1927] 1960

Debreu, G.: *The Theory of Value: an axiomatic analysis of equilibrium economics*, Cowles Foundation Monograph, no. 17, 1959

Douglas, P.H.: *The Theory of Wages*, 1934

——: 'Are there Laws of Production?', *American Economic Review*, 1948

Dowling, Edmund T.: *Mathematics for Economists*, Schaum Outline Series, 1980

Edgeworth, F.Y.: *Mathematical Psychics: an essay on the application of mathematics to the moral sciences*, 1881

Friedman, M.: 'The Quantity Theory of Money: a restatement', *Studies in the Quantity Theory of Money*, pp. 3–21, 1956

Glass, J. Colin.: *An Introduction to Mathematical Methods in Economics*, 1980

Hahn, F.H.: *The Share of Wages in the National Income: an enquiry into the theory of distribution*, LSE Research Monographs, 1972

Hall, A.P.: *Philosophers at War: the quarrel between Newton and Leitniz*, 1980

Hansen, A.: *A Guide to Keynes*, 1953

Harcourt, G.C.: *Some Cambridge Controversies in the Theory of Capital*, 1972

Heathfield, D.: *Production Functions*, Macmillan Studies in Economics, 1971

Henderson, J.M. & Quandt, R.E.: *Microeconomic Theory: a mathematical approach*, International Student Edition, 3rd edition, 1980

Henry, S.G.B.: *Elementary Mathematical Economics*, Students Library of Economics, 1969

Hicks, J.: *Value and Capital: an inquiry into some fundamental principles of economic theory*, [1932], 2nd edition, 1939

——: *A Theory of Wages*, 1932

Hollis, M. & Nell, E.J.: *Rational Economic Man: a philosophical critique of neoclassical economics*, 1975

Hutchinson, T.W.: *On Revolutions and Progress in Economic Knowledge*, 1978

James, D.E.: *Introduction to Quantitative Methods in Economics*, 1973

Jevons, W.S.: *Theory of Political Economy*, 1934 edition [1871]

Johnson, H.G.: *International Trade and Economic Growth: studies in pure theory*, 1967

—: *Macroeconomics and Monetary Theory*, Lectures in Economics no. 1, 1978

Jones, Hywel: *An Introduction to Modern Theories of Economic Growth*, 1975

Kahn, R.F.: 'The Relation of Home Investment to Unemployment', *Economic Journal*, June, 1931

Kaldor, N.: 'Alternative theories of distribution', *Review of Economic Studies*, vol. 23, pp. 83–100, 1955–6; repr. in Kaldor, N.: *Essays on Value and Distribution*, Duckworth, 1980

—: 'The Irrelevance of Equilibrium Economics', *Economic Journal*, vol. 82, pp. 1237–55, 1972; repr. in Kaldor, N., *Further Essays on Economic Theory*, Duckworth, 1978

Kennedy, C. & Thirlwall, A.P.: 'Import Penetration, Export Performance and Harrod's Trade Multiplier', *Oxford Economic Papers*, vol. 31, pp. 303–23, July 1979

Keynes, J.M.: 'Can Lloyd George Do It: the pledges examined' (with H. Henderson) 1929, in *Essays in Persuasion*, vol. 14 *Collected Writings of John Maynard Keynes*, 1972

—: *Essays in Biography*, 1933

—: *The General Theory of Employment, Interest and Money*, 1936

Koutsoyannis, A.: *Modern Microeconomics*, 1975

Kregel, J.: *The Theory of Economic Growth*, Macmillan Studies in Economics, 1972

Lancaster, Kelvin: *Introduction to Modern Microeconomics*, 1969

Lerner, A.: 'Geometrical Comparison of Elasticities', *American Economic Review*, vol. 37, p. 191, 1947

Lewis, J.P.: *An Introduction to Mathematics for Students of Economics*, Macmillan Student Editions, 2nd edition, 1969

Machlup, F.: *The Economics of Sellers Competition*, 1952

—: 'Equilibrium and Disequilibrium: misplaced concreteness and disguised politics', *Economic Journal*, vol. 68, 1958

—: 'Operational Constructs and Mental Constructs in Models and Theory Formation' in *Selected Writings of Fritz Machlup*, 1976

Marshall, Alfred: *Principles of Economics*, 5th edition, 1907 [1890]

Mishan, E.J.: *Introduction to Normative Economics*, 1981

Morley, R.: *Mathematics for Modern Economics*, Fontana Introduction to Modern Economics, 1972

Nath, S.K.: *A Reappraisal of Welfare Economics*, 1969

Naylor, T.H. & Vernon, J.M.: *Microeconomics and Decision Models of the firm*, International Edition, 1969

Olson, M.: *The Logic of Collective Action: public goods and the theory of groups*, 1965

Peacock, A. & Shaw, G.K.: *The Economic Theory of Fiscal Policy*, revised edition, 1976

Pearce, I.F.: *International Trade*, Book I, Macmillan Student Editions, University of Southampton Economics Series, 1970

Peston, M.H.: *Elementary Matrices for Economics*, Students Library of Economics, 1969

Pfouts, R.W.: *Elementary Economics: a mathematical approach*, 1972

Quincey, R.W. & Neal, F.: *Using Mathematics in Economics*, 1973

Reekie, W.D.: *Managerial Economics*, 1975

Robbins, L.: *An Essay on the Nature and Significance of Economic Science*, 1932

Robinson, J.: *The Economics of Imperfect Competition*, 1933

—: *Economic Philosophy*, 1962

—: *Contributions to Modern Economics*, 1978

— & Eatwell: *An Introduction to Modern Economics*, 1973

Russell, R. Robert & Wilkinson, Maurice: *Microeconomics: a synthesis of modern and neoclassical theory*, 1979

Samuelson, P.A.: *Foundations of Economic Analysis*, Harvard Economic Studies, vol. 80, 1948

—: *Economics: an introductory analysis*, 1980 [1948]

—: 'The Simple Mathematics of Income Distribution', in *Income, Employment and Public Policy: essays in honour of Alvin Hansen*, pp. 133–55, 1948

—: 'What Classical and Neoclassical Monetary Theory really was', *Canadian Journal of Economics*, vol. 1, pp. 1–15, 1968

—: 'Paul Douglas's Measurement of Production Functions and Marginal Productivities', *Journal of Political Economy*, vol. 87, pp. 923–39, October, 1979

Schumpeter, J.: *History of Economic Analysis*, 1954

Shackle, G.L.S.: *An Economic Querist*, 1973

Simpson, D.: *General Equilibrium Analysis: an introduction*, 1975

Solow, R.M.: 'A Skeptical Note on the Constancy of Relative Shares', *American Economic Review*, vol. 48, pp. 618–31, 1958

Stafford, L.W.T.: *Mathematics for Economists*, M & E Handbooks, 2nd edition, 1978

Tangri, O.P.: 'Omissions in the Treatment of the Law of Variable Proportions, *American Economic Review*, vol. 56, pp. 484–93, 1966

Thompson, S.A.: *Calculus Made Easy: being the very-simplest introduction to those beautiful methods of reckoning which are generally called by the terrifying names of the Differential Calculus and the Integral Calculus*, 3rd edition repr., 1965 [1910]

von Thunen, J.H.: *The Isolated State*, 1826

Townsend, H.: *Price Theory: selected readings*, 2nd edition, 1980

Walras, M.E.: *Elements of Pure Economics*, translated by W. Jaffe, 1954 [1874]

Walsh, V.: *Introduction to contemporary Microeconomics*, 1970

—: & Gram, Harvey, *Classical and Neoclassical Theories of General Equilibrium: historical origins and mathematical structure*, 1980

Wicksell, K.: *Lectures*, 1901

Wicksteed, H.: *An Essay on the Coordination of the Laws of Production*, 1932 [1894]

Wildsmith, J.R.: *Managerial Theories of the Firm*, 1973

Williamson, O.E.: 'Peak Load Pricing and Optimal Capacity Under Indivisibility Constraints', *American Economic Review*, vol. 56, pp. 810–27, 1966

—: *The Economics of Discretionary Behaviour: managerial objectives in a theory of the firm*, 1973 [1967]

Index

A-level economics, 4
absolute price level, 26
absolutist view of economics, 6
addition, 13
additive utility, 85—6
Adelman, Irma, 126
adjustment, 19
aggregate production function, 95
Allen, R.G.D., 38, 127
Archibald, G.C., 127
auctioneer, 19
average-marginal relations, 69—74

Bacharach, M., 127
balanced budgets, 35
Ball, R.J., 125
Baumol, W., 114, 128
Becker, G., 127
behavioural equations, 10
Black, R.D., 6, 129
Blaug, M., 6, 89
Blinder, A.S., 126
Bowley, A.L., 126
budgets, 7, 108, 110

calculus: brink of, 41—2 (*see* differentiation, derivatives); integral, 119—25; notation, 37, 43, 67, 97, 121
capital, 90—5, 99, 105, 108
cardinal utility, 85—6
ceteris paribus, 19
chain rule, *see* differentiation
Chamberlin, E., 114
Chiang, A.C., 128
choice, tyranny of, 84, 107
chord, 40, 104
Clark, J.B., 89
Coates, A.W., 6, 129
Cobb, C.W., 90
Cobb-Douglas functions, 89—95
Cognoscenti, 16, 18, 22, 24, 26—30, 32, 38—9, 41, 46, 51, 58, 68, 88, 95, 100, 104, 107, 114

comparative statics, 8, 19
competition: perfect, 53, 62, 76, 90—2, 94—5, 108; imperfect, 53, 60; monopolistic, 114
concave, 115
constant, defined, 9; revenue, 63; shares, 90
constraints, 106
consumer theory, 7, 110—11
consumption, 9, 27; function, 28
contours, 98—9, 101
convex, 115
co-ordinate geometry, 39, 101
cost, 10, 41—6, 73—4, 108; average, 73—4; fixed, 51; marginal, 42, 44—6, 51—2, 64, 77, 121; total, 42, 51, 115, 121—22; variable, 51
Cournot, A., 8, 38
cross-partials, 116—18
Curly Dees, 84—103, 108—11, 116, 126

Debreu, G., 7
Delta notation, 33
demand: excess, 19; equation, 10, 17, 39—40, 53, 57, 95—7; law of, 18; theory, 8, 102
denominator, 31
derivatives: dance of, 51—67; first, 69, 77, 80, 114; higher order, 58—9; negative, 69, 75, 79; partial, 87—9, 100—12; second, 74—6, 78, 93—5, 97, 114, 116, 118; third, 115; zero, 69, 75—7, 114
differentiation, 46—50, 114; addition, 66; chain rule, 111—12; constants, 50, 88; functions, 49, 52; inverse, 61, 67; partial, 87—9, 100—12; quotients, 70; subtraction, 66; variables, 50
diminishing returns, 93—4
diminishing utility, 86

disequilibrium, 28
disposable income, 32
distribution of product, 6
divider rule, 70
division, 13
dodges, 23, 26, 31
Douglas, P.H., 90, 101
Dowling, E.T., 127

Eatwell, J., 6
econometrics, 92
Edgeworth, F.Y., 20, 126
elasticity, 38—40, 42, 57—8, 60—3, 115
Engel, E., 38
equations, 9—11, 20, 95; straight line, 15, 39
equilibrium, 7—8, 21—2, 24, 26; condition, 10, 19—20
equimarginal principle, 7, 102
examiners, 35, 40, 58
ex ante, 27
exogenous variable, 30
ex post, 27

Ferguson, C.E., 1
firm, theory of, 11, 103
Fisher, I., 8
fixed costs, *see* costs
Friedman, Milton, 126
functions, 10, 17, 44—6

general equilibrium, 7, 126
ghosts, 18—19
Glass, Colin, 128
Goodwin, C.D.W., 6
government expenditure, 32—6
Gram, Harvey, 126
growth, 126

Hahn, F.H., 127
Hansen, A., 33
Harcourt, G.C., 95, 127
Heathfield, D., 89
Henderson, J.M., 127

Index

Henry, S.G.B., 127
Hicks, Sir John, 7, 38, 89, 103
higgling, 20
Hollis, M., 19
Hutchinson, T.W., 26

identity, 10, 27
income, 95–7; determination, 27–36
indefinite constant, 123–4
indices, rules of, 67, 91
indifference curves, 101–2
inequalities, 25
inflexion points, 68, 82, 115
integration, 119–25
intercept constant, 16, 18–19, 23, 33
interest rate, 92, 94, 102, 108
inverse functions, 38; quadrille, 61
investment, 9, 11, 27–35
isocost, 107–9
isoquant, 99, 102, 105–9

James, D.E., 128
Jevons, W.S., 6, 20
Johnston, Harry G., 126–7
Jones, H., 127

Kahn, Lord, 30
Kaldor, Lord, 7, 127
Kennedy, C., 125
Keynes, Lord, 26, 28–38, 88
Koutsoyiannis, Anna, 1, 43, 127
Kregel, J., 125

labour, 70, 90–5, 105, 108
Lagrange, J., 107–9; multipliers, 107–9, 119, 126
Lancaster, K., 1
Leaning Lambda, 107–11
ledges, 68
Leibniz, G.W., 114
Lewis, J.P., 128
limiting values, 41–2, 100
Lipsey, R.G., 127
literary economics, 2, 85, 102

Machlup, F., 8, 17
Malthus, T., 6
marginal productivity, 89–95, 103–6, 109
marginal propensity: to consume, 29, 31, 33; to save, 31, 102; see also cost, revenue, utility
marginal rate of technical substitution, 106
markets, 20, 64

mark-up pricing, 64, 66
Marshall, Alfred, 1, 6–8, 17–19, 21, 26, 38
mathematics: convention, 17–18; collective memory, 49; code, 13; mountains, 3, 8, 10, 12, 14, 68, 81, 83–5, 98, 113, 115, 125; palsy, 21; union, 4, 84
Marx, K., 6, 26, 76, 126
maxima, 68, 74, 78, 80–1, 83, 114–17; constrained, 106–11, 115
Menger, Carl, 6
microcomputers, 55–6
Mill, J.S., 6
minima, 68, 74, 77, 83, 107–8, 114, 116–17
Mishan, E.J., 126
models, 8, 19, 22, 25–6
money supply, 10, 26, 88
multiplication, 13
multipliers, 22, 26–36

Nath, S.K., 125
national income, 9, 102
Neal, F., 128
necessary conditions, 79, 114
negative signs, 24–5
neoclassical economics, 6, 43–4, 64, 75–6, 85, 91, 102, 108, 114
Newton, Isaac, 114
notation, 22, 26, 58, 88, 90; Greek, 102, 108, 114
numerator, 31

Ohm's Law, 3, 15
Olson, Mancur, 125
optimisation, 115
output, 99–5, 103, 108

parametric constants, 22
partial differentiation, 85, 96–7
partial equilibrium, 7
Peacock, Alan, 2, 126
Pearce, I.F., 126
Peston, M., 1, 59, 128
Pfouts, R.W., 127
philosophy, 7, 84
Pigou, A.C., 26
positive signs, 24–5
price, 9–10, 109; level, 26
product 70–3, 89–95, 109, 115; functions, 89–95, 103, 105; reel, 59 (see differentiation); see also marginal productivity

profit: defined, 10, 94–5; maximisation, 54–6, 64–5, 76, 78, 80, 91, 114, 116
public works, 30
publishing, 55, 80

Quandt, R.E., 127
quantity theory of money, 126
quest for calculus, 6, 37
Quincy, R.W., 128
quotient rule, 70

radical economics, 89
Reekie, Duncan, 127
relative shares, 92, 94
relativism, 6
revenue: average, 11, 120; marginal, 53, 55, 58, 62, 77, 115, 120; total, 11, 55, 78, 115, 120–2
Ricardo, David, 6
Robbins, Lord, 84
Robinson, Joan, 6, 26, 38, 58–9, 85
rock-bottom models, 26–8, 30, 32, 39

saddle point, 118–19
sales people, 14, 64; maximisation, 114
Samuelson, Paul A., 88, 90, 125–6
savings, 11, 27–8, 32, 102
scarcity, 84, 106
Schumpeter, J., 6, 126
Shackle, G.L.S., 9
Shaw, G., 2, 126
Simpson, David, 126
slope constant, 17–18, 28
Smith, Adam, 6, 126
Solow, R.M., 126
specialist, 84
Stafford, C.W.T., 128
stationary points, 74, 81–3, 104
student power, 79
substitution, 11, 106
subtraction, 13
sufficient condition, 79, 114
summation, 121
Summing Sids, 119–25; see also integration
supply, 8, 10, 17, 19, 39–40
surface, 98, 104

tangency, 41, 109, 114
Tangri, O.P., 116
taxation, 32–6
Thirwall, A.P., 125

Thompson, S.P., 128
Throsby, C.D., 128
Thunen, von, 89
total dees (derivatives), 95, 103–6, 111–12, 126
total diffs (differentials), 98, 100–3, 126
Townsend, Harry, 127
training, 63–6

unintended investment, 28
Utilitarianism, 7
utility: marginal, 7, 43, 85–9, 101, 106; total, 7–8, 85–9, 101, 110

variables, 8, 20, 30, 113
video-cassettes, 79–80

wages, 90–2, 94
Walras, M.E., 6–7
Walsh, V., 1, 7, 126
Wicksell, K., 89
Wicksteed, H., 89
Wildsmith, J.R., 116
Williamson, O., 126

Mathematics for Innumerate Economists

Gavin Kennedy

Many economics students choose to ignore mathematics while pursuing their course of study, in spite of the fact that mathematics is increasingly important in the understanding and application of economic theory. It is an invaluable shorthand if understood.

This clear and simple handbook is an indispensable guide for both beginning and advanced students, bringing even the most abstruse elements of calculus within their grasp. Those previously confounded by figures and formulas will be grateful to the author—who himself had to learn the hard way—for lightening their load and perhaps removing some longstanding prejudices about the difficulty of mathematics. Long after studies have been completed, the economist is likely to return to *Mathematics for Innumerate Economists* as a reliable tool.

Gavin Kennedy is Senior Lecturer in Economics at the University of Strathclyde. This book is based on ten years' experience in teaching remedial mathematics to economists. Dr. Kennedy's other books include *The Military in the Third World, The Economics of Defense,* and *Burden Sharing in NATO.*

ISBN 0-8419-0777-3
      0-8419-0789-7 (pbk)

Holmes & Meier Publishers
IUB Building
30 Irving Place
New York, N.Y. 10003

HB135
.K47
1982

Kennedy

Mathematics for innumerate
economists

DATE DUE